CORPORATE SOCIAL INVOLVEMENT

*Dedicated to the memory of my father-in-law
and dear friend, Harry Hughes*

Corporate Social Involvement

Social, political and environmental issues in Britain and Italy

MICHAEL MARINETTO

Ashgate

Aldershot • Brookfield USA • Singapore • Sydney

Published by
Ashgate Publishing Ltd
Gower House
Croft Road
Aldershot
Hants GU11 3HR
England

Ashgate Publishing Company
Old Post Road
Brookfield
Vermont 05036
USA

British Library Cataloguing in Publication Data
Marinetto, Michael
   Corporate social involvement: social, political and
   environmental issues in Britain and Italy
   1.Social responsibility of business - Great Britain
   2.Social responsibilty of business - Italy 3.Business -
   Environmental aspects - Great Britian 4.Business -
   Environmental aspects - Italy
   I. Title
   658.4'08'0941

Library of Congress Catalog Card Number: 98-72804

ISBN 1 84014 189 1

Printed and bound by Athenaeum Press, Ltd.,
Gateshead, Tyne & Wear.

Contents

Acknowledgements

I would like to record my gratitude to the many people who helped me during this study, which originally formed part of my doctoral research undertaken at the University of Westminster between 1992—95 in the School of Economic and Business Studies. First of all, I would like to mention my supervisor, Robin Theobald, who was of great assistance during the course of this research. Robin carefully guided the research work and offered me a great deal of sound advice during the drafting stage. I should also like to mention my second supervisor, John Stanworth, who commented perceptively on draft chapters and also kindly provided me with some of the research money at his disposal for my study trips to Italy. I would also like to thank Nick Zafiris, Head of the School of Economic and Business Studies, for offering financial assistance for my travelling expenses to Italy. I am indebted to the Norman Hart Educational Foundation which kindly contributed to my travelling expenses for my first research trip to Italy.

This research would not have been possible without the many individuals in companies and organisations that gave up their time to be interviewed about their work. I am particularly grateful to those company representatives from British Telecom, Shell UK, Unilever, BAT Industries and their various subsidiaries. I would also like to thank representatives from the following organisations who agreed to be interviewed: the Policy Studies Institute, Business in the Community, Lambeth City Challenge, LENTA (London Enterprise Agency), Association for Business Sponsorship of the Arts, Action Resource Centre, Charities Aid Foundation, Brixton Enterprise Centre.

There are numerous people who were integral to the Italian phase of my research. Bryn Jones at the University of Bath provided me some very useful contacts. In Italy, I was assisted by Professor Mirella Giannini at the University of Bari, who led me to some useful people. Dr Maurizio Brioni from Reggio Emilia went beyond the call of duty in helping me with the cooperative movement in Italy. Giuseppe della Rocca of Main Management and Beatrice

Lentati were also invaluable. I would like to extend a special thanks to all those representatives from Fiat, Olivetti, ENI and their subsidiaries who agreed to be interviewed and for tolerating my clumsy Italian; as well as those that I interviewed from the following banks and small companies: Banca di Roma, Banca Popolare di Milano, Angelini Pharmaceuticals, Cassa di Risparmio di Firenze, Cariplo, Fratelli Dioguardi, Istituto Bancario San Paolo di Torino. My gratitude also extends to those representatives from the Associazione Mecenati Italiani, BIC Liguria, BIC Trieste, Comitato (Comitato per lo Sviluppo di Nuova Imprenditorialita' Giovanile), Fondazione Adriano Olivetti, Fondazione Giovanni Agnelli.

I am also indebted to all at Ashgate, especially Sarah Markham and Ann Newell. Without their assistance this book would never have seen the light of day. My final word of thanks and most significant acknowledgement goes to Debbie who was a constant source of encouragement. Any mistakes are of course my own. The credit for any achievement is shared.

Preface

This text examines the issue of corporate social responsibility (defined here as business engagement in social action concerned with the general well-being of society). This study initially focuses on Britain. In recent years, there has been growing interest in businesses rendering themselves more socially active and involved in addressing social problems. A number of British companies has adopted the community practices characteristic of corporate life in America since the early 1960s. The first part of the analysis focuses on Britain, but the second part of the text examines whether similar developments have occurred in Italy.

The study employs a variety of sources: historical texts, secondary studies and detailed case studies of the social programmes organised by different corporations (Shell, BT, Unilever, and BAT Industries in Britain, and Fiat, Olivetti, ENI, IRI and Dioguardi in Italy). These case studies are based on in-depth interviews of relevant personnel and on the study of company documents.

The aim is to provide a qualitative explanation of why companies go beyond their commercial remit to engage in philanthropic action. A socially informed analysis is furnished: this area is located in its historical and political context. Any explanation of contemporary advances in corporate social responsibility needs to stress the role of the modern state in society. In particular, it must emphasise the development of relations between the state and the business community. It is argued that, in Britain, as a response to the political and economic crisis of the 1970s, the links between the business and state sectors became ever closer. This created the institutional opportunities for active business involvement in areas such as environmental protection, small firm development and urban regeneration. Italy has seen less political impetus given to active corporate involvement in society. The most significant achievements have come from within the state sector.

Political and economic events external to the business community are highly significant. These provide the necessary external jolts and opportunities for business involvement in areas which, since in the postwar period, have been colonised by the state. At the same time, company policies are not solely shaped by external events and developments. Company involvement in social activities is also a product of certain internal dynamics: the perceptions and concerns of key actors, and the culture within companies. Managers and directors are undoubtedly influenced by what happens in society but they perceive and actively choose particular responses to external events. This is underlined by the case studies of the social policies organised by companies in Britain and Italy.

As well as explaining the phenomenon of corporate responsibility, this study assesses the actual contribution made by the private sector to the well-being of society. This is an important point to consider. In Britain particularly, corporate social activism has come to be equated as a private solution to public problems. It is shown during the course of the analysis that there are limits to what companies can achieve on a social front. It is concluded that corporate social responsibility must emphasise the need for companies to observe social and legal restrictions in their pursuit of commercial goals.

1 Introduction: Issues in the Study of Corporate Social Responsibility

The central purview of this study is to examine corporate social responsibility in Britain and Italy. In theory, this should be a straightforward and uncomplicated task. As defined by British company law, the public company is primarily responsible and accountable to its owners, who, in effect, are the shareholders (Donnelly, 1987). Directors, as the custodians of shareholder assets, are under no legal obligation to use company resources for social activities, the reason being that such activities are not directly related to the overarching objective of maximising financial returns.

The orthodox view of the company and its responsibilities has its philosophical advocates. Postwar liberal economists Milton Friedman (1962) and Frederick Hayek (1969) argue that, apart from creating wealth, businesses have no wider social obligations. These theoreticians introduce an important notion, borrowed from Adam Smith, into the contemporary debate on corporate social responsibility: that the selfish pursuit of profit has beneficial repercussions for the rest of society. This argument is based on the concept of the 'invisible hand', first introduced by Adam Smith in *The Theory of Moral Sentiments* (Goyder, 1987). This concept is a metaphor describing the process whereby the accumulation of wealth automatically benefits wider society through consumption and investment. Hence it follows that a business, by seeking to fulfil its commercial obligations, secures its own survival and contributes to the overall wealth and prosperity of society (Levitt, 1979).

We would expect the classical view of corporate responsibility to have widespread credence and support in modern capitalist economies. However, there are alternative perspectives to the classical view. American business leaders and academic writers were at the forefront of the contemporary debate on corporate social responsibility. Indeed, the likes of Friedman, Hayek and Levitt were galvanised into producing a critique of corporate philanthropy by the

1

advent of what Epstein terms the '"modern era" of interest in corporate social responsibility' in the United States (1989, p. 585).

The 'modern era' was signalled in 1950 by the Supreme New Jersey Legislature ruling that firms should be allowed to make contributions for the purposes of social betterment. The debate was later given scholarly credence when New York academics Bowen (1953) and Clark (1957) published their seminal apologias on the social responsibilities of companies (Walton, 1982). From the mid-1960s to the mid-1970s a consensus regarding the importance of company-led social action emerged among leading American businesses (Epstein, 1989). By the 1980s the corporate social responsibility debate in the United States moved on to the strategic terrain. Business managers and academics examined whether company involvement in dealing with social problems could benefit mainstream commercial activities.

In postwar Britain, efforts to reconcile the commercial and social responsibilities of firms witnessed brief advances in the early 1960s. The Jenkins Committee on Company Law Reform in 1962 maintained that charitable gifts by businesses would be acceptable before the law courts. It was concluded by the Committee that such giving would endear companies to the public (Sheikh, 1990). The modern debate on corporate social responsibility did not gain any real prominence until the 1970s. Executives, academics and government ministers used various platforms to pontificate on the wider responsibilities of business.

The spectre of America, where, by this date, corporate responsibility was a mature research field in university departments (Epstein, 1976, p. 215; Jones, 1983), was influential. Undoubtedly, American practices held a definite bearing on early British discussions of corporate philanthropy (see Fogarty, 1966). These developments also established an important precedent for the expansion of corporate social involvement during the 1980s. It was in this period that companies actively participated across a wide range of areas. For practitioners researching corporate responsibility, initially in America (Jones, 1980) and later in Britain (Beesley and Evans, 1978), the subject matter under scrutiny generated several problems of definition.

Defining corporate social responsibility

So far, a definition of corporate social responsibility has remained largely implicit. It is assumed, in so doing, that the reader already holds a definition of the term which is congruent with its present usage. This is a problematic assumption, not least because, as writers on the subject have observed, no definitive version of the concept exists. Hargreaves and Dauman describe the predicament as a matter of 'one man: one definition' (1975, p. 15), and McAdam (1973) notes that there are over 150 potential areas where a company might disclose information of a social nature (cited in Gray *et al.*, 1987).

The concept is elusive. However, it has not stopped researchers from trying to come up with an operational definition of corporate social responsibility. One of the most useful attempts to define the subject area comes from Hargreaves and Dauman (1975). These authors provide a procedural explication of the term, with three distinguishable levels of responsibility. The first level covers 'basic responsibilities', referring to technical and routine obligations, such as paying taxes and ensuring scrupulous dealings with customers. At the second level, 'organisational responsibilities' are intended to secure the well-being and needs of those under the aegis of the company, whether employees, suppliers, managers or shareholders. When a company adopts 'societal responsibilities' — the third level in the classification — it becomes involved in the wider community by assisting the creation of a 'healthy overall environment' (Hargreaves and Dauman, 1975, p. 19). What distinguishes societal responsibilities from the other categories is that it covers a wider constituency, emphasising the welfare and prosperity of society.

In view of this, the aim of this study is not to focus on those responsibilities within the parochial animus of the company — welfare and social services for employees, pension schemes, health and safety. Rather the objective is examine the implications for companies of wider social responsibilities. Here, our analytical interests coincide with Hargreaves and Dauman's third level category or what the CBI (1973) terms a company's responsibilities to 'society at large' — the government, national and local communities.

Providing a definition of the concept is not the only problem generated by this particular field of research: there is also the pressing analytical matter of explaining why corporate responsibility rose to prominence in Britain during the 1970s. When it comes to making decisions about corporate social involvement, a company does not operate in a social vacuum. In this respect, it is influenced by broader developments. The main predicament for the present study is to try to pinpoint these general social factors.

The search for an explanation

There have been some laudable attempts by social scientists to locate corporate philanthropy and social action in a wider social context. Most notably these have come from two main sources. Firstly, managerial theorists have linked corporate social responsibility to the rise of industrial society. Secondly, there are thinkers for whom corporate philanthropy is a functional-defensive strategy on the part of commercial organisations. Each perspective is outlined separately below. The rationale is to assess whether they provide a sound theoretical framework for understanding the emergence of corporate responsibility, especially in Britain.

The managerial thesis

The managerial thesis is the generic term applied to a distinctly American tradition of social science research popularised during the 1950s and 1960s. This intellectual trend spawned a substantial body of literature on the nature of capitalism in the postwar era, and the role of business institutions within society (see Jones, 1983). More importantly, it seems, initially, to have provided theoretical grounding for understanding corporate social action.

The main assertion of those working in the managerial tradition is this: the material basis of class distinctions in capitalist society — the close, umbilical relationship between the ownership and control of capital — has been made redundant by the modernising forces within the postwar economy and society. Galbraith (1974) argues that the emergence of new technology, coupled with the wider distribution of share ownership, has resulted in the growth of business enterprises. This has led to the decline of individually- or family-owned enterprises, thus severing the links between the ownership and control of capital. In the new industrial state, non-owning, salaried managers preside over the operations of business organisations. For Galbraith, capitalist societies have converged towards a common industrial structure, replete with advanced technologies. As such, it is imperative for non-partisan, technical specialists to assume control of commercial enterprises.

According to other theoreticians, the rise of managerial specialists, following from the divorce between ownership and control, has facilitated a greater interest in social issues (Ewing, 1970). As non-propertied controllers of the means of production, managers no longer have a vested interest in the narrow, instrumental pursuit of financial gain. Consequently, the leaders of industry can aspire to broader social and humanitarian objectives. Kaysen has argued that the new managerial class of modern corporations, no longer tied to propertied interests, is responsible to a broader constituency:

> Its responsibilities to the general public are widespread: leadership in local charitable enterprises, concern with factory architecture and landscaping, provision of support for higher education, and even research in pure science, to name a few. (1957, p. 313)

4

A similar point was made by Berle (1959) who noted that, with the separation of ownership and control, the private company has become accountable to a broad range of interests.

Although influential during its time, there are notable difficulties with the theoretical claims made by managerial theory. For the present analysis, this perspective does not furnish an entirely satisfactory explanation for the prevalence of corporate social responsibility. These misgivings stem from views concerning the development and nature of modern capitalism. Historically, the transition from small family-owned units to large, shareholder-owned companies has not facilitated a greater sense of social duty amongst managers. Evidence shows that this development has concretised the objectives of expansion and profit-making. Indeed, for some managerial theorists, the new structure of ownership has generally allowed managers to pursue their own personal interests rather than those of wider society (see Scott, 1985, pp. 19—20).

Economic considerations are still important because links between ownership and control in modern enterprises remains intact. The only changing feature is the identity of the owners: the family enterprise of the Industrial Revolution was replaced, in the twentieth century, by an impersonal, shareholder system of ownership dominated by financial institutions (Scott, 1986). Rather than creating a dispassionate class of managerial technocrats, the dominant form of capital ownership in modern society has reinforced the rights of property holders. Moreover, in legal terms, the maximisation of financial returns on capital investments is a legal requirement for companies.

This critique of the managerial thesis still leaves unaddressed an important issue: that of explaining the flourishing interest surrounding corporate responsibility in Britain. On the whole, the literature that has expressly tackled this subject lacks useful insights. Much of it has been characteristically practical in emphasis, either advising managers on how to organise social action programmes or providing voluntary groups with ideas on corporate fund-raising (Clutterbuck, 1981; Knox and Ashworth, 1985; Norton, 1987, 1989; Carmichael and Drummond, 1989; Clutterbuck and Snow, 1990; Fogarty and Christie, 1990; Christie *et al.*, 1991). Most of these writings are bereft of analytical vigour and valuable observations. Nevertheless, there are some notable illuminations made by British theoreticians and researchers. The most interesting ideas are those that have conceptualised corporate social responsibility as a defensive response in the face of economic and political instability.

The defensive thesis

For subscribers to this thesis, commercial survival in modern society is contingent on enterprises addressing social problems. Writing from their experience of pioneering a corporate social programme for IBM in Britain, Hargreaves and Dauman (1975) view social responsibility as an indispensable element of modern business strategy. The authors make this assertion because commercial activities and the external environment have coalesced into an interdependent and dynamic relationship.

One influential feature of contemporary society, mentioned by the authors, concerns the increasing size and importance of the central state bureaucracy. The state apparatus controls institutions and functions vital to the reproduction and maintenance of society — for instance, the provision of health and educational services or the safeguarding of industry. Hence, unless businesses are prepared to actively participate in society, their influence and position will be marginalised. Hargreaves and Dauman are not alone in expressing concerns over the level of state involvement in society and the possible repercussions for business activity. A number of texts and reports written in the 1970s, during a time of economic and political crisis, expressed similar concerns. These reports argued for self-imposed social regulation instead of government intervention to protect the wider social good (Ivens, 1970; CBI, 1973; Beesley, 1974; BIM, 1974; Kempner et al., 1974; Beesley and Evans, 1978).

Hargreaves and Dauman (1975) further observed that modern commerce is taking place in an unstable social environment: finite energy resources, hyper inflationary pressures, urban poverty and industrial disputes have undermined the aims and philosophy of the liberalised market. The panacea offered by the authors is for business organisations to invest their resources in social and community action:

> ...we find that the long-term profit-making potential of every individual company and of free enterprise as a whole, and indeed their very survival, will be jeopardised unless all companies substitute their token handouts, often made with muddled motives, for heavy investments in public and social affairs. (Hargreaves and Dauman, 1975, p. 39)

The above arguments are mainly prescriptive in their intent. Yet they provide a theoretical framework for understanding the modern era of corporate social responsibility in Britain. The hypothesis that is forwarded is very much in the tradition of American writings on the subject (Ackerman, 1975; Logsdon et al., 1990). The central claim of these writers is that interest in corporate responsibility is essentially symptomatic of commercial organisations responding to their social environment. These active responses are made in order to secure legitimacy and commercial success.

There may be some validity to the contingency view. When corporate responsibility came to the fore in Britain during the mid-1970s, there was a deep economic and industrial relations crisis. For the private sector, this crisis was exacerbated by the possibility of increased government scrutiny over commercial activities (see Chapter 3). But there are questions over whether these strategic responses by the business sector to wider social events sustained the expansion of corporate social responsibility throughout the 1980s. The contingency thesis is undoubtedly correct in its assertion that enterprises are required to modify and adapt, organisationally, to changes in society. Nonetheless, it is prone to conceptualising the relationship between society and business organisations in functionalist terms. Harvey *et al.* write as such:

> Corporations are treated as if they simply adapt to their 'environments', and writers try to relate corporate social responsibility mechanisms and responses to organisational characteristics and effectiveness with the apparent lack of appreciation of 'structural' conflicts of interest implied in their unitarist themes. (1984, p. 157)

The contingency view simplifies the agency of business organisations in society. Corporations, as organisational bodies, may be forced into adopting defensive strategies to external events. Yet these very same organisations — particularly large corporations that have extensive resources at their disposal — can assert their own interests with varying degrees of success, and negotiate with other institutions (Utton, 1982). This study attempts to go beyond this simplistic functional theory. The aim is to provide a fuller explanation of corporate philanthropy.

Corporate responsibility and philanthropy in and across capitalist societies

The emergence of corporate social responsibility can be explained by recourse to a socially informed analysis. This requires a sharper, more focused examination of the political and social circumstances that give rise to a general interest in corporate social activism. As part of this analytical strategy, a historical examination will be outlined. Chapters 2 and 3 trace the emergence of the modern capitalist economy in Britain and its influence on the social and philanthropic aspirations of commercial agents and institutions. In particular, these chapters focus on the emergence of large, corporate-owned, industrial conglomerates and their repercussions for philanthropic activities.

The 'modern era' of corporate social responsibility, dating from the mid-1970s onwards, introduces new factors for consideration. Most notably, these are concerned with the relationship between enterprises and other relevant institutional agents, especially the state. In Britain, such relations have played a key role in the ushering in the modern era. Owing to the concentration of the business sector in Britain, the government has traditionally established direct relations with commercial institutions. During the 1970s, this trend accelerated as both government departments and businesses made provision for closer relations (Grant, 1993). Closer ties between business and government, together with radical changes in the balance between private and public provision of social services, have been crucial. They have created greater awareness of corporate responsibility, and they have opened up opportunities for private intervention in areas of society dominated, since the Second World War, by public authorities.

Chapters 4 and 5 cover this analytical terrain in greater detail. Each chapter examines, in turn, those areas of society — urban and local economic renewal, and the environment — in which corporate social action has featured most prominently. These chapters demonstrate how close links between government and business established an institutional conduit for corporate social involvement. In addition, they also underline the way in which an explicit government agenda to expand the opportunities for business engagement in social policy had a crucial influence on key corporate players. Throughout the 1980s policy-makers adopted private sector mechanisms to organise the public services and to devise solutions for modern social problems (see Beck, 1983 for business influence on education reforms; and Strong and Robinson, 1990, pp. 22—6 for business contribution to NHS reforms). A related feature of these reforms was the emphasis placed on the private sector expertise in dealing with social problems and in developing public policy.

This sociological analysis of corporate social action shares certain parallels with Mintzberg's and Pettigrew's respective works on strategic organisational change. Their research has shown that fundamental or strategic change in the private sector is brought about by environmental events located externally to the organisation, such as national and global economic movements. This study places a similar emphasis on the significance of external developments. The argument followed is that political developments outside the business community were crucial in precipitating a movement of general interest in corporate social involvement during the 1980s. However, Pettigrew warns that emphasising the primacy of external or environmental forces in strategic change can lead to structural determinism. It is a position which neglects the contribution of individual intentional agents in deciding crucial strategic matters.

Any adequate framework for examining strategic change must include not only objective changes in economic and business forces, but the role of executive leadership and managerial action in intervening in the existing concepts of corporate strategy in the firm... .(Pettigrew, 1985, p. 453)

Similar analytical concerns apply to understanding how companies become involved in social action. While the political factors considered above are important, research should not ignore the action of key actors in companies and the cultures in which they operate. Such arguments are explored in case studies, found in Chapters 4 and 5, of the social programmes organised within BT, BAT Industries, Shell and Unilever. The studies show that key actors in these companies actively respond to external political developments. In so doing, they have a crucial and influential role in developing social programmes.

As already mentioned, the objective of this thesis is not simply to concentrate on Britain. It is also to examine corporate responsibility across societies by focusing on Italy. Some of the themes covered in the course of the first two sections, particularly the interface between external forces and internal agency within companies, will be critically examined in the context of Italy. Although there is a growing body of cross-cultural research on corporate social involvement (Dierkes, 1980; Rey, 1980; Farooq Khan and Atkinson, 1987; Orpen, 1987), very few have studied Italy (see Mauksch, 1982, ch. 5; Lentati, 1991). The objective of analysing corporate social involvement in Italy, and contrasting it with Britain, is to understand more fully part of the more structural argument at the centre of this study: that the general development of corporate philanthropy is contingent upon proximate social and political factors within society. Of special significance is the political status of the business sector and its relationship to government.

The dominant expressions of corporate philanthropy within a particular society are partly shaped by wider social, political and economic considerations. These factors, at the same time, are specific to that national configuration. However, the proclivity of recent academic research has been to overlook differences between capitalist states. Features of distinct societal entities have been subsumed under general movements in the global capitalist economy. One of the main underlying themes of the third section of our study is to assert the distinctiveness, particularly in terms of historical trajectory, of societal configurations. Global economic integration has undermined the autonomy of individual national societies. However, institutions and processes specific to particular societies continue to have an influence over the way capitalism operates in different regions. As argued by the likes of Worsley (1983), the distinct historical and political paths charted by societies should not be discounted — a salient point when trying to understand corporate-led social action in capitalist societies.

As part of this analytical objective, the historical origins of business philanthropy in Italy are examined (Chapter 6), and it is shown that traders and commercial institutions were active in the civic communities of pre-industrial Italy. The industrialisation of Italy, however, did not result in a greater expansion of industrial philanthropy, as happened in Britain. While some isolated instances of industrial philanthropy began to emerge in the early years of the twentieth century, as Italy's economic prospects improved, it was the state that played a central role in both the economy and society.

This sets the scene for the analysis in Chapter 7, which looks at the nature of modern corporate philanthropy. The main point here is this: because of various political and economic factors, state-owned corporations assumed a prominent role in Italian society during the early postwar period. These companies have been at the forefront of reforms and have brought social considerations into the commercial sphere. It is clear that the issue of corporate social responsibility has become dominated by public enterprises in Italy. Through economic and political mobilisation, the private sector commandeered a more prominent social position.

Unlike the situation in Britain, Italian philanthropic corporations operate in isolation with little support from within the business community or government. Despite this, the cause of preserving Italy's cultural heritage, as detailed in Chapter 8, has elicited active support from the business community. Such proactive intervention has come to resemble the development of corporate activism in Britain and America during the past 20 years. And it was management figures in companies such as Fiat and Olivetti who were prominent in developing notable private sector-led cultural programmes. Again, this underlines the fact that the actions and decisions of company actors should not be ignored.

A methodological framework

Theoretical discussions concerning the relationship between business and society have been in circulation since the 1950s. A corresponding body of empirical research on corporate social action and philanthropy has emerged only in recent years, with American academics leading the way. Much of this early research employed quantitative methodologies — mainly statistical forms of analysis and surveys (Post and Andrews, 1982).

Aldag and Bartol (1978) found that researchers working in a quantitative empirical tradition have utilised a variety of devices to measure business sensitivity towards social action and philanthropy. The measures included the following indices: responsiveness versus non-response to social surveys; proportion of lines in annual reports devoted to social responsibility; independent ratings of social responsiveness; and pollution ratings. Studies which have attempted to produce objective measures of social responsibility in this way demand some caution when it comes to interpreting their results (Aldag and

Bartol, 1978, p. 168) since these taken-for-granted measures are susceptible to the influence of other variables: they could be measuring activities other than corporate social responsibility. For instance, they could reflect a company's efforts to improve its image or attract ethically-conscious consumers.

Alternative methodologies have been put forward. Harvey *et al.* (1984) suggest that empirical research in this field should adopt a qualitative case study approach over survey research methodologies. Indeed, Post and Andrews (1982) note that quantitative analysis is still prevalent in corporation-society research. There is, nevertheless, an increasing number of qualitative-based studies that use the case approach, providing as it does a detailed examination of a limited number of instances concerning the area under study (see Shenfield, 1971; Neubeck, 1974; Ackerman, 1975; Merenda, 1981; Harvey *et al.*, 1984). This does not discount the utility of the survey approach which has produced important general findings about corporate social action in Britain (see Adams *et al.*, 1991). Increasingly, though, qualitative methodologies have gained prominence in this research field. For proponents, these are better able to deal with important questions about corporate social involvement and the many complex issues that are generated by this field.

These research activities have established a significant corpus of literature, demonstrating that research design determines areas and questions covered in the study of corporate responsibility. The number of companies included in the research, the type of organisations contacted in the course of the study and the choice of method to obtain empirical information all have an important bearing on the type of areas or issues that are examined.

There are two general objectives in this research. Firstly, one of the main preoccupations of this study is to analyse the social, politico-economic and historical factors responsible for shaping the dominant expressions of corporate philanthropy within Italian and British society. Secondly, the research, through a range of case studies, scrutinises the internal dynamics which lead companies to establish social programmes. Detailed analysis will also be made of the programmes developed by different corporations. This raises questions about the consequences of corporate social involvement for wider society.

In view of these objectives, the present research strategy deploys a hybrid methodology. It utilises a combination of primary sources, based around detailed case studies, and secondary material. The case studies are based on detailed examinations of the social and philanthropic activities of a limited number of companies, with extensive social and philanthropic commitments. This was mainly achieved by conducting in-depth interviews with a number of relevant personnel from each of the institutions chosen for the research (see the Appendix for further details). In addition, company literature relating to the field of corporate philanthropy was examined (see the bibliography of company documents). As

11

we have noted above, the advantage of such qualitative analysis over survey methods is that it furnishes detailed information about corporate social involvement. As such, it is better able to deal with some of the complex issues covered in the study.

The actual number of firms involved in the study was different for the British and Italian phases of the research. In order to furnish the qualitative evidence required for carrying out detailed case studies of company practices, much of the primary material for the British part of the research was based on four major British corporations: BAT Industries, British Telecommunications (hereafter, BT), Shell UK (hereafter, Shell), and Unilever (see the Appendix for a brief profile and an outline of the commercial activities of each company). The four organisations that agreed to participate in the research were all major British corporations. Each has distinct commercial activities, but these are mainly confined in the service and commodity industries. Since the early 1980s each of these companies has cultivated an active concern for corporate responsibility and, during this period, all four corporations have institutionalised social initiatives. Symptomatic of this was their formalisation of social and charity policies. For each institution, several managers and company personnel responsible for administering community affairs and social action programmes were contacted and interviewed.

The Italian phase of the research employed a similar methodology. However, the main difference was that the actual number of commercial organisations used was larger — around 24 in total. A larger company sample for the Italian case work was included to compensate for the dearth of primary and secondary information on corporate involvement. (Greater emphasis, though, was placed during the course of the research on the larger companies, such as Fiat, Olivetti, ENI and IRI.) In addition, a number of non-business organisations relevant to the area under study were contacted. Assembling primary evidence from a wide variety of sources helped create a general picture about the nature and incidence of corporate social involvement in Italy.

In the main, the companies represented in the study are among some of the largest enterprises in Europe. They have numerous operating concerns under their control and profits in the billions. This reflects the general development of corporate philanthropy in modern society. Research shows that larger firms are more likely than smaller firms to be actively involved in philanthropic and social action (Useem, 1987, p. 341). These findings reflect the fact that corporations have the financial wherewithal at their disposal to expend resources on social initiatives not directly related to commercial interests (Aldag and Bartol, 1978, p. 173). Furthermore, most of the companies included in the research, although spanning a variety of sectors, are broadly confined to the commodity or service industries rather than primary industries. Fry *et al.* (1982) note that the service sector is more likely to adopt social and charity giving programmes. The main reason suggested is that it has a higher level of contact with the public at large than primary industries.

Thus, from previous research (see Aldag and Bartol, 1978; Useem, 1987), the companies selected for the present study seem representative of those businesses which normally become embroiled in social action. It could be argued, however, that relying on detailed studies of a relatively small number of organisations does not provide a sound basis for making wider assertions or generalising on a broader range of cases. A number of strategies, though, can be used extrapolate broader assertions from the research material and to check the typicality of these detailed case studies (Hammersley, 1992).

A hybrid methodology is employed, whereby the empirical evidence is supplemented by a variety of other sources — historical studies, statistical information and existing research. This has made it easier to check and substantiate primary findings. In addition, secondary interviews were conducted, where possible, with representatives of non-profit-making organisations that had participated alongside sample companies on social projects or had been the beneficiaries of support. These interviews produced a more rounded array of views. They also provided a glimpse behind the information contained in official reports, leading to a more realistic assessment of the contributions made by businesses to social schemes.

Part One
A History of Corporate Philanthropy in Britain

2 The Early Foundations of Commercial Philanthropy

What follows is not intended to be a definitive or final authoritative history of business philanthropy in Britain. Histories are essential reconstructions (Tudor, 1989). This does not mean that any attempt to write a history of the said subject would inevitably be rendered too partial to have any analytical utility. Within the limitations of historical sources, the conditions and ideas that have guided business philanthropy throughout the ages can be examined. Such a history is required. Much of the literature on corporate social responsibility has characteristically lacked historical insight. The exception to this is a scattering of texts that have traced the development and expansion of business philanthropy in the United States (Walton, 1967, ch. 2; Handel, 1982, ch. 4; McCarthy, 1982; Bremmer, 1988, ch. 8; Dobkin Hall, 1989; Mitchell, 1989; see Cannon, 1992, ch. 2 for a British perspective).

Historical research is also useful in that it affords analytical depth: it establishes the basis for comparing the incidence and relative extent of corporate social involvement at distinct temporal junctures and, by implication, in different social settings. The historical analysis in this chapter focuses on the early origins of business philanthropy. It starts with the guilds of the Middle Ages, covers the philanthropists of late Victorian Britain, and ends in the post-Second World War period.

Business philanthropy during the Tudor and Elizabethan period centred around the endeavours of individual company owners, many of them inspired by religious doctrines. These religious influences, however, were by no means universal and were subject to modification over time. Indeed, after the seventeenth century, the rise of religious humanitarianism influenced the philanthropic activities of business owners. The point is that commercial philanthropy in this period was driven by a combination of social, economic and ideological factors which were encompassed in the responses of company owners to developments in wider society. Business leaders became prominent contributors to the private system of welfare — a system which was regarded, especially in the Victorian period, as the most acceptable way to tackle poverty. After the Industrial Revolution, reformers, including some notable industrialists, began to campaign for a statutory system of welfare provision, but it was not until the twentieth century that the public provision of welfare services became more comprehensively available. Hence, in the closing sections of this chapter, we explore how the development of public services helped redefine the social role of industrialists.

The guild system of the Middle Ages

Possibly the earliest historical recollection of commercial social involvement is the guild system of the Middle Ages. As a trade regulating body, the guild was not unique to medieval Europe; similar organisations existed in ancient Rome and Greece and on the continent of Asia. In Europe, though, the guild system was ubiquitous and the dominant institutional means for regulating trade.

The foremost organ of this system was the merchant guild. As a central association of town merchants, including artisans who sold their products directly, the merchant guild was granted monopoly powers over trading activities. This organisation appeared soon after the Norman Conquest and spread rapidly thereafter throughout England. The earliest known guild reference in a town charter is that of Burford (1087—1107). By the twelfth century, around 100 towns in England, and 70 in Ireland and Wales, had a merchant guild (Lipson, 1937). Originally the town burghers organised themselves into merchant guild associations, but membership was opened up to traders, even to those hailing from neighbouring towns.

The guild organisation was distinct from the municipal body, responsible for governing the town, raising taxes and devising legal regulations. The merchant guild, by contrast, under the auspices of municipal officers, presided over commercial activities within medieval town communities. To this end, it would systematise markets, fix prices and wages, arrange communal purchases, impose regulations over its members, collect tolls and discipline any violations of its regulations.

In addition to their commercial responsibilities, merchant guilds carried out a number of social functions: they organised relief for the poor, funerals, prison visits and care for the sick; their members also benefited from mutual assistance during times of adversity. This was an age when the Christian religion constituted an integral part of the social fabric. As such, guildsmen did not separate their commercial responsibilities from their religious and moral obligations towards the well-being of those around them.

If anything, the craft guilds showed an even greater commitment to charitable and religious activity. These were originally integrated within the merchant guild until they steered an independent course after the expansion of trade in the twelfth century. Many craft guilds began as religious fraternities, becoming involved in commerce only at a later date (Clune, 1943). Once engaged in commerce they acted as Christian-inspired mutual aid associations, mainly focusing on protecting wages and securing reasonable prices for commodities and materials. Apart from guaranteeing mutual assistance for members, the craft guilds handed out doles to needy inhabitants. In some instances, members were obliged to make weekly contributions for the relief of the poor. Other craft associations obtained funds through ad hoc tax measures. At Winchester, an officer was employed by the guild of St John to collect two handfuls of corn from every market trader as a way of funding care facilities for the poor (Clune, 1943, pp. 74—5). The craft guilds were also instrumental in founding alms-houses, schools and hospitals through bequests made by their members.

As part of their religious commitments, the merchant and craft guilds subjected their commercial and economic activities to rigorous moral scrutiny. Tawney describes how the subjective moral guidance of the guilds contrasts with the commercial strategies of modern enterprises:

> An age in which combinations are not tempted to pay lip-service to religion may do well to remember that the characteristic, after all, of the medieval gild [sic] was that, if it sprang from economic needs, it claimed, at least, to subordinate them to social interests, as conceived by men for whom the social and the spiritual were inextricably intertwined. (1984, p. 40)

Integral to this ethical exercise was the introduction of regulations to determine a just price for goods being sold by guild members. Hence, unrestrained free trade was regarded as being at variance with the interests of the community. Even so, competition was not suffocated by regulations or the monopoly position of guilds within local town economies (Clune, 1943). In several instances, traders outside the guild fraternity were given access to markets on major trade days. Moreover, if the guilds abused their monopoly privileges, the municipal authorities would import products, especially staple products such as food, from other localities.

Still, the strict regulations over trade provided a necessary bulwark against some of the commercial transgressions of the day. One notable misdemeanour concerned the artificial inflation of prices by manipulating the market. To prevent excessive increases, the merchant and craft guilds organised communal purchases of commodities to be sold off at fixed rates. In certain districts, the guild office held the exclusive right to deal in particular commodities. Any profits subsequently made found their way into the communal purse. Integral to this regulatory armoury was the payment of a toll by external traders. Indigenous town guildsmen had to scrutinise carefully the actual payment of tolls; it was a punishable offence — incurring a fine or even expulsion — for guildsmen to establish commercial relations with toll evaders (Clune, 1943).

The monopoly and regulatory powers of the guilds, used to effect moral trade relations, were not inviolable. By the 1300s the regulatory control enjoyed by the guilds over trade was beginning to diminish — a factor that led to the eventual dissolution of the guild system (Ashley, 1894).

The dissolution of these monopoly and regulatory powers can attributed to various factors. Commentators have blamed the expansion of parochial town economies after the twelfth century, when the protective barriers of town economies and the internal self-sufficiency of the guild system proved incompatible with the first stirrings of the modern economy, which required open markets and access to capital. There is some justification for this argument: the pressures building up against the guild system began to gain impetus between the fourteenth and fifteenth centuries. This was a period that coincided with a liberalised and expanded trade market. Such expansion struck at the heart of the intricate system of regulations presided over by the guilds. For instance, some towns passed special charters so that external traders could avoid toll payments and other restrictions.

The regulatory and administrative authority of the guilds was further undermined by the signing of trade agreements with foreign powers, the most prominent being the statute of Edward III in 1335, allowing foreign merchants to trade without restriction in England (Ashley, 1894, pp. 83—4). All these developments contributed to the breakdown of local economic regulations — the very *raison d'être* and source of authority for the guilds.

On a temporal scale, however, it would be a misplaced assumption to suggest that economic growth was directly responsible for the dissolution of these regulations. First, from the time it was instituted, the guild system had been subject to market pressures. Despite this, the system still maintained a pre-eminent role within the public arena up to the seventeenth century, since the authorities relied on guilds as sources of emergency taxation (Hickson and Thompson, 1991). Moreover, the livery companies of the City of London, which originated from the medieval guilds, continued to operate after the seventeenth century, mainly as charitable bodies (Ditchfield, 1904).

Undoubtedly, the penetration of local town economies by non-guild and foreign traders eroded the administrative and economic powers of guild organisations. But such economic explanations tend to neglect the importance of political developments: it was the wider transfer of economic power from the guild masters and journeymen to the new class of merchant entrepreneurs which

20

proved crucial. The ascendent merchant traders actively dismantled guild regulations and monopoly powers. Roll (1992, pp. 78—9) notes how joint-stock colonial companies deposed the original, guild-operated, export merchant companies. Furthermore, the specialised craft guilds were eventually usurped by embryonic commercial enterprises controlled by wholesale merchants and semi-industrial capitalists (Cunningham, 1922).

By attaining a secure foothold in the economy, this new socio-economic grouping was ideally placed to chip away at the regulatory powers of guild monopolies. A particular set of regulations that became the focus of entrepreneurial concern were those that existed to protect wage labourers, such the prohibiting of Sunday and night work. The first volume of Karl Marx's (1976) magnum opus, *Capital*, catalogues how industrial owners embarked on the task of stripping away these protective regulations, with the intention of intensifying the manufacturing process in order to maximise commercial returns.

As shown, the dominant model of business philanthropy in the Middle Ages was characterised by the collective intervention of traders and merchants. With the break-up of the guild system, this style of intervention was gradually transformed. The wealth generated by merchant activity created a class of independent traders who could adopt philanthropic causes on their own terms. In this respect, commercial philanthropy was transformed into a more individualised activity than it was under the guild system. Andrews comments with regard to this point:

> Wealthy individuals, too, were beginning to make their own gifts, for purposes of their own devising. As the individual became philanthropist, giving took on individuality — sometimes constructive, sometimes merely amusing. (1950, p. 37)

The merchant class and the relief of poverty

Merchants played a vital part in the economic and social affairs of pre-industrial society. They used the newly created wealth at their disposal for alms and other forms of poverty relief. These contributions, far from being marginal, carried some weight in a society experiencing increased vagrancy and deprivation.

One of the main causes of mendicancy in the pre-capitalist epoch of the sixteenth century was the commercialisation of agricultural production (Tawney, 1967). Under the monarchal system of medieval society, the lord would allow farmers to use his land as a way of building paternal ties with tenants (Birnie, 1955, p. 72). By contrast, much of the land freed after the confiscation of Church property during the Reformation was purchased by city merchants as a commercial investment. The rules of lucre that came to govern agriculture transformed the whole milieu of rural communities: the substitution of arable farming for the more profitable, but less labour-intensive, activity of sheep grazing resulted in wholesale evictions of tenants from their land (Birnie, 1955). These problems were exacerbated by general increases in farm rents. The only option for unemployed agricultural workers was to obtain employment in town areas; but the fledgling cotton industry of the town economies did not have the capacity to absorb rural migrants into the workforce (Ashley, 1914).

The emasculation of Church property during the Reformation undermined ecclesiastical programmes of poverty relief. Indeed, throughout the medieval period, Church institutions, especially the monasteries, failed to utilise the resources at their disposal for social purposes (Hartridge, 1930). Even though a number of poor laws were passed during the Elizabethan era (1561—1600), government measures against deprivation proved generally insufficient and sparingly enforced (Eden, 1928).

The impotence of both Church and government allowed private charity to become the dominant institutional vehicle for the provision of welfare and social security (Hartridge, 1930, p. 156). If the main contributors to private charity are broken down in terms of occupational status, the members of the emerging merchant class were among the foremost benefactors.

This assessment can be made with a degree of confidence because of the findings from Jordan's (1964) historical study concerning the incidence of giving by different social groups during the pre-industrial period. While not constituting a universal analysis of the subject, Jordan's survey of charitable giving from 1480 to 1660 is highly comprehensive. It examines the extent of charitable giving across ten of the major English counties at the time — Bristol, London, Yorkshire, Lancashire, Hampshire, Kent, Norfolk, Somerset, Worcestershire and Buckinghamshire. Using historical records originating from these ten counties, Jordan generated a sample of 34,963 donors, which collectively gave a total of £3,102,696 between 1480 and 1660. (Around 82 per cent of this total was generated by endowments.)

The main archival source for making these estimates were the wills left by donors. These gave an indication of charitable giving across the main social groups — yeomen, merchants, professionals, clergy — during this period (Jordan, 1964, ch. 2). The urban merchants constituted a small socio-economic group but it assumed much of the charitable burden in this period. The figures obtained by Jordan are self-explanatory. Included in the survey are 369 merchant donors whose estates can be accurately valued. This group gave away 17.25 per cent of its wealth to charitable causes, compared to the next highest of 7.12 per cent given by the upper gentry. The merchants constituted one-tenth of all sample donors, but their donations formed around 43 per cent of the total endowed by all the groups in Jordan's archival survey (Jordan, 1964, p. 349).

If we analyse the final destination of these donations, an influential pattern emerges. Jordan estimates that 40 per cent of merchant charitable giving from the sample was used to meet the needs of the poor. In contrast to previous ages, the merchants distanced themselves from direct almsgiving. Instead, greater deliberation was given to the benefactions that were made. Most of their charitable donations came in the form of large capital aggregates. These sums were carefully distributed to provide permanent welfare facilities for the most vulnerable groups in society. Facilities, such as hospitals, were also built for rehabilitating the poor. It could be said that merchant traders were responsible for some important advances in charitable action by the end of the Elizabethan period, the most conspicuous being the replacement of personalised almsgiving with endowments and long-term benefactions.

The commitment of this class to traditional religious causes proved less marked. Merchant giving for religious activities amounted to 13 per cent of the total benefactions furnished by this socio-economic grouping. This made the merchants the most secular category in the survey (Jordan, 1964, p. 387). By contrast, the conservative husbandmen dedicated 44 per cent of their benefactions to ecclesiastical purposes. Their benefactions suggested that the merchants were clearly distancing themselves from the established Church. Moreover, one of the few religious causes favoured by them was the funding of Puritan lectureships. As a sectarian religious group, the Puritans distrusted the ecclesiastical authorities of the realm.

If Weber's Protestant Ethic thesis is anything to go by, the active support of Puritan religious activities by merchants during the sixteenth and seventeenth centuries comes as no surprise. It was this strand of the Protestant faith that sanctioned both wealth creation and charitable action. The argument put forward by Weber is that Protestant doctrines, notably the concept of the calling (1985, ch. 3) and the Calvinist teaching of predestination (1985, ch. 4), exalted a diligent approach to work. These credos largely supported and provided some justificatory logic for the merchant lifestyle. At the same time, Protestant doctrines condemned the pursuit of wealth for its own sake and the enjoyment of possessions through luxurious living. Puritan religious ideals generated a conflict within the individual believer: it was perfectly legitimate to endeavour for material prosperity, but wealth was perceived to be a temptation (Weber, 1985, p. 172). Authors have pointed out that charitable activities provided a solution to this moral conundrum in that they demonstrated an individual's righteous stewardship over wealth (Handel, 1982).

During the seventeenth century, a considerable body of literature was produced, valorising the ideals of charity and benevolence (see Jordan, 1961, pp. 406—7). Moreover, the merchant class, as a relatively new socio-economic configuration, was uncertain of its status. Merchants thus relied on charitable activities to improve their social position. This might partly explain the significant charitable contribution made by this socio-economic group, outstripping, as Jordan demonstrated, the benefactions of other classes.

During the latter part of the seventeenth century, certain doctrinaire strains of the Protestant faith, such as Puritanism, began to wane as a religious force. However, business involvement in society and philanthropic action generally continued to flourish beyond this date. Private charity had expanded considerably and could not be easily dismantled. The growing influence of humanitarianism through all sections of society provided popular ideological support for private munificence. Humanitarianism, though inspired by religious convictions, assumed largely secular preoccupations: it encouraged individuals, particularly merchants, to empathise with suffering and poverty. The rise of humanitarian thought, thus, forms an integral part of philanthropic activities in the years leading to the Industrial Revolution.

The humanitarian impulse and business philanthropy

The declining influence of Puritanism and its replacement during the eighteenth century with humanitarian religious ideals had a profound affect on charitable aspirations. Humanitarian thought is viewed as diametrically opposed to the doctrinaire teachings of Calvinism. Closer scrutiny reveals that its origins can be traced within and not without the Protestant movement. In Weber's thesis, Protestantism declines as a result of the forces of secularisation and rationalisation after the eighteenth century, but historical evidence suggests that Weber failed to negotiate the development of Puritan thought after the seventeenth century (Campbell, 1987). In this period, sections within the Calvin-inspired Puritan movement reacted against some of the its strict doctrinaire excesses — particularly predestination. This largely undermined Puritanism as a force in society.

The first major break with Calvinism took place in the Puritan communities of Holland during the 1850s. In contrast to the previous doctrine, Arminianism advocated the notion of free will rather than predestination as the basis of salvation. The influence of this new doctrine went beyond Holland: by the mid-seventeenth century Arminian-inspired philosophy was widespread in England. Concerted opposition against Calvinism came from the influential liberal scholars of Emmanuel College, Cambridge, known as the Cambridge Platonists who, as indicated by their nomenclature, drew upon philosophical writings to construct an alternative theological doctrine to Calvinism. While they originated from a Puritan background and retained some of its moral earnestness, they rejected predestination, emphasising the goodwill, love and grace of God (Cragg, 1968).

What gave the Platonist theology popular credence, especially amongst the clergy, was its critique of the empiricist tradition, represented by the likes of Thomas Hobbes. Religious spokesmen stressed the ideas of morality and the inherent goodness of man against Hobbes's view of the egotistic individual driven by self-interest (Campbell, 1987). As Owen acknowledges, charitable effort in general took its cue from this ambiguous, yet simultaneously popular, ethic of Christian sentimentalism:

> Modern humanitarianism took its rise in the course of the century [seventeenth century], and the benevolence and sensibility associated with it, though sometimes no more than emotions which it was fashionable to display, had a good deal to do with forming the social temper of the time...Yet it is impossible to miss the compassion with which certain members of the middle and upper classes could view the misfortunes of the lower or to suspect the disinterestedness of their efforts to mitigate them. (1964, p. 14)

This new humanitarian sensibility was largely responsible for the most conspicuous achievements in philanthropy after the Restoration in 1660. A quintessential example of humanitarian ideals inspiring progress in charitable action was the hospital movement. Unlike the medical almshouses of the Middle Ages, the new medical institutions of the eighteenth century catered specifically for the sick and physically incapacitated. The clientele of these new hospitals consisted mainly of the burgeoning number of sick-poor located predominantly in urban centres. Here rapid population growth, coupled with poor sanitation, had resulted in the spread of epidemics and disease. Many of those responsible for establishing specialist infirmaries were religious-inspired humanitarians. Humanitarian clerics, such as Reverend Dr Alured Clarke of Winchester and the Reverend Philip Doddridge of Northampton, were responsible for new hospitals in their respective localities. In London, the five general hospitals established during the 1719—46 period allied humanitarian action to new methods of charitable fund-raising (Owen, 1964, pp. 39—40).

The prevailing orthodoxy in religious thinking and charitable action found some faithful adherents within the business community. While humanitarianism was undoubtedly a factor in the philanthropic activities of such entrepreneurs as Thomas Firmin, it was amongst the newly emerging group of textile manufacturers where humanitarian doctrines of philanthropy gained an important foothold. Quakerism, a humanitarian influenced denomination, was especially significant in this respect. As will be shown below, Quaker business leaders were responsible for some of the most extensive and generous demonstrations of philanthropy during this turbulent period of British history.

Humanitarian industrialists

Throughout this period of transition, disruption to the fabric of society was felt most keenly in urban centres. Even up to the mid-eighteenth century, the schisms generated by economic expansion were confined to a few city districts such as London and Bristol (Owen, 1964). The industrial age, as it was launched in the early nineteenth century, gave unrestrained momentum to the process of urbanisation. Many population centres experienced rapid growth, as sweeping labour migration from rural to urban districts progressed unremittingly. The population of greater London increased from just over 1 million in 1801 to over 5.5 million in 1891. Equally dramatic was Manchester: a population of 53,000 in 1801 increased to 505,000 by 1891; and Birmingham's population in the same period grew from 71,000 to 478,000 (Mitchell, 1988). The first report by the Registrar-General in 1839 provided statistical information on the life-chances of the new urban working class. The report estimated that, in the rural districts of Yorkshire, Durham and Cumberland, 204 out of 1,000 inhabitants reached the age of 70, whereas in urban centres like London, the figure stood at 104 individuals per 1,000; in Manchester it was 63, and in Birmingham the figure stood at 81 (Owen, 1964, p. 135).

Despite the deteriorating living conditions, authorities in early Victorian Britain continued to rely on private charity. Government intervention of any sort was treated with suspicion. The legislative measures that were made available proved unsatisfactory on the whole. For example, the Poor Law of 1834 placed resources in the agricultural south rather than in the urban regions. Whilst agricultural areas experienced mendicancy, with the advent of industrialisation, the most severe cases of pauperism had shifted to urban centres. Overall, only limited statutory protection and insurance to the poor was provided by the Poor Law. The Law was preoccupied with abolishing outdoor relief for the able-bodied as opposed to dealing with the true causes of poverty (Prochaska, 1988).

The reluctance of central government to make systematic provision for poverty relief helped stimulate private philanthropy (Prochaska, 1988, p. 35). A proliferation of charitable activity, whose temper was shaped by the repercussions of growing urban indigence, took place throughout the nineteenth century. Charitable initiatives assumed various imaginative forms (district nursing, orphanages, houses for the homeless, industrial schools) and covered a spectrum of social problems (child poverty, delinquency, illiteracy and unemployment). Such was the surge in philanthropy that the memoirist, Charles Greville, observed: 'We are just now overrun with philanthropy, and God knows where it will stop, or whither it will lead us' (quoted in Prochaska, 1988, p. 21).

Amidst this expansion of charitable activity, entrepreneurs built significant philanthropic reputations to rival their commercial achievements. Britain enjoyed several advantages — including the availability of investment capital, low transport costs, developing technical skills — that facilitated an early industrialisation of its economy, and a number of business owners managed to amass considerable fortunes (Supple, 1973).

The wealth generated by this process provided civically-minded business owners with the necessary wherewithal to fund magnanimous acts of charity. However, economic development was not in itself responsible for these philanthropic expressions. There were also ideological factors at work. In particular, humanitarian religious ideals, popularised by the reaction against Puritanism, had a profound bearing on philanthropists throughout the nineteenth century. These ideals were readily expressed by a number of new denominations, which emerged out of the Christian evangelical revival of the late eighteenth century. Many of these denominations viewed charitable involvement as a profound expression of faith.

Among the complex changes sweeping Britain in these years none was more important in its effects on philanthropy than religious revival. Christians of all denominations espoused charitable ideals…Some denominations were more active in philanthropic causes than others, and most had particular charitable interests growing out of doctrinal interpretation and social circumstances. (Prochaska, 1988, p. 21)

The revival of Christian worship, together with its effect on charity, was not lost on the emerging business community. Throughout the nineteenth and early twentieth centuries, the Quaker denomination, for instance, contained within its congregations some of the most celebrated industrial philanthropists of the age. This was not a coincidence. The social status of the Quaker sect, together with its unique beliefs, encouraged an ardent commitment among its members to the wider social good.

The founder of this idiosyncratic, Nonconformist, Christian denomination was the shoemaker George Fox, who hailed from a Puritan background. At twenty-three he began a concerted preaching campaign, and was able to gather around him a loyal band of followers. By 1650, the Society of Friends, scornfully known as the Quakers, was officially established under Fox's leadership. Although the Quakers adopted the Puritan traits of simplistic living and

27

frugality, their beliefs strayed towards the humanitarian end of the doctrinal spectrum. The Quakers stressed that believers could actively seek a relationship with God. Wagner notes: 'The central doctrine of the new movement was the belief that in every man there was the seed of God and that knowledge of God came through direct communication with his spirit' (1987, p. 38).

These doctrinal commitments, which saw them refusing to pay tithes, and their seemingly strange form of contemplative worship, turned the Quakers into pariahs. Most notably, they found themselves excluded from attending English universities and pursuing many distinguished professions. Consequently, the only viable livelihood left for them was the world of commerce. Their involvement in business passed through distinct phases. During the early years of the movement, from 1650 to 1700, Quakers showed a distinct tendency towards small-scale trading. In fact, most of the early Friends were drawn from the artisan workshops and yeoman farms. By the end of the seventeenth century, Quaker entrepreneurs headed the first technical and mechanical businesses (Wagner, 1987).

In all their business activities, the Quakers regarded wealth for its own sake as sinful. Because of this, they subjected their own commercial activities to rigorous moral scrutiny. Moreover, business activities were viewed as a form of service to the community whereby individual participants could earn a frugal living (Raistrick, 1993). Apart from running a business equitably and treating their customers fairly, Quaker businessmen were actively involved in the community through acts of charity and benevolence.

The Quaker businessman, Richard Reynolds, was one of the first individuals to finance philanthropic activities through the ownership of a heavy industrial company. From his background as the son of an iron merchant, Reynolds became a partner in an iron works near the Severn Valley, where revolutionary advances in iron production had been achieved. Much of his career was spent managing a furnace at Ketley, but, after the 1760s, the parent establishment at Coalbrookdale came under his auspices. Although heavy industry was potentially harmful to localities and the environment, Raistrick (1993) maintains that Reynolds presided over an enlightened company which dealt fairly with customers and workers.

As an impassioned Quaker, Reynolds was preoccupied by charitable action throughout his life. The objects of his benefactions included schools located near the work furnaces, and eventually in other parts of the country. On his relocation to Bristol in 1804, he virtually became a full-time philanthropist. In this new vocation, orphan asylums and almshouses benefited from his donations. Outside Bristol, Reynolds granted support to various metropolitan charities. One estimate has it that he was regularly distributing an average of £8,000 per annum — a substantial amount by early nineteenth century price indexes. Many commercial philanthropists, particularly those from the Quaker denomination, followed Reynolds's example throughout the nineteenth century.

By the Victorian period, the Quakers had given up their missionary zeal, becoming more introverted in the process. Their adherence to the strict obligation of marrying within the denomination isolated many Quakers, resulting in dramatic falls in membership. The Friends, nevertheless, continued to exert economic and political influence through successful and enlightened Quaker business owners, such as George Cadbury and Joseph Rowntree. One of the most important Quaker firms was the York-based grocery business under brothers Joseph and John Stevenson Rowntree. The Rowntrees were committed Quakers, but they questioned those doctrines responsible for isolating numerous members within the Quaker community. John Rowntree contended that the Quaker Church had become introverted at the expense of helping the poor in society.

The Rowntrees acted upon these liberal beliefs within their business. In the workplace, with Joseph at the helm, an enlightened programme of industrial welfare was established. This included relocating the company from the city centre to a greenfield site on the outskirts of York, the introduction of one of the first employee pension schemes, and the building of the New Earswick community to house employees. Indeed, throughout the century several enlightened employers had introduced welfare facilities within their factories and living residences for their workers (Niven, 1978; Joyce, 1982; Meakin, 1905). One of the first employers to establish staff residences was Robert Owen, the founding father of the cooperative movement, in New Lanark during the early nineteenth century (Lawrence, 1988). Owen's example was subsequently followed later in the century by William Lever at Port Sunlight (Jeremy, 1991), Titus Salt at Saltaire, George Cadbury at Bournville Village (Williams, 1931) and, of course, the Rowntree housing complex of New Earswick in York.

Quaker firms, such as Rowntrees, also looked to exercise their religious and humanitarian beliefs beyond the confines of the factory. Joseph Rowntree, the founder of the company, unwittingly built a reputation around his topical campaign for the amelioration of poverty. Initially, he went about this by collecting statistics about the incidence of poverty in his native York. This soon evolved into a personal campaign for concerted state intervention in tackling deprivation. Rowntree became dissatisfied with what he termed the 'charity of emotion' — a reactionary form of philanthropy that dealt only with superficial manifestations of social deprivation. To remedy this misplaced emphasis, Rowntree established three trusts in 1904, each with distinct aims (Owen, 1964, p. 450). The Joseph Rowntree Village Trust was to run the New Earswick complex and organise studies of housing conditions; the Joseph Rowntree Charitable Trust funded social research, Quaker projects and adult education;

and finally, the Joseph Rowntree Social Service Trust was used to fund social and political campaigns.

Victorian philanthropy: Nonconformist and Liberal credos

It would be a mistake to assume from the above that industrial philanthropy was the sole preserve of Quakers. Enlightened entrepreneurs from this age came from a diverse range of Nonconformist Christian backgrounds — Baptists, Congregationalists and Unitarians. In addition to these humanitarian denominations, business philanthropists were prompted to action by the dominant political values, which, during the Victorian era, were influenced by Liberalism. Free trade, social responsibility and the importance of self-improvement in relieving poverty were the central traits of the Liberal agenda.

> Victorian Liberalism stood for free trade, self-help, minimal government interference and internationalism — all values calculated to appeal to industrialists and employers. It also stood for generosity and tolerance, for democracy and popular representation and for radical social reform, carried out by public authorities if necessary but preferably by the spontaneous voluntary actions of individuals and communities. It stressed the moral responsibilities of those with wealth and power towards those without it and...it had a strongly redistributionist and egalitarian flavour. (Bradley, 1987, p. 5)

Typifying this nineteenth-century tradition of industrial philanthropy was Samuel Morley (1809—86), who headed the London and Nottingham-based hosiery firm J. & R. Morley. The company made the transition to factory production relatively early. At its height, J. & R. Morley had seven factories in the Midlands employing 7,000 workers, and it was this commercial expansion that allowed Morley to fund his philanthropic interests. Owen writes: 'If hosiery supplied the material for Samuel Morley's philanthropy, it was Nonconformity that largely prescribed the conditions of its expenditure' (1964, p. 403). As a committed Nonconformist, Morley saw philanthropy as a lifelong vocation.

The dissenting Church and Nonconformist reform activities were the main objects of his early benefactions. As a philanthropist, he liked to be intimately involved with his projects. One of his favoured methods was to provide struggling churches with incentives for raising money by agreeing to double the sums already collected. Overall, his giving to Nonconformism was consistently generous. Between 1864 and 1870 he put £15,000 into chapel building. He was also known for making spectacular one-off donations, such as the £5,000 that he bestowed for the purchase of Exeter Hall for the Young Men's Christian Association (Owen, 1964, p. 404). However, he did not give indiscriminately to the Church: he refused a request for a donation made by his local church on the grounds that the poor should take precedence (Hodder, 1887, p. 308).

Later in his career, Morley's philanthropic horizons broadened to include secular concerns. The most important cause to which he dedicated the last 20 years of his life was as a Liberal MP for Bristol. His political burdens led him to become an active supporter of free trade, the temperance lobby and the Financial Reform Association (Owen, 1964, pp. 404—5). Morley also supported the universities of Nottingham and Aberystwyth and the Old Vic during its incarnation as a working-class recreation centre. He approached these secular projects with the sort of purposeful attention reserved for benefactions to religious causes. As his biographer observes, Morley accorded to all these charitable commitments, whether secular or religious, the same importance as to his commercial activities (Hodder, 1887, p. 310).

Not all Victorian philanthropists were galvanised into civic action by a sense of religious obligation. For some industrialists, the Liberal sense of social responsibility was sufficient justification. To this secular category belonged a number of illustrious names: Thomas Holloway, who traded in medicines, financed the Royal Holloway College; the publisher Passmore Edwards was noted for establishing library facilities; and Josiah Mason, the manufacturer, championed the vulnerable in society. In contrast to Samuel Morley, Mason was resolute about his lack of faith (Bunce, 1882, p. 72) and became involved in charitable work at the end of his business career — running a pen and electroplating manufacturing enterprise. Mason limited his charities to children, the aged and higher education, financing — to the tune of £500,000 — the building of a small almshouse for aged women, an orphanage for girls, both located at Erdington, and Mason College which later became the University of Birmingham. Despite renouncing Christian ties, Mason's view of the steward-ship of wealth echoed the views of Christian humanitarians: 'The wealth he acquired was valued by him chiefly as the means of doing good on a great scale' (Bunce, 1882, p. 63).

The common thread running through the philanthropic efforts of these benevolent magnates was their concern regarding the impact of industry, whether in the workplace or in the surrounding community. The deleterious repercussions felt throughout society when Britain industrialised elicited magnanimous acts of benevolence from entrepreneurs and industrial owners. However, at the turn of the century, it became evident that welfare and social care facilities could not wholly depend on the contributions of private philanthropists. This resulted in a growing campaign to bring about concerted state intervention to alleviate poverty. These developments need to be scrutinised more closely because of their impact on business philanthropy in the twentieth century.

A question of public versus private welfare

The prevailing orthodoxy in Victorian Britain was for indigence to be viewed largely as the result of moral permissiveness. The task of ameliorating genuine poverty was seen as the responsibility of voluntary agencies, including industrial philanthropists. However, the spectacle of deprivation and hardship was the most powerful testimony against the pre-eminence bestowed on private charity as the purveyor of public welfare services.

The advancement of social policy research and statistical surveys on the incidence of poverty carried some import in bringing the extent of deprivation in society to public attention. Not all these studies originated from officially sponsored bodies. Socially aware business owners made pioneering and highly informative contributions to the study of poverty. The shipowner, Charles Booth, carried out a paradigmatic inquiry into the extent of poverty in London. The final study, *Life and Labour of the People in London* (1902—1903), spanning a mammoth 17 volumes, concluded that 30 per cent of Londoners were existing below a bare level of subsistence. In the course of his research, Booth suggested that, to eradicate poverty, the state should make greater provision for the poor and the elderly.

Booth's observations about the appalling living conditions of the working population were confirmed by Seebohm Rowntree in his seminal study, *Poverty: a Study of Town Life* (1922). Using statistics collected by his father Joseph, Seebohm Rowntree estimated that 15 per cent of York's wage earners could be legitimately classified as belonging to the ranks of the primary poor. Significantly, Rowntree's research was used by Beveridge to calculate subsistence standards for his final report on the establishment of a nationwide public welfare system.

In addition to the growing number of studies on poverty, the system of private philanthropy was increasingly shown to be unreliable. This applied particularly to commercially funded charities. The ability of companies to provide lasting solutions to the problem of industrial poverty was circumscribed by the fact that not all company owners or industrialists showed the same willingness to release their wealth for charitable purposes. In a moment of Victorian nostalgia, Harrison writes:

> If the Cadburys and Rowntrees had been more widely imitated, public welfare in Britain — instead of being financed through compulsory taxation

— might have been voluntarily conceded, and channelled by the employer through the wage packet, with all the consequences for industrial relations flowing from that. (1982, pp. 220—1)

By and large, charitable action in the business community, like philanthropic action in general, was confined to a limited number of entrepreneurs. Hodder acknowledges this: 'Lord Shaftesbury was wont to say that the great givers of London could be enumerated on the fingers of both hands, and that every subscription list was a proposition of another' (1887, p. 301). Moreover, as a system dependent on the whims and fancies of individual donors, whether business owners or private benefactors, incoming financial resources for charities were too variable and inconsistent over time to provide comprehensive protection against poverty. For example, the city of Liverpool between 1905 and 1920 saw a near trebling of its charitable income, because of the dramatic increase of benefactions made through legacies. However, such gifts proved a less stable form of charitable giving than subscriptions. Hence, the distribution of finances among agencies was uneven, and there were considerable fluctuations from year to year (Owen, 1964, p. 467).

Added to the problems over resources was the inconsistent behaviour of certain business philanthropists. In the harsh social world of the nineteenth century, some benevolent entrepreneurs would discredit their own philanthropies by committing major indiscretions. The *Northern Star* ran a report in 1842 disclosing that employers were funding philanthropic activities by deliberately underpaying their employees (Harrison, 1982). The nineteenth century Chartist, George Harney, was aware of the contradictions inherent in the world of business philanthropy:

I discovered that a good many manufacturing 'philanthropists', whose sympathies had been enlisted on the side of the negroes, had been quite oblivious to the sufferings of women and children in their own factories, and had opposed...champions of the factory workers...to redeem the white slaves of England from what was, in some respects, worse than Jamaica or Barbados slavery. (*Newcastle Weekly Chronicle*, 15 November 1890, quoted in Schoyen, 1958, p. 8)

In a similar vein, Keir Hardie, during the 1890s, mounted a concerted attack against what he saw as the hypocrisy of Lord Overtoun, the Scottish industrialist and Liberal. The Labour MP revealed that Overtoun, who was apt to publicise his philanthropic achievements, subjected his employers at the Sawfield chemical factory to labour for 12 hours a day, seven days a week, without meal breaks.

For Hardie, Overtoun's life was the manifestation of 'a living lie' (Benn, 1992, p. 138).

The obvious shortcomings of relying on private charity or employers as the primary means of poverty relief made the cause for systematic public intervention more resounding. Throughout the nineteenth century, state intervention of any sort was distrusted. Nevertheless, the idea of government provision within the ambit of social welfare was given an important fillip by the embryonic legislative forays of local municipal authorities. The 1835—88 period constituted a veritable municipal revolution. The legislative overhaul of local government facilitated the movement towards extensive statutory services. The Public Health Act (1872) created local statutory authorities to inject a degree of uniformity into the system of public health administration.

The increasing contribution of municipal authorities to poverty relief was the result of Victorian pragmatism rather than a commitment to redistribution. There were local councils that found themselves forced into taking responsibility for welfare services by public opinion, which included the views of local magnates. By the end of the 1860s, the local council in Bristol was pressurised to intervene on behalf of the city's poor by the local business families, Frys and Wills (chocolate and tobacco producers respectively). These demands came after they had observed for themselves the living conditions of the poor in their missionary ventures among such groups (see Frazer, 1979, p. 118).

The incidence of high unemployment in the late nineteenth century once again called upon the pragmatic tendencies of Victorian authorities to intervene in society. The depression years of the 1880s and 1890s challenged the dominant assumption that poverty was simply the product of individual malaise. It was a heartless and exceptional person who suggested that the jobless poor were morally culpable for their predicament. The Liberal Joseph Chamberlain was one of the first politicians to organise government support for the unemployed. In a circular released in 1886, Chamberlain authorised local councils to provide work for the unemployed (Birch, 1974). However, the prescription was not enforced because Chamberlain only remained in government for three months following an electoral defeat.

Despite this set-back, the movement towards a state organised and funded welfare system at the turn of the twentieth century gained further momentum. This gradually helped dislodge the emphasis on voluntary modes of poverty relief, such as those provided by charities or commercial benefactors. The main legislative provisions in this period were preoccupied with the problem of unemployment. One notable achievement was the Liberal government's introduction of the National Health Insurance Act (1911). The measure insured against the loss of health and covered subsequent treatment of any sickness for employees. During the interwar period, social welfare was still largely selective and privately operated. With unemployment in the 1930s reaching the 3 million mark, the Labour government eradicated the Poor Law, introducing supplementary aid for the unemployed.

Ultimately it was the experience of the Second World War that brought Britain nearer to a national system of welfare (Birch, 1974). Using the report by the Interdepartmental Committee on Social Insurance as its blueprint, the Labour administration introduced a series of welfare reforms that formed part of a national system of social and welfare provision. At the heart of the postwar welfare reforms was the National Health Service Act and the National Insurance Act, both passed in 1946. The former created a comprehensive system of health care without charge, while the latter established a unified insurance scheme. Further legislative measures paved the way for a nationwide system of care and assistance: the Children's Act (1948) provided services for children without a proper home life; the National Assistance Act (1948) filled the gaps in the Insurance Act; and the earlier Education Act (1944) extended secondary schooling (King, 1987, pp. 52—3).

Generally, the introduction of the welfare state rendered the voluntary sector peripheral to the state services. On closer inspection, however, the voluntary sector was not superfluous in the postwar era and, in fact, continued to flourish after the establishment of the welfare state, as shown by Green and Murphy (1954) in an early postwar study of charities. Prochaska writes:

Though little reported, voluntary traditions carried on with considerable vigour after 1945, shifting ground where necessary and pioneering terrain which the state dared not enter. Moreover, a concentration of attention on those charities fulfilling welfare services obscured the many other voluntary campaigns which prospered. (1988, pp. 1—2)

This suggests that there were still opportunities for enlightened business owners and industrialists to support social projects. Indeed, during the early part of the twentieth century, there is evidence of commercial benefactors adopting social causes that were not directly covered by the state sector. Religious doctrine came to exercise less of an influence, as did the individual business owner, in philanthropic activities. In fact, throughout the twentieth century, especially in the post-Second World War period, the nature and extent of business involvement in the non-profit sector was influenced by developments in the structure of business ownership. The aim of the next chapter is to explore these developments further.

3 The New Corporations and their Responsibilities

The development of a comprehensive system of public welfare meant that business owners came to play a marginal role in basic social services. While the government assumed a dominant position in social welfare, it did not prevent enlightened business leaders from contributing to the well-being of wider society. The voluntary sector continued to grow and devise important innovations, even though certain welfare functions had been colonised by the state.

The aim of the first half of this chapter is to explore the nature and extent of philanthropic action by business owners and industrialists from the late nineteenth century onwards. The contention is that business philanthropy was shaped by the new structure of proprietorship that was coming to the fore in the twentieth century: namely, the emergence of the oligopolistic commercial organisation under the impersonal proprietorship of shareholders. For some analysts, this emerging structure began to separate the close umbilical links between ownership and control of business enterprises. This helped create a non-sectional managerial class, sensitive to the needs of society. Historically, the development of capital during this period did not produce the type of humanitarian business organisation postulated by certain managerial theorists. If anything, business enterprises became more commercially focused.

During the mid-1970s, however, there was a discernable growth of interest in corporate social responsibility, continuing throughout the 1980s. Such developments are explained in terms of social and political processes which transformed the relationship between business and government.

The beginnings of the corporate economy and enlightened businesses

The growth of the modern corporate economy is normally traced back to industrialisation. Equating both processes in Britain is not straightforward:

36

industrialisation did not automatically require or lead to the wide-scale formation of oligopolistic enterprises (Hannah, 1983). Initially, industrial expansion was isolated to specific areas of the economy. The first sector to capitalise on new machine technology and steam power was the textile industry. These innovations transformed textile production from a domestic craft industry into a highly intensive, factory-based form of production. The rapidity of this transformation proved phenomenal. Between 1858 and 1861 the number of power looms in Britain rose from 298,847 to 399,992 (Marx, 1976, p. 561). The expansion of textile companies did not lead immediately to a monopoly control. This scenario was avoided because the expansion of textile firms was matched by further market expansion which allowed small-scale specialisation, both on a commodity and geographical basis, to take place. Similar patterns of development in other traditional industries — pottery, brewing, chemicals, iron smelting — occurred as technological innovations enabled companies to produce for a mass market at a profit.

These new forms of technology and the larger number of employees needed to operate machine units necessitated higher levels of financial investment. The levels required went beyond the capacity of traditional resources, such as family wealth or yearly profit margins. Industrial owners encountered considerable difficulties in trying to attract external investors. The Stock Exchange, in the early nineteenth century, lacked dynamism and there was no national legislative framework covering joint-stock ownership. This legal void was rectified in the 1844—62 period, as legislation sanctioned the formation of joint-stock and limited liability companies. This is not to say that joint-stock commercial entities did not exist before the mid-1800s. The distinctive feature of this legislative foray, according to Penrose, was that it 'removed the most important limitation on the growth and ultimate size of the business firm when it destroyed the connection between the extent and nature of a firm's operations and the personal financial position of the owners' (1968, p. 6). The actual funding of a business was rendered more equitable and attractive. Shareholders were now liable for company debts according to the size of their holding.

Legal provision for joint-stock ownership and limited liability was in place by the mid-1800s. Yet the expected growth in the size of businesses was delayed. It was common for existing company owners to adopt private registration, whereby limited liability was assumed whilst the original owners retained control. This development, in Payne's words, amounted to a 'fearful and hesitant' step towards larger business organisations (1967, p. 520). Matters began to change, however, at the turn of the century when a whole spate of new limited liability firms emerged: for instance, during the 1898—1900 period, 650 firms, valued at £42 million, were absorbed in 198 separate mergers (Hannah,

1983, p. 21). Hart and Prais (1956) observe that a fully conscious and deliberate movement towards amalgamation took place in the heavy industrial sector.

The merger movement in this period did not result in levels of industrial and capital concentration comparable to that of Britain's foreign competitors. As a number of commentators have noted, at the turn of the century, the most important areas of the American economy were under the auspices of large industrial combines (see Mitchell, 1989). One of the obstacles that stood in the way of wider corporate growth in Britain was the disinclination of individual owners to sell their companies (Payne, 1967, p. 526), although this is not to deny the impact of the merger wave at the turn of the century. However, industrial concentration was mainly confined to heavy industry, whereas in America concentration covered a wider constituency of business sectors (Hannah, 1983, p. 22).

Efforts to overcome this reluctance to expand gained momentum during the interwar years. The industrial practices introduced throughout the First World War challenged the dominance of the family-owned enterprise, paving the way for the wider expansion of commercial and industrial enterprises. Furthermore, the government, through the Ministry of Munitions, made unprecedented strides to intervene in the economy and the manufacturing process. Among its many influential recommendations, the Ministry discouraged industrialists from product diversification. It promoted, instead, the mass production of commodities and the amalgamation of enterprises to meet government munition targets.

Attempts to rationalise industrial units continued after the war with the onset of recession and high unemployment. By the early 1920s the joint-stock enterprise had turned into a generalised feature of the economy (Tawney, 1920). Increasingly, family owners were opting to sell their businesses to other quoted companies or to float them directly on the issues market. In addition, direct competition from large and technologically advanced foreign (mainly American and German) combines forced business owners into forming defensive amalgamations within their sector groupings. I. G. Farben's attempt to acquire British Dyestuffs propelled three of Britain's foremost chemical businesses to combine forces, resulting in the formation of the ICI company.

Banks and financial houses that had invested in British industry exerted intense pressure for industrial expansion. In 1929 the Bank of England established the Bankers' Industrial Development Company (BIDC) as a formal financial agency to promote rationalisation within the industrial sphere. A major achievement of the BIDC's work was the formation of the Lancashire Cotton Corporation. This new textile holding company absorbed almost 100 separate firms, occasionally under duress, between 1923 and 1932.

The changing face of ownership during the interwar years was indicated by the increased number of firms quoted on the Stock Exchange: in 1907 there were 569 domestic manufacturing and distribution firms quoted on the London Stock Exchange; by 1924 the number had risen to 719 and in 1939 the figure stood at 1,712 quoted companies (Hannah, 1983, p. 61). A number of family businesses used investment from the securities market to expand their operations enormously during this period. In 1919, 30 years after being floated on to the stock market, the textile company, J. and P. Coats, was one of the first family enterprises to achieve corporate status (Hannah, 1983). Ten years later, it was being joined by the likes of Unilever, Imperial Tobacco, ICI, Courtaulds and Guinness. Although large commercial entities had existed before the 1920s, the interwar merger movement covered a wider range of industrial sectors. Acknowledging this point, Scott writes: 'By the Second World War "big business" was a more diverse, and more powerful, sector of activity, and it was increasingly determining the conditions under which smaller enterprises had to operate' (1985, p. 200).

This restructuring inevitably affected the strategies of capitalist enterprises. Saliently, the remodelling of company structures established new sectional interests and constitutional frameworks. These contributed to a redefinition of the social expectations of business in modern society.

For shareholder-owned companies that were gaining prominence during these years, philanthropy and charitable giving was rendered problematic. Directors of a joint-stock enterprise, unlike the owners of a small family company, were not in a position to expend shareholder resources on non-commercial activities, such as philanthropy. There are records of shareholders taking legal action against executives who had used the funds for charitable purposes. Although the actual litigations were few in number, they demonstrated that shareholder-owned entities were problematic for business philanthropy.

Taunton v. Royal Insurance Co. (1864) was one of the earliest legal cases regarding the discretion of executives to support philanthropic causes. The action was brought before the court by a shareholder who objected to the directors offering compensation for houses damaged by a gunpowder explosion on board a vessel. The point of contention was that the insurance policy did not compel the company to compensate for these losses. The court intervened to prevent the expenditure of these funds for purposes not related to the interests of the company, but stated, nevertheless, that directors should not, on the whole, be prevented from making gratuitous payments to their customers, especially when such payments would enhance a company's reputation (Sheikh, 1990). In the *Hutton v. West Cork Railway Company* lawsuit of 1883, an early legal precedent was established over whether directors could utilise finances for non-commercial purposes. The case was specifically brought to decide whether a company had the mandate 'to expend a portion of its funds in gratuities to servants or directors...' (*Law Reports*, 1883, p. 654). In his summary, Lord

Justice Bowen maintained that charity is not the responsibility of business. Philanthropy and charitable donations, however, could be justified providing they are, in some way, congruent with commercial interests.

Although this ruling established strictures for philanthropic activities, industrialists and company owners continued to make benefactions throughout the early twentieth century. Historical evidence shows that modern joint-stock companies were not indifferent to the needs of society. A report presented to the House of Commons in 1909 on the charitable contributions of railway companies in 1908 is revealing. It demonstrates that some of the new industrial corporations appearing at the turn of the century supported a variety of mainly secular welfare and social causes. The most favoured areas included hospitals, which gained £7,699, schools and technical institutions which were given £1,107, and benevolent societies which were granted £1,051 (Board of Trade, 1909, p. 19).

The continuation of philanthropic activity can be explained in various ways. One factor is that the shareholder-owned firm did not develop into a generalised phenomenon until the interwar period — the majority of companies were owned outright by individuals or families up to this date. Consequently, industrialists and company owners could pursue their charitable aspirations without the prospect of shareholder opposition or court interference. Furthermore, modern philanthropy edged towards the parameters established by the *Hutton* case. Here, emphasis was placed on making philanthropic action relevant to the interests of the commercial benefactor. For shareholders, this would be deemed more acceptable than straightforward charity. One prominent cause seen to embrace both motives of charity and self-interest was education, especially technical and higher education.

Industrialists, corporations and university education

Towards the end of the nineteenth century, the university system in England expanded from the ancient cloisters of Oxbridge to several metropolitan centres. In this period, no less than ten new university colleges were formed to provide undergraduate studies up to degree level. The origins of provincial universities such as Manchester (1851), Leeds (1874), and Reading (1892) could be traced to local medical schools, colleges for technical training and university extension classes (Evans, 1975, p. 247). A number of industrialists participated in the provincial university movement as a response to the perceived chasm between the scholastic field and the requirements of industry (Armytage, 1955). While the efforts made by local authorities to promote higher education should not be overlooked, the university movement at this early stage had not gained the full attention of public authorities. This, in turn, gave local business owners the latitude to assume a pioneering role in the provincial university movement. Many of these industrial leaders felt excluded, on cultural and religious grounds, from the elitist enclaves of Oxbridge (Owen, 1964). To combat the exclusivity of the ancient universities, local industrialists attempted to promote educational institutions that would be both progressive and relevant.

The University of Sheffield is a typical example. The university began life as Firth College in 1879, the brainchild of a local manufacturer, Mark Firth. Firth had already recorded some conspicuous philanthropic achievements: 36 almshouses and a college for the training of Methodist ministers were singlehandedly endowed prior to his involvement with the university. Firth's interest in building a higher education college was stimulated during a course of university extension lectures given between 1875 and 1877. In response, he bought some land and constructed a building at a cost of £20,000. His untimely death in 1880 did not bring the work that had been initiated to a premature end: in 1905 the college was officially named the University of Sheffield. Even without Firth's contributions, financial support was forthcoming. The largest donations, during the interwar period came from Sheffield's business leaders and local firms. Chapman's (1955) statistical analysis reveals the extent of business contributions to the university: between 1902 and 1920 Vickers Ltd made contributions amounting to £16,979; from 1920 to 1948 the United Steel Companies Ltd made donations totalling £30,400; its counterpart, the English Steel Corporation, gave £2,500 to the building fund in 1936 and £22,400 to the development fund in 1947; and, finally, the Staveley Coal and Iron Co. donated £50,000 towards chemical research laboratories.

Business leaders and enterprises were found to be active at every stage of the process in the establishment of Leeds University. One historical account of the university revealed that, from the turn of the century to around 1950, the university managed to attract the support of over 40 companies (Brown, 1953, pp. 36—7). Members of the Yorkshire business establishment not only provided financial assistance, but also actively participated in the university's administration. For example, the Tetleys, one of Yorkshire's better known commercial families, contributed to the long-term development of the university. Dr Charles Tetley was a life governor of the university and a member of its council from 1904 until his death in 1934. His concern for student welfare led him to contribute towards the building of a sports hall. Shimmin observes that the Tetleys' 'help belongs in the main to a period when public grants were very limited and it was a courageous thing to help University education and to invite others to do the same' (1954, p. 104).

A number of individuals with business and industrial backgrounds contributed to Leeds University's progress without taking up official posts. Lord Brotherton, an important figure in the British chemicals industry, contributed £220,000 and his company made a donation of £39,000. The merchant tailor, Sir Montague Burton, endowed a chair of industrial relations (Owen, 1964, p. 366). However, it would be wrong to assume that it was solely eminent industrialists or the representatives of large enterprises that dominated the private sector's contribution to the university. When an appeal was made in 1925, the £500,000 generated over four years included donations from smaller companies in textiles, mining, agriculture, engineering, chemicals and leather.

In the modern business environment, the benefactions furnished by firms to higher educational institutions could not be made dispassionately. There had to be some return (Shimmin, 1954). For philanthropically inclined corporations, financial contributions made to higher education seemed to traverse the divide between social goals and commercial interests. This was confirmed by the *Evans v. Brunner Mond* (1921) case. The action was brought by a disgruntled shareholder who attempted to obtain a court injunction to stop his company from distributing £100,000 to various universities and scientific bodies. In the end, it was decided that using the sum to sponsor education and scientific research was the most advantageous way in which corporate funds could be expended for non-commercial purposes (Sheikh, 1990).

The funding of research in general stood out as an educational activity in which business leaders recognised a direct benefit. With Leeds University, local businesses consistently provided research grants and facilities. There were numerous instances of such benefactions: the ICI company from 1945 to 1954 gave around £78,000 towards research fellowships and additional funds for departmental equipment. The textile industry, a mainstay of the Yorkshire industrial economy, was a staunch supporter of research. The Wool Industry Surplus Cloth Corporation endowed a chair in textile engineering. The International Wool Secretariat gave around £60,000 towards equipment and research for textile departments. In a different, yet traditional Yorkshire industry, the West Yorkshire Coal Owners Association donated £60,000 for the study of coalmining (Shimmin, 1954, pp. 109—10).

The active presence of business interests was a distinctive feature of the history of Leeds University. Yet, from 1905 onwards, the university came increasingly under the administrative aegis of Leeds Education Authority. For its own financial well-being, it also became reliant on Treasury grants — a symptom of the burgeoning presence of public agencies in the affairs of society generally (see Chapter 2). The constituent elements of the university's income, when broken down in percentage terms, reinforce these observations: for the 1903—4 academic year, Treasury grants constituted 10 per cent of the university's income, fees 39 per cent, local authority grants 25 per cent, and other income 26 per cent, including business donations. By 1952, the corresponding figures showed a number of changes: Treasury grants had risen to 69 per cent, fees had fallen to 14 per cent, local authority grants to 5 per cent, and business gifts to 12 per cent (Shimmin, 1954, p. 214).

The growing importance exercised by public funds was not unique to Leeds University. Much of the increasing public involvement in higher education was directed towards the expansion of the whole system, necessitated by the growth of statutory education after 1945 (Sanderson, 1972). Hence, higher education now depends on public resources and intervention. While industry no longer has a central, innovatory part to play in universities, it continues to fund research not only in technical and scientific areas, but also in the field of management studies.

The modern corporate economy

With the end of the Second World War, Britain's political leadership undertook the task of rebuilding British society along social-democratic principles. There was bipartisan agreement in Parliament over the need for concerted state intervention in the economy to achieve full employment and maintain a comprehensive welfare system (see Chapter 2).

The changing nature of postwar society reverberated in the business sector. During these years, major companies consolidated the rationalisation of their organisational structures. This led to an intensification of the expansionary trends that had taken place within Britain's major industries during the years leading up to the Second World War. But what made the postwar rationalisation movement distinct was the involvement of financial institutions as both investors and shareowners in private companies.

Like the industrial sector, financial institutions had experienced a merger wave through joint ventures and take over bids. Such concentration enhanced the ability of these financial institutions to exert an influence over external investments. Aaronovitch (1955) provides statistical data revealing the extent of financial concentration. The 1890—1920 period saw a reduction in the number of deposit banks from 104 to 20 (1955, p. 47). By 1951, five banks held 86 per cent of the total deposits and current accounts. Alongside deposit banks, insurance firms also grew in stature: between 1913 and 1951 their assets increased seven times, from £550 million to £3,500 million. These assets came under the aegis of a limited number of companies. Thus, by 1951 11 organisations controlled half the assets outlined above, and one-sixth of the total was owned by the Prudential insurance company (Aaronovitch, 1955, pp. 47—8). This powerful financial bloc developed into a prominent supplier of investment capital to industry and commerce. Indeed, financial houses bought shares and placed their own representatives on the company boards where they had financial stakes. Scott estimates that the proportion of shares held by families and individuals declined from 65 per cent in 1957 to 28 per cent in 1981. During the corresponding period, the holdings for financial institutions increased from 21 per cent to 57 per cent (1985, p. 78). Financial institutions cultivated networks both in other financial houses and in industrial complexes to retain strategic control over their investments.

How did the growth of business enterprises influence the philanthropic contribution of the commercial sector? This is pertinent issue and one that will be considered in the next section.

Corporate social action in postwar society

The oligopolistic corporation in the postwar era came to be the dominant economic institution in many Western capitalist nations. It presided over the most critical areas of the economy. As noted in Chapter 1, several American social scientists made particular extrapolations about the emergence of corporate ownership. They noted that the postwar expansion of businesses, and the concomitant increase of minority share ownership, abrogated the links between the ownership and control of capital. For some writers, the separation brought managerial specialists to the helm of modern companies. These specialists were not shackled to class interest groups and thus aspired to ideals of social responsibility (see Chapter 1).

In the heady days of the postwar economic boom and early years of the welfare state, the managerial thesis, on the surface, seemed to have credence. On closer inspection, many of its claims are questionable. Assumptions that new forms of ownership instilled a concern with broader social responsibilities has not been substantiated by historical evidence.

One of the few British academics to test these claims was Theo Nichols (1969). Industrial and company managers were endeavouring, as claimed by managerial theorists, to render companies accountable and responsible to society. In a study of businessmen from 'Northern City', Nichols scrutinised many of the themes relating to the managerial hypothesis — business ideology, ownership and control and corporate social responsibility. The study was based on a survey of 65 business managers selected from 15 companies based in 'Northern City'. Nichols found that the sample of businessmen were motivated more by long-term company interests than by social responsibility and concluded that 'the conception of social responsibility held by most Northern City businessmen was some distance removed from that advocated or implied in much of the management literature' (1969, p. 239). The sample of businessmen obtained from 'Northern City' was not entirely representative of private sector managers in this period. At the same time, Nichols's findings have some credence in that modern-day businesses have not wholeheartedly aspired to social and political goals as envisaged by some managerial thinkers.

The erroneous assertions made Kaysen, Berle, Bell and other managerial theorists concerning the emergence of ethically motivated companies derive from this: their lack of real insight into the nature of modern capital ownership. Recent studies of ownership patterns in Britain and America have shown that capital is not strictly under managerial control (Scott, 1985, 1986). The modern corporation, like its family-based predecessor, is still owner-controlled. However, the owners have changed. Most companies are controlled through what John Scott terms a 'constellation of interests'. The constellation has increasingly come to include institutional shareholders and financial intermediaries. This development has had portentous implications for industrial and commercial philanthropy.

The expansion of businesses after the Second World War, and the presence of powerful financial interests in this sector, only served to restrict the opportunities for philanthropic involvement. A survey of charitable donations in 1964 found that larger companies were likely to give away a smaller percentage of their pre-tax profits than their medium-sized counterparts (Shenfield, 1969). From a sample of 442 firms, the largest institutions gave 0.12 per cent of their profits to charity. Middle-range firms, by contrast, gave 0.25 per cent. This was confirmed by American research. Green, from analysing company contributions according to company size in 1968, notes that 'the larger a company becomes, the lower its contributions as a percent of net income' (1973, p. 57n.). Prominent voluntary leaders, commenting in *The Times*, claimed that business expansion had contributed directly to the decline in company giving: 'The national trend of business mergers, reducing the number of local businessmen accustomed to supporting the charities of their district, has left a serious gap' (*The Times*, 1968, p. 2).

Modern corporations, however, did not disregard socially responsible activities *tout court*. Undoubtedly, the legal ownership claims of individual and institutional shareholders established well defined parameters for corporate giving to charity. But within these legal and financial limits, companies still reserved funds for charitable causes and voluntary organisations. Indeed, the 1962 Jenkins Committee on Company Law Reform asserted that directors should be able to make charitable donations without the threat of court action. These contributions were justifiable, argued the Committee, because they preserved a sense of public goodwill for their businesses (Sheikh, 1990, p. 16).

A study by the Economist Intelligence Unit (1957) provided a thorough examination of business philanthropy during the early postwar years. The

Intelligence Unit approached a total of 900 British firms across a wide range of sectors. Out of 381 replies, only 232 were suitable for statistical analysis, but these respondents covered all 16 of the sectoral categories used by the researchers. Ninety per cent of respondents claimed an interest in philanthropy, but it was 'apparent very early on in the survey that the majority of companies had no clearly conceived policy regarding their charitable donations' (Economist Intelligence Unit, 1957, p. 10). Only 12 of the 381 companies examined actually had definite policy guidelines outlining suitable organisations and preferred causes for charitable gifts. The companies in the study used a range of informal criteria when making contributions: for a substantial number of respondents (60 per cent), the rationale for charitable giving was guided by the possible benefits they would bring to the company and its employees.

This study showed that philanthropy was not ruled out by modern economic conditions. Yet the emergence of large, predominantly shareholder-owned corporations restricted the financial autonomy of company heads in making donations. In addition, it placed pragmatic criteria on giving policies: that charitable gifts should in some way promote commercial interests. Compared to the philanthropists of the Victorian period, all this made for a fairly staid and passive approach to corporate social responsibility.

Throughout the early postwar years, corporate involvement was equated with formal donations to the subscription lists of charitable organisations. This contrasted with the proactive approach adopted by American corporations in the late 1950s and 1960s. Heald notes:

> Formal monetary contributions, of course, were by no means the only form of corporate assistance to community and philanthropic agencies. Loans of company personnel, gifts in kind and services, use of company clerical and other facilities, payroll deduction plans, sponsorship of community activities, advertising, and a host of similar services added untold amounts to the values actually contributed by business firms. (1970, pp. 259—60)

During the 1960s American corporations were prepared to tackle major social problems. Neubeck (1974), for example, studied corporate initiatives to rejuvenate the urban district of St Louis in Washington.

The 'modern era' of corporate social responsibility

Significantly, the social policies of British corporations did not remain in a conservative rut indefinitely. The early 1970s witnessed the beginning of a modern era of corporate social activism. Many of the practices were inspired by the policies of American corporations. Much of this interest was not due to a fundamental transformation in the essential nature of British capitalism. Any explanation must be grounded in the proximate social and political developments of this period — more specifically, the social and political repercussions following the economic recession of the 1970s which made corporate social responsibility a relevant issue of public debate.

After 20 years of near uninterrupted growth, the early 1970s were marked by the beginning of long-term economic decline. This economic recession proved to be a deep-seated international crisis of confidence afflicting all OECD countries. British governments found that they could no longer rely on economic growth to sustain the central pillars of the postwar consensus. Furthermore, alternative forms of state financing had the potential to threaten popular support for the social services:

> More public expenditure meant higher taxation for it could no longer be financed out of growth. The liability to income taxation slipped dramatically down the income distribution: the traditional middle-class hostility to income tax spread to the working class. (Heald, 1983, p. 7)

Historical texts locate this economic collapse to a specific event: the quadrupling of international oil prices in 1973 caused by the oil producers cartel, OPEC. Although contributing to the intensity of the recession, the OPEC incident was a symptom of deeper structural faults. These structural defects have their origins in the growing integration between different national economies. This process gained substantial momentum under the aegis of the United States which organised trade liberalising agreements after the Second World War such as OEEC (later OECD), IMF and GATT.

The steady integration of national economies by the early 1970s had created unprecedented demands for goods. This in due course drove prices up sharply: the general price index for OECD countries rose from 5.5 per cent in 1972 to 15 per cent by the spring of 1974 (Harris, 1983, pp. 75—6). Ultimately, this surge in demand allowed the OPEC cartel to destabilise the world economy through its decision to raise the price of oil. In the industrial world, prices rose dramatically, while output fell. For Britain, this meant a marked growth in inflation and unemployment. The dramatic injection of inflation into the British economy curtailed the range of policy prescriptions to stimulate growth and protect welfare (Currie, 1983, p. 95). This meant that the ability of British governments to uphold the political consensus surrounding the social democratic state was rigorously circumscribed by these economic conditions.

One of the most damaging features of the economic crisis was its impact on the souring of industrial relations. Prior to this, relations between governments,

47

trade unions and employers could be described as fairly cordial. In the 1964 general election, the issue of industrial relations did not feature with any prominence during the campaign. As the postwar economic boom faltered, the government found it difficult to maintain institutions and services established under the postwar democratic consensus, all of which strained relations between the Labour government and public sector unions.

Successive governments throughout the 1970s, but initially starting with Wilson's Labour government in 1968, attempted to solve this problem through legislation (Davies and Freedland, 1993). For Wilson, this meant restricting free collective bargaining and the introduction of incomes policy to hold down inflationary pressures (ibid., p. 349). The Heath government took a different legislative course by following the dictates of the right-wing Selsdon Man strategy which sought curbs on the political power of trade unions. Consequently, the Industrial Relations Act (1971) attempted to curb the legal privileges of trade unions in order to render incomes policy unnecessary. The Act created immense turmoil as a total of 23 million working days were lost due to strike action in 1972 (Kavanagh, 1990). The subsequent 1974—79 Labour government was then forced to adopt a 5 per cent norm for wages and salaries to combat inflationary pressures, leading to the so-called 'winter of discontent' — a spate of strike activity, often unofficial and mainly located in the public sector. A series of industrial disputes organised by core public sector employees in January 1979 affected numerous services.

In this climate of unstable industrial relations, political parties became increasingly concerned with the issue of making companies more accountable. The Labour Party's industrial strategy, *Labour's Programme for Britain*, broached the subject. Significantly, it was integrated in the election manifesto of February 1974 (see Beck, 1983; Benn, 1989). The main objective was to halt the long-term decline of British manufacturing through concerted state intervention. But this was not a Soviet-inspired nationalisation plan. The proposals in the strategy attempted to combine state intervention with democratic controls over the private sector. The main institutional vehicle for realising the strategy was the National Enterprise Board (NEB) whose specific role was to conduct selective nationalisation and to organise subsidies, thereby increasing the level of investment in the manufacturing sector. The strategy also proposed 'planning agreements', in which financial assistance from government would be provided in return for public control and democracy in the workplace. Although this proved a radical agenda for Britain, similar discussions took place within the Conservative Party. Heath's government had already produced a White Paper on Company Law Reform (DTI, 1973) which recommended a code of conduct to engender a wider sense of responsibility in the business community (DTI, 1973, pp. 19—20).

When Labour came into power after the 1974 election, the proposals for the NEB and planning agreements faced intense opposition from the private sector. Companies and their representative organisations mounted a virulent campaign of opposition against the 1974 White Paper on industrial regeneration. The business-sponsored Aims of Industry launched a £100,000 campaign against nationalisation, and sections of industry canvassed European Community officials in Brussels to prevent the British government from assuming control of industries (Browne, 1983, p. 227).

The private sector response to these proposals was not entirely confrontational or negative. Business leaders and academics published a number of texts on corporate social responsibility, all within a relatively short space of time (Ivens, 1970; Beesley, 1974; BIM, 1974; Kempner *et al.*, 1974; Robertson, 1974; Fogarty, 1975; Epstein, 1976, 1977; Humble, 1976; SSRC, 1976; Beesley and Evans, 1978). Possibly the most significant publication was the CBI's Company Affairs Committee report on *The Responsibilities of the British Public Company* (1973).

The Committee generally welcomed the notion of social responsibility; but disapproved of any external interference in company affairs to secure compliance with social objectives. Instead, the CBI report opted for a policy of self-regulation: 'The business of private enterprise is capable of working out its own programme of self-reform, as this and other initiatives by the CBI and other bodies show' (CBI, 1973, p. 5). Business enterprises, it was argued, should consider the interests of groups, other than shareholders — namely, employees, suppliers, trade unions and the community. The CBI's admission that business should demonstrate sensitivity to a broader constituency of interests came with qualifications:

> In return, we hope and expect that those who have a relationship with the board and the company which it controls, will seek to reciprocate by re-examining their own standards of conduct and applying them to their relationships with the board and the company. We certainly include the Trade Union movement in this context. (CBI, 1973, p. 43)

Thus, the business community was willing to build consensual relationships within certain limits and conditions. While the CBI accepted the need for socially responsibility, it did not concur with the idea that companies should be made accountable to these parties (Fogarty, 1975, p. 13).

The worst fears of the private sector, however, did not materialise. The Labour leadership did its utmost to dilute the plans for industrial development, adopted by the party while in opposition. The provisions of the Industry Act, passed in November 1975, was a pale version of the original NEB planning agreements strategy. After the Act, planning agreements were organised on a purely voluntary basis. In the event, the only agreement conducted by the NEB was with the Chrysler company at the end of 1978. In fact, many subsidies were handed over without planning agreements or conditions placed on public and democratic control (Forester, 1978).

A revised version of the industrial strategy was formally presented in November 1975. This plan emphasised the importance of cooperation between government, industry and trade unions in achieving industrial regeneration. However, the approach of this new tripartite forum was mainly confined to those deemed acceptable to the private sector. In accordance with the CBI's recommendations (see Adamson, 1975), the government established 40 sectoral working parties to improve industrial performance. These sectoral plans made no mention of nationalisation or planning agreements.

The new policy resulted in the augmentation of direct links between government and business. Civil servants stepped up their contacts with companies. Corporate representatives, in turn, liaised with a range of government departments. One senior civil servant observed:

...in the 1970s there has been a greater realisation that government must also have contact with individual companies, to complement its relations with industry's collective representative bodies. That principle is now generally accepted and quite a lot of progress has been made. (Mueller, 1985, p. 105)

Such direct contact was of strategic importance. For the Labour government, it provided a symbolic demonstration that its new industrial strategy was succeeding; for business, there was the opportunity to influence opinion within government.

The interlocution between government and business gave crucial impetus to corporate social involvement. The government transposed the tripartite model of partnership for industrial policy to social legislation. There was the 'perception of a relative shift from government to companies as the source of social improvement and the means to promote specific items of social welfare' (Beesley and Evans, 1978, p. 13). Hence, semi-public bodies, such as the Department of Industry's Industry/Education Unit (1978), were established to involve the private sector in policy formation. These developments led a number of large companies to form specialist in-house departments for government relations (see Mitchell, 1990; Chapter 1, methodology section). In many instances, these government liaison departments became responsible for a broad range of external functions. They were given suitable, often non-descriptive, titles, such as external affairs or corporate relations, and, inevitably, responsibility for organising and implementing social programmes was devolved to such departments.

To summarise: the economic crisis of the 1970s undermined the postwar welfare consensus and resulted in a gradual shift in dominant political ideas. In this unstable climate, corporate social responsibility was the focus of public and political debate. Moreover, the instability of these years and the political solutions offered increased the frequency and importance of direct links between government and business. The transformation of government and business relations generated the institutional opportunities for businesses to become actively involved in areas of public and social concern.

Studies at the time confirmed the general raising of awareness among companies over corporate social action. Webley (1974) canvassed the opinions of 180 chief executives, and found that 90 per cent of respondents agreed that companies had obligations besides profit-making. Moreover, 50 per cent of those questioned rejected the view that profit is the sole priority of business. In a study of company policy statements, Melrose-Woodman and Kverndal (1976) demonstrated how enterprises took seriously the notion of social responsibility. Out of the 130 companies studied by these authors, 66 gave an affirmative response to the idea of a written code for social interventions. From this number, 40 already had written codes, a further 13 were planning to write a social policy, and another 13 favoured such a policy in principle but had not devised such a code. According to Melrose-Woodman and Kverndal, most of the policy statements in the study were published after 1970: '...since 1970 there seems to have been a small but significant number of companies turning their attention to the production of a code' (1976, p. 21). Although 60 of the companies questioned did not support written policies, a significant proportion of them still donated resources for use in non-commercial ventures.

A series of community programmes undertaken by a number of major corporations during the early 1970s seemed to confirm these findings. These initiatives indicate that corporate social responsibility was not only becoming a generalised phenomenon, it was also being reinvented as a solution to modern social problems such as unemployment, urban degradation and low educational standards. The foremost protagonist was the British subsidiary of the American computer hardware company, IBM. The schemes pioneered by IBM emphasised business assuming a creative and enterprising approach to social involvement. Such practices were essentially modelled on the social interventions characteristic of American firms.

The company helped established two ground-breaking projects. The first project was the Trident Trust, established in 1970 through the work of IBM's public affairs director. The Trust functioned as a progenitor for vocational schemes under local education authority management. Its aim was to provide

51

work experience for pupils close to school-leaving age by linking them with local companies. A close relation of this scheme was the Action Resource Centre (ARC), founded again with the assistance of IBM's public affairs director in 1973. It was formed principally to act as a clearing house for business secondments to community and voluntary groups. The organisation also aimed to promote partnerships between the government, voluntary groups and the private sector (*New Society*, 1973).

IBM's social lead was subsequently followed by several other British-owned corporations. These companies actively organised and funded social schemes, many of them directed at prominent social problems of the day. In 1978, a senior chairman of Shell UK, C. C. Pocock, created the Shell Small Business Unit to provide entrepreneurial advice to those wishing to start small enterprises. Pocock viewed small businesses as being the institutions most likely to create jobs in the future. Following Shell, the Midland Bank announced in 1979 a financial support package for the small business sector. In addition, the Midland supported the ARC and furnished secondments to the GLC London Industrial Centre. The British Petroleum Company (BP) contributed to job creation schemes with the ARC and the Pilkingtons venture capital trust (DOE, 1980).

The various initiatives outlined above could not have been envisaged two decades earlier. An important shift in British society and politics had taken place. This became increasingly entrenched throughout the 1980s, culminating in extended opportunities for business engagement throughout society.

Business and society in the age of the New Right

The sharp decline of Britain's economic fortunes was a *coup de grâce* for the postwar democratic consensus. The political and economic events of these years, as we have seen, legitimised more extensive private sector involvement in society. Symptomatic of this was the Labour government's attempt to embrace the market in response to economic and political pressures (King, 1987, p. 68). Policies developed by the Labour government set the pattern for economic strategies employed by Conservative governments throughout the 1980s (Kavanagh, 1990). Public borrowing, the control of the money supply and the constriction of public expenditure: these key monetarist concerns became more prominent after the late 1970s.

The Labour government's dalliance with the market proved a decisive turning point in British politics. However, whereas the adoption of monetarism by Labour was an expedient response to crisis, for the incoming Conservatives, monetarism was a strategy in its own right (Richardson, 1989, pp. 12—13). After four successive terms of Conservative office, the onus in macroeconomic policy has been on money supply, requiring the government to traverse the rubicon of consensus-Keynesian politics on many policy fronts. Successive Conservative governments eschewed tackling inflation through income agreements and opted for widespread cuts in government spending.

A key element was the increasing emphasis placed on the use of market mechanisms in organising public utilities and social services. As part of this, the Conservatives envisaged greater opportunities for business involvement in community action and in shaping public policy (see Kelly, 1991). Governments of these years systematically consolidated interest that had developed in corporate social responsibility during the mid-1970s. Concerted efforts were made to create further opportunities for corporate involvement in society. Here, corporate-led social action was imbued with ideological and political significance.

Developing links between business and government proved significant. They helped extend the institutional outlets for active corporate involvement in society. Joint initiatives taken by civil servants and business representatives led to the creation of coordinating bodies, the most notable of which was Business in the Community (BITC). This organisation was founded in 1981 to organise business involvement in local enterprise agencies — a nationwide network of support agencies for small enterprises. BITC's membership went up from 20 companies in 1981 to over 400 member corporations by the early 1990s (see Chapter 4). In addition, the government proved instrumental in creating policy-making forums for the private sector. This was evident in areas such as job training and inner-city rejuvenation. During the 1980s, a number of independent research agencies also began to publish information and practical advice on corporate social action. Among the most prominent organisations were the Directory of Social Change, the Policy Studies Institute, and private firms such as Bain and Company.

As well as organisational support, fiscal assistance was at hand for socially active companies. Throughout the 1980s, governments introduced new fiscal measures for company giving. These measures were introduced by the Conservatives immediately on entering office: there was a reduction in the minimum period of charitable covenants from seven to four years in 1980. In 1983 employers were given tax relief on salary costs for those employees seconded to charities. The 1986 Lawson Budget introduced a £70 million package of fiscal reforms for charities. According to its author, this package 'had one principle running through it, which I frequently enunciated, and which informed my other concessions in this field in other Budgets: namely, that the best way to make such concessions is to assist, not the charities themselves, but the act of charitable giving' (Lawson, 1992, p. 380). To encourage corporate donations, the 1986 Budget gave companies tax relief of up to 3 per cent of their annual dividend to shareholders for single donations. Moreover, employers were encouraged to institute payroll giving, in which charitable donations worth £120 per year would attract tax relief (Fogarty and Christie, 1990, p. 64). Encouragingly for policy-makers, the past few years have seen marked increases in the level of corporate giving: in 1977, the charitable contributions of the top 200 companies totalled £13.9 million. In 1990 this total rose to £190 million (Lane and Saxon-Harrold, 1993, p. 24).

The following two chapters explore more fully the modern era of interest in corporate social responsibility. They examine two of the most significant and prevalent areas of corporate intervention: local economic development, especially in urban areas, and the environment. Indeed, one survey of the community policies of 230 firms provides evidence on the specific causes adopted by socially active companies. Both the environment and local economic development were popular areas of intervention: 75 per cent of the companies identified the environment as an issue of active concern, while 58 per cent indicated an involvement in economic regeneration (Gillies, 1992).

These chapters focus in part on the social and political forces which encouraged corporate intervention in these areas. These wider social factors do not provide a complete picture of corporate social involvement. It is necessary to consider the interface between these external factors and the internal dynamics of agency within companies. Detailed case studies assess how agents within companies respond to a political context which encourages greater corporate social involvement. The case studies are based on the social programmes organised by four major British corporations — BAT, BT, Unilever and Shell. These corporations typify, to a great degree, the way in which social responsibility has been embraced by companies. All of them, over the past 15 years, have formally instituted departments for administering social interventions. They have also participated actively in areas such as local economic development and the environment. Such case studies will underline an important analytical point: the implications of corporate community involvement for society. In particular, they will highlight the extent to which corporate social intervention can provide solutions to public problems.

Part Two
The Modern Era

4 Rejuvenating Local Economies through Enterprise

Britain's faltering position within the global economy had a direct and uneven bearing on the fortunes of local economies throughout the country. While regional economic decline is not unique, the systematic deterioration of particular city areas during the 1970s was dramatic. The local economy thus became the object of numerous policy initiatives (Lawless, 1987). Most of the efforts made to tackle this problem at that time were state-centred. In the 1980s, however, private sector-led initiatives were seen to offer alternatives to this prevailing policy orthodoxy. Throughout the early 1980s, the private sector was seen to embody an alternative institutional strategy to state intervention. Indeed, urban decline and unemployment were perceived to be among the most pressing issues for corporate attention.

The concern of this chapter is threefold. Firstly, it examines the changing social and political through which companies became more closely involved in urban initiatives. This has certain parallels with the analysis in Chapter 3, which traces the modern era of corporate social involvement. Secondly, it details the actual attempts made by companies to engage in and develop urban programmes. Case studies of projects organised by BAT Industries, BT and Shell highlight the significance of key company players and their involvement with government agencies. Finally, the chapter explores the extent to which commercial practices and enterprises are seen to offer expert insight to policy solutions for urban areas.

Local economic decline and the response of government and business

The initial pioneering forays of corporate intervention into urban regeneration were precipitated by the onset of economic instability and recession during the early 1970s. The failings of the national economy were immediately transmitted to local city economies through factory closures and disinvestment. Older urban industrial districts — unsuited to the requirements of modern production — were susceptible to widespread plant closures (see Massey and Meegan, 1982). The local economies within these urban areas experienced structural dislocation, retarding, or at least postponing, the prospects for recovery.

Some firms organised institutional provisions to reduce the social impact of mass redundancies. For example, a number of companies carried out social audits to assess the wider social and economic costs of forcing redundancies (Craig *et al.*, 1979). In 1969, having been forced to rationalise its production process, the British Steel Corporation formed a Social and Regional Policy Department which carefully scrutinised the implications of redundancies and plant closures prior to making final decisions (Jones, 1974, p. 18). The glass-making company Pilkingtons established an enterprise agency, the St Helens Community Enterprise Trust, in the wake of large redundancies at its St Helens plant in 1978. This drew together representatives from local employers in the area to advise the unemployed on setting up small businesses.

Although these corporate contingency programmes were influential, it was the development of government policy for urban areas which proved more decisive. This secured the momentum of interest and the institutional opportunities for extending private sector involvement in local economic regeneration.

When Peter Shore became Secretary of State for the Environment in 1976, there ensued a conspicuous revision of postwar planning strategies. Since the late 1960s, governments had largely relied on district-based policies to revitalise urban areas. These interventions, however, were characteristically fragmented: local and central government agencies were implementing measures for communities with little or no cooperation and often in isolation (Hambleton, 1981). By 1976 leading figures within the Department of the Environment (DOE) set in motion new proposals for urban redevelopment. This resulted in the creation of an interdepartmental committee of junior ministers, under the chairmanship of Peter Shore, to review inner-city and local economic policy.

The committee's findings resulted in the publication of the White Paper, *Policy for the Inner Cities* (DOE, 1977). The document acknowledged the socio-economic and structural causes of urban deprivation and recommended that the existing policy measure for urban renewal, the Urban Programme, should be bolstered. Consequently, it was suggested that the Urban Programme be widened to include economic, environmental and social projects and that its funding should be increased from a projected £35.2 million in 1977—78 to £165 million in 1979—80. In terms of institutional provisions, the White Paper recommended that partnerships should be established between central government and designated local authorities. A more expansive role for selected local authorities in economic development was envisaged. This included the power to declare industrial improvement areas, prepare industrial sites and provide loans to small businesses (Hambleton, 1981).

The recommendations of the White Paper were placed in the Inner Urban Areas Bill of 1978. As the Bill made its way through Parliament, the Labour government was in the midst of economic and political turmoil (see Chapter 3). It responded by reneging on some of the radical industrial policies, devised in opposition, and by making a series of concessions to the private sector. The Inner Urban Areas Bill was not unaffected by these events. Some of the funding provisions made available by the Bill were circumscribed. Many authorities faced reductions in rate support, as public spending was constricted in response to economic pressures. In addition, the government attempted to impose controls over inner-city and local economic policy, contradicting the plans of the Inner Urban Areas Bill to devolve certain powers to local authorities. Symptomatic of this was the use of the urban development corporation model, initially used for depressed areas within Scotland. The introduction of the Scottish Development Agency into Glasgow and other inner-city areas in the Clydeside conurbation 'brought a strong central policy thrust into local projects influencing the objectives and focus of urban projects' (Moore and Booth, 1986, p. 362).

A further dilution of this legislation came during the committee stage. Here, the Bill was widened in scope to include considerations of commercial interests (Hambleton, 1981, p. 56). Hence, it was no coincidence that James Callaghan pressed Peter Shore to examine the possible contribution of the small firm sector in the reconstruction of urban areas (Fieldwork interview, senior DOE official, 23.3.93). Callaghan seemed to be echoing the arguments being put forward by some senior executives — such as the chairman of Shell Transport and Trading Company, C. C. Pocock — on the need to promote the small business sector as an alternative form of employment and economic rejuvenation.

The micro-capital sector soon became a cause that helped stimulate private sector interest in urban development. Some officials within the DOE began to petition corporate executives about their willingness to assist small firms in economically depressed locations. Initially, DOE officials at Under-Secretary level were loath to involve large firms in this policy area, because the Inner Urban Areas Bill had unequivocally singled out local authorities as the 'natural agencies' of urban policy (Fieldwork interview, senior DOE official, 23.3.93).

Despite these reservations, a coterie of DOE mandarins, members of the London Chamber of Commerce and representatives of leading corporations — BP, Shell, Marks & Spencer, Sainsbury and Tesco — went ahead. They met informally to discuss the details of establishing a corporate-sponsored agency for small entrepreneurs, similar to the St Helens Community Enterprise Trust founded by Pilkingtons. To give the proposals some degree of momentum, the Under-Secretary at the DOE persuaded Peter Shore to organise a special dinner

59

with the heads of leading British companies. The dinner was held at the Foreign Secretary's special residency at Carlton Terrace in a bid to attract a full attendance. A working party, under the auspices of the London Chamber of Commerce, was formed as a result of the event. It was subsequently instrumental in bringing together Tesco, Marks & Spencer, Shell, Barclays, Lloyds, Midland and BP to form the London Enterprise Agency (LENTA) in April 1979.

Shortly after the formation of LENTA, plans were afoot to form similar organisations in Bristol, Birmingham and Manchester. With hindsight, the LENTA model was of considerable significance to the modern era of corporate responsibility. By the mid-1980s, the enterprise agency phenomenon would take on national proportions, and it provided the first attempt to create a systematic and nationwide movement for corporate social involvement.

Business involvement in the local enterprise movement

In 1979 Britain once again entered into a period of recession which was to last throughout much of the early 1980s. The decline of manufacturing industries was particularly acute. Most OECD countries suffered falls in industrial production, but the constriction of manufacturing employment and output was more serious in Britain than in other advanced capitalist nations (Judge and Dickson, 1987). Because the industrial sector was mainly implicated, the regional impact of the recession proved uneven: areas in the Midlands and the north, where manufacturing industry was an integral part of economic life, saw greater economic and social decline than the south. The north and other regions, such as Scotland, lost 10 per cent more manufacturing jobs when compared to areas in the south (Fothergill and Guy, 1990, p. 13). Over time, the deepening recession led influential authorities to look towards the private sector as a possible solution to urban decay.

On the eve of what proved to be one of the worst recessions in 50 years, the incoming Conservative government conducted a policy review. The new Secretary of State for the Environment, Michael Heseltine, finally made a statement on government plans for inner cities in September 1979. Although the statement pledged to continue the Urban Programme, it indicated a change of approach. Heseltine stressed the limits of public sector intervention in solving the economic problems of urban areas and stated that greater efforts had to be made by local authorities to attract private sector investment (Hambleton, 1981).

The tenets of exploratory statements gradually turned into the central planks of legislation. Government policy in these early years gradually shifted the content of urban policy. There was less emphasis on social provision for assisting underprivileged groups and onus was placed instead on economic measures aimed at creating wealth and invigorating private sector activity in deprived geographical areas (Hambleton, 1981, pp. 57—8). Here, wealth creation was hailed as the panacea for social problems left in the wake of economic recession.

The creation of enterprise zones by the 1980 Local Government, Planning and Land Act provided an early indication of this change in emphasis. The enterprise zone scheme provided designated areas with an array of fiscal concessions for a period of ten years. The most important concessions included exemptions from rates and 100 per cent capital allowances on commercial properties. The first zones to benefit from the initiative were within deprived Urban Programme areas. By the mid-1980s the scheme had been extended beyond these locations. According to Lawless, the enterprise zone strategy held on to the assumption 'that by reducing physical and financial controls within selected areas, enterprise would flourish, output expand and jobs be created' (Lawless, 1987, p. 126).

As part of the general review of urban policy that saw the creation of enterprise zones, the small firm sector was raised to a position of prominence. Under Margaret Thatcher this sector was imbued with ideological significance: the micro-sector was perceived to be better equipped than monolithic state-owned entities for the task of stimulating enterprise in local communities. Towards this end, the Thatcher administration, during its first four years of office, delivered 108 separate administrative, fiscal and advisory measures to assist the small firm sector (Goss, 1991).

For those DOE officials who had endeavoured, since the late 1970s, to promote enterprise agencies, this was a welcome development. The debate surrounding the small business sector was used to consolidate interest in corporate social responsibility. Senior figures within the DOE, in conjunction with prominent corporate heads, established a national coordinating body, Business in the Community (BITC), for enterprise agencies. Later in the 1980s, the organisation would extend its remit to provide a forum for debate and practical leadership in corporate social activism. Because of its importance to corporate social involvement, events surrounding the establishment of BITC require analysis.

Projects such as LENTA and the ARC from the 1970s (see Chapter 3) provided a ready-made network of parties interested in corporate social involvement from both government and the private sector. These close associations proved integral to the acceleration of corporate intervention in local economic policy during the early 1980s. After the 1979 election, the same civil servants involved in the formation of LENTA embarked on the task of winning over their new Conservative Secretary of State, Michael Heseltine, to the idea of local enterprise agencies. Heseltine proved himself receptive to the overtures being made by the DOE mandarins, and subsequently agreed to visit the St Helens Community Trust, one of the first local enterprise agencies to be established. After the visit, Heseltine was suitably impressed by the Trust and launched plans to create 30 enterprise agencies by the end of 1980 (Heseltine, 1987, p. 165).

The Secretary of State at the DOE played an important part in trying to enthuse business associations such as the CBI and the Chambers of Commerce, as well as individual businesses. He was keen to point out the contribution which businesses could make to urban and local economic regeneration by supporting enterprise agencies (see Richardson, 1983, p. 1). To help the process, an Anglo-American conference on corporate social involvement was organised in April 1980 by the Department of Trade and Industry (DTI) and the DOE. The conference gave company representatives, mainly from the United States, an opportunity to share their experiences about corporate social action (DOE, 1980).

The conference concluded that a national umbrella organisation was required to promote local enterprise agencies throughout the country. A working group on community involvement, comprising DTI and DOE officials, senior managers from BP, Fison, the Coal Board and high profile executives — Marcus Sieff from Marks & Spencer, and Alastair Pilkington — considered the possibilities. Four months later, a report containing a proposal for a Business in the Community Unit was published by the working party. By 1 June 1981, BITC was officially constituted, with two full-time administrators seconded from the DOE and Shell overseeing this initial phase. The organisation soon attracted major figures from the corporate world to act as executive board members. For instance, Tiny Milne of BP assumed a position as part-time director.

Once formed, BITC continued to promote partnerships between government and business representatives to sustain the local enterprise agencies. In this formative phase, BITC was assisted by a number of seconded assistants who operated in tandem with the Small Firms Minister, David Trippier. These people helped establish enterprise agencies in specified areas. The agencies shared similar aims: that of providing jobs and developing economically depressed areas by stimulating the growth of small businesses.

As organisations, they were far from homogeneous. Each agency was created as a separate, autonomous company, which in turn was required to attract funding from private and public sources. In Cheshire, Business Link Ltd was founded by Cheshire County Council, Grosvenor Estates, Holton Borough Council and ICI Mond. There was also assistance from the Midland and National Westminster banks. In Merseyside, Unilever, together with the local authority and Chambers of Commerce, helped form the enterprise agency, In Business Limited. Helped by BITC's coordinating work and the provision of tax concessions for local enterprise agencies, the rate of formation grew dramatically from 40 agencies in 1981 to 100 by May 1983. By the late 1980s this figure had increased to 250. In the early 1990s there were over 300 local enterprise agencies operating in Britain (Richardson, 1983; Deakins, 1993).

What is most significant about BITC and the local enterprise agencies has been their contribution towards mobilising corporate support in local economic rejuvenation. For instance, two and a half years after being founded, BITC's membership rose from 20 to 200 companies. The number of businesses sponsoring enterprise agencies also grew appreciably: within the space of a year, between 1984 and 1985, the sum total of businesses actively engaged in furnishing monetary support for enterprise agencies rose from 1,477 to 2,242. The actual contributions from these companies totalled £10 million for that year (Metcalf *et al.*, 1989, p. 12).

In view of the events that had taken place around BITC, a number of enterprises established specialist in-house units for supporting economic regeneration schemes (see Chapter 3; Mitchell, 1990). Such organisational provision allowed companies to go beyond impersonal largesse by actively assisting local enterprise agencies. Shell's involvement in the enterprise agency network provides an apt illustration of modern corporate involvement. It also highlights the way in which key agents in companies not only responded to the expanding opportunities for business input in local economic regeneration but also contributed to the development of enterprise agencies.

Shell representatives were prominent figures in the setting up of BITC and the local enterprise movement. In fact, Shell was one of the first companies to embrace small enterprise creation. The company's support of this area was initiated by a senior chairman, C.C. Pocock, when he delivered the 1977 Ashridge Lecture. Following company-sponsored research on the creation of small businesses, the Shell Small Business Unit was established in July 1978. Initially, the Unit assisted such organisations as LENTA and the ARC, but, during the 1980s, it made a bold move to organise an enterprise initiative at its own behest, rather than rely exclusively on schemes managed by external bodies.

The programme began in 1982 as a competition for young people in the Strathclyde region. The competition was initiated by two local employees, galvanised into taking action by the high levels of youth unemployment in the area (Livewire, 1992/93). The Livewire scheme, as it was called, involved placing contestants who had devised plans for an enterprise under the tutelage of experienced business counsellors who helped them refine their business proposals for the final stages of the competition. The underlying objective of Livewire was to make young people aware of the job prospects available through self-employment. The success of the scheme led Shell to organise a national Livewire competition in 1985. A year later, Livewire expanded to such an extent that it could no longer be managed in-house by Shell. The management of the scheme was subsequently placed under Project North East, a Newcastle-based enterprise agency founded in 1980 to cater for young business owners (PNE, 1990), although Shell continued to be the scheme's principal financial backer. In 1993 the Enterprise Unit allocated around £624,000 — 60 per cent of its annual budget — to fund Project North East's management of the Livewire scheme (Fieldwork interview, Shell UK, 23.4.93).

Under the management of Project North East, Livewire was transformed into a national enterprise advice service for 16 to 25 year-olds. By the early 1990s it had 17 full-time staff based at Project North East headquarters and a network of 80 local coordinators. Through this network, enquirers were put in contact with suitable advisers, garnered from a pool of 2,000 professional and voluntary business counsellors. From its inception in 1982, the scheme has provided advice and support to over 55,000 young people. Since going national in 1986, enquiries have increased dramatically: in a three-year period between 1989 and 1991, UK enquiries rose by 146 per cent (Livewire Bulletin, 1992). These sharp increases tend to reflect national trends, particularly regarding unemployment: in 1989, 39 per cent of enquirers were unemployed, but this rose to 62 per cent by 1992 (Livewire, 1993).

Shell's Livewire project shows how the local enterprise agency network has supported corporate involvement in local economic regeneration. The flexibility offered by the enterprise agency network has given companies like Shell a certain degree of latitude over the form and extent of their contribution.

By the mid- to late 1980s there were further opportunities for the private sector to engage in economic issues. The Conservative government was making concerted efforts to stimulate entrepreneurial activity in local economies and achieved this by opening up urban policy to private sector influence. Companies were increasingly allotted functions both in the formation and implementation of policies to redevelop urban areas. This needs to be given fuller consideration, as corporations were made central to the future development of local and urban city areas.

Urban policy and the corporate contribution

It is not unknown for companies and business associations to engage and influence public policy. In the late 1970s there were sectoral trade agreements, in which business associations negotiated, unofficially, on behalf of the government (Grant, 1993). For successive Conservative governments during the 1980s there was a strategic and ideological thrust to the delegation of policy responsibilities to business organisations. Thus, certain industries were allowed to regulate their own activities rather than have to face the bureaucratic mechanisms of the state. Some of the most prominent instances of self-regulation have occurred in the financial, newspaper and dairy industries. More importantly, the private sector has been involved in the actual devising and implementation of social polices. One of the most prominent areas where this has taken place is in the regeneration of local economies and urban areas.

The involvement of business in local economic policy formed an integral part of the Conservative government's perceived solution to urban decline. Such participation, which required the private sector to define and present solutions for urban problems, was a significant step up from supporting local enterprise agencies (Harding, 1990, p. 109). Several factors facilitated this development: the links between government and business, much of it confined to the largest firms (Mitchell, 1990), were already extensive; and both sectors had collaborated on all manner of issues. On social matters, organisations such as BITC ensured that these links were sustained. Furthermore, throughout the 1980s, a number of businesses had installed external relations functions that could deal with government ministries on social policy issues.

Among the most significant institutions harnessing the private sector for local economic policy are the urban development corporations. These semi-public agencies were introduced in 1980 to organise market and economic renewal of specific urban locations. The Local Government, Planning and Land Act (1980) introduced the powers needed to designate urban development corporations. Two such bodies were immediately created for urban areas in Liverpool and London. Firstly, the Merseyside Development Corporation (MDC) was given the task of regenerating 865 acres of redundant dockland on the Merseyside waterfront (Parkinson, 1988); and secondly, the London Docklands Development Corporation (LDDC) presided over 5,100 acres of central and east London, including docks previously owned by the Port Authority of London (Barnekov et al., 1989). Private business managers and executives, at the government's insistence, were given prominent and influential representation on the urban development corporations. Such participation has generally complemented and added symbolic value to the Conservative government's early market reforms in the urban arena (Robinson and Shaw, 1991). The presence of business representatives was also a deliberate ploy to maximise private resources through the use of matching public grants. The 1984—85 LDDC *Annual Report* announced that public funding of £149 million had been used to lever in £821 million of private investment (Barnekov et al., 1989, p. 195). The urban development corporations demonstrated the government's intent to expose the process of local economic and urban renewal to private sector influence. Moore and Booth comment: 'The role of the private sector has moved from that of client or consumer of the benefits of initiatives to an equal partner in policy formulation and implementation' (1986, p. 374).

The urban development corporations were an institutional conduit for engaging the private sector in prominent policy matters. The opportunities for such involvement increased during the mid- to late 1980s. For instance, in 1987, a further nine urban development corporations were created in the Black Country, Trafford Park, Tyneside, Teesside, Manchester, Bristol, Cardiff, Sheffield and Leeds (Parkinson, 1988). In all these new bodies, specially appointed officials and senior business leaders dominated the executive boards.

The Action for Cities Initiative of 1988 invited private industry, particularly construction firms, to participate in subsidised property renewal schemes within urban areas. As a result of Action for Cities, 11 of the largest civil engineering and construction firms joined forces to redevelop derelict city sites. Out of this policy there emerged a pattern of public-private partnership in which the interests of the private sector are uppermost. This became the dominant model for urban policy. As Barnekov *et al.* write: 'That model implies that the city, first and foremost, is a place to do business and that politics, government, and administration must...rely on the initiatives of the private sector to direct the process of urban change' (1989, p. 211).

The City Challenge partnership: the case of BAT Industries and the London Borough of Lambeth

The onus placed on the private sector only served to marginalise the position of local authorities in the urban area. By the early 1990s, with Michael Heseltine back at the DOE, there were some modest attempts to address concerns over the pariah status of local government in relation to urban policy. The most notable initiative was the City Challenge funding scheme, announced in May 1991. This new funding programme signalled a slight break with the prevailing orthodoxy of Conservative urban policy in that local government was given a prominent position in the City Challenge process. Here, authorities would receive funding directly, without the interlocution of an intermediary body. Moreover, the City Challenge scheme was deliberately linked to a broad strategy involving 'local authorities, local communities, and business, voluntary groups and other organisations active in the area, backed by Government support' (DOE, 1991).

The scheme took the form of a competition which, in the first round, was opened to 15 of the 57 local authorities with special Urban Programme status. All these local bodies were invited to bid for a DOE grant package worth £37.5 million over five years. In the end, 11 authorities were successful in the first round. A second round of the City Challenge was announced in 1992, and on this occasion all 57 Urban Programme authorities were invited to make bids.

Subsequently, 20 more authorities gained City Challenge funding. Exemplifying the influence attained by the corporate sector over the policy process for urban development, the private sector was given a central part in the City Challenge competition (De Groot, 1992). The DOE conditions for the competition stipulated that an essential prerequisite for successful bids was the ability to build effective partnerships with businesses. Local authorities also had to attract private funding through public sector grants.

In the following, a case analysis is carried out of the City Challenge bid made by the London Borough of Lambeth in the second round of the competition. The bid is worth scrutinising because it gained close support from the London-based tobacco and insurance conglomerate, BAT Industries. Prior to the City Challenge bid, BAT had already established close links with Lambeth Council through its support of an enterprise centre in the Brixton area.

The campaign from the very start was problematic because of Lambeth's reputation for political extremism. A senior participant in the proceedings commented: '[Heseltine made it clear that] there was no point in Lambeth even asking for the application form, because they wouldn't win a City Challenge grant' (Fieldwork interview, confidential). This was certainly the outcome in the first round of the competition, but BAT's close links with the government proved decisive in the Borough's ability to organise another City Challenge campaign. Prior to the second round of City Challenge in 1992, BAT had a senior official seconded to the Inner Cities Unit of the DOE. One of the Under-Secretaries encouraged the BAT representative to assist Lambeth in putting together a bid for City Challenge. The chairman of BAT was informed of the conversation. An informal lunch was organised for DOE officials, Lambeth representatives and senior managers from BAT (Fieldwork interview, BAT Industries, 25.9.92). Subsequently, it was decided that Lambeth should produce a bid for the second round of City Challenge. To support and promote the bid, BAT agreed to second a public relations manager from its Eagle Star insurance subsidiary.

A funding proposal was marshalled by a steering group consisting of four councillors, members of the private sector, including BAT Industries, and representatives from community groups. The funding strategy outlined details of 65 potential schemes, requiring an investment of £170 million over five years. It was estimated that the investment would create 2,000 jobs and 8,000 training places for local people. Improvements to the quality of life would be made through environmental improvements, health care facilities and better housing. Conditions established by the DOE demanded that authorities should demonstrate an ability to 'lever in three times as much money from other sources as is available from City Challenge' (Lambeth City Challenge, 1992).

In its bid, Lambeth demonstrated a leverage ratio of 3.1 to 1, so that total investment was forecasted as £170 million over a five-year period.

BAT's efforts to secure a City Challenge funding were not in vain, as the authority obtained funding worth £37.5 million over five years. The involvement of BAT Industries was an indispensable component in this successful bid. Throughout, the company interceded with relevant authorities — primarily with government departments such as the DOE. This became part of a concerted public relations exercise to promote Lambeth.

The City Challenge policy exemplifies, as with other initiatives, the extent to which the private sector figured in urban regeneration policy. The importance attached to the private sector continues even today with new funding initiatives such as the Single Regeneration Budget. In view of this, it would be worth considering whether the private sector has made an effective partner in reversing urban decline.

Prospects for economic regeneration

Lying at the centre of the rationale to engage the private sector in urban renewal is the following supposition: that businesses can help invigorate local economies and improve the prospects of these areas. In fact, the debate surrounding corporate social responsibility in recent years has been influenced by the idea of enlightened self-interest. The concept implies that business social involvement is of mutual benefit to both companies and communities (Bennett, 1990; L'Etang, 1994). These claims, like the government policies for economic regeneration examined above, are based on the conviction that the private sector plays a crucial role in bringing about the renewal of urban and inner-city areas (see CBI, 1988). These claims may be evaluated by singling out two broad areas of proactive corporate engagement: firstly, those corporate-led interventions in the local economy that have been coordinated by intermediary bodies and, secondly, policies involving direct action on the part of business.

The intermediary role of local enterprise agencies

As already noted, early advancements regarding corporate involvement in economic regeneration focused on support for the small enterprise sector. From the early 1980s onwards, much of the social activity in this area was coordinated by local enterprise agencies. These organisations contributed to small enterprise creation through the provision of advice, training, business support clubs and occasionally by making work spaces available. The agencies were also established to provide a focal point for private sector involvement and public-private partnerships in local economic development. An important aspect of this partnership, so far as the enterprise agencies are concerned, was financial: most of these bodies have gained financial support through a combination of private and public sector sources, although the actual ratio between both tends to vary quite considerably.

The enterprise agency movement has not placed strict definitions and requirements on the types of firm that can be involved in small business and local economic development. Much of the private sector support has tended to emanate from larger companies (Smallbone, 1990, p. 18). There are variations in terms of the quality and length of corporate support. Metcalf *et al.*, in a study of 200 local enterprise agencies and 400 businesses, found corporate assistance was generally stable. It was the provision of long-term support to enterprise agencies by corporations that was problematic (1989, p. 173).

During the early 1990s, companies such as BT and Shell scaled down their support for enterprise agencies, after becoming involved in this support network during the halcyon days of the 1980s. BT's Economic Regeneration section, forming part of the company's central Community Affairs Division, reduced the number of agencies under its sponsorship from 120 to 50 between the late 1980s and early 1990s (BT, 1991). One manager in the section explained the reasoning behind this gradual rationalisation of support:

> This was a decision by our Board of Charities Committee [the executive committee over community affairs at BT]. They don't like leaving things open-ended where every year we are committed to giving so much money to all these agencies. It doesn't matter who it is. They'll support a programme, but they want to know what the end is. At the end they'll want to get out of it. (Fieldwork interview, BT, 7.1.94)

Moreover, the Economic Regeneration section subsequently adopted new schemes with the Training and Enterprise Councils and Action for the Rural Communities of England. Without commensurate increases in the department's yearly budget, this has meant reducing support for local enterprise agencies.

The Shell Enterprise Unit, as mentioned earlier, used the Newcastle-based enterprise agency, Project North East, to organise and implement the Livewire scheme. The funding for the Livewire scheme was a reliable source of annual income for Project North East — making it one of only 60 per cent of enterprise agencies which possessed guaranteed funds for a full year (BITC, 1987). When Shell withdrew from the project at the end of 1993, the agency was prompted to consider whether it could provide for-profit advisory services to generate funds (PNE, 1990). Diversifying into these profit-making areas may result in enterprise agencies being less willing to assist those who are economically marginalised and in need of most help (Metcalf *et al.*, 1989).

The action taken by BT and Shell reflects the way in which corporate support for enterprise agencies has developed over the years. In a study of local enterprise agencies within Greater London, Smallbone (1990) found that business funds for local enterprise agencies were concentrated in the successful and high profile agencies. The following trend was identified: 'The growing concentration of private sector resources in the high profile LEAs is part of a national trend, and the consequences may be even more serious in other parts of the country' (Smallbone, 1990, p. 31). The pattern reflects regional differences: those agencies which have failed to attract sufficient private sector support and are dependent on public assistance have been concentrated in areas that have experienced serious economic decline, such as Northern Ireland or Scotland. In Greater London, enterprise agencies are predominantly private entities, showing little dependence on public funds (Smallbone, 1990, p. 19).

The uncertainty over private funding causes difficulties for enterprise agencies. A considerable number rely on single sponsors as their principal source of finance (Metcalf *et al.*, 1989, p. 4). Various funding safety nets are available from public sources in those instances where private sector support is withdrawn. Since 1986, the Department of Employment has operated the Local Enterprise Agency Grant Scheme, enabling approved agencies to obtain grant aid to match private sponsorship. In Urban Programme authorities, the Local Enterprise Agency Project (LEAP) was established for specific projects.

Researchers have demonstrated the importance of public funding for local enterprise agencies, especially those in economically depressed areas (see Moore *et al.*, 1985). One senior executive from LENTA — an enterprise agency totally funded from the private sector — was highly scornful, when interviewed, of reliance on public sector funds, simply because the enterprise agencies were originally established to act as conduits for private sector support (Fieldwork interview, LENTA, 16.11.92). Gibb and Durowse make an important observation about the injection of public funds into the enterprise agency network:

> Without public support of this kind, it is possible that the impetus of enterprise agency generation will die out and many of the agencies will disappear, thus weakening the number of channels available for large company participation in community initiatives. (1987, p. 15)

It should be concluded from this that corporate involvement in the enterprise agency movement has proven to be uneven. Agencies have relied more on public sector assistance than originally envisaged. It would be worth exploring in view of this whether the enterprise agency model has effectively promoted the advancement of the micro-business sector.

Organisations have been involved in monitoring the services provided by local agencies and their impact upon job and enterprise creation. But, as Gibb and Durowse observe, this is far from a straightforward task:

> Some individual enterprise agencies have attempted to evaluate their activity, but their results can be taken as no more than broad indications of performance, given the great difficulties in relating interventions such as counselling or training or advice to 'outputs' in terms of employment, income or jobs. (1987, p. 14)

In addition, researchers have pointed to the distinct paucity of firms regularly monitoring the effectiveness of their activities.

One exception to this is the Shell Livewire scheme. The Project North East enterprise agency collated regular information on the number of young people using the business start-up advice service. The information was published by Project North East or reported in the Livewire newspaper, *The Link*. The agency also collected information on the characteristics of enquirers: their regional location, gender and the commercial sector they envisage entering. These figures usefully demonstrated how the enterprise culture is affected by socio-economic differentials between social groups and regions. For instance, Northern Ireland represents 8 per cent of Livewire registrations in the UK, compared to 76 per cent for England (Livewire, 1993, pp. 1—2). The Livewire figures also showed that only 33 per cent of UK enquiries were made by women, reflecting their lack of representation in the small enterprise sector.

Support for these categories has to be targeted. However, Deakins' study of 150 enterprise agencies found only a minority of these organisations had a policy or strategy towards different groups of clients on the basis of age, gender and ethnic grouping (1993, p. 65). Because support strategies tend to be non-targeted, as Deakins demonstrates, enterprise agencies may end up reproducing the inequalities that already exist in the world of small businesses.

Turning from training to the vital task of job creation, there are certain difficulties in assessing the performance of local enterprise agencies in this respect. This problem is exacerbated by the characteristic reticence of enterprise managers to quantify their efforts in terms of jobs being created (Moore, 1988). From their point of view, they are simply facilitating the process of job creation by assisting the expansion of small firms. However, some assessments are more optimistic about the job creation capabilities of the local enterprise agencies: in a press release, BITC announced that the local enterprise agencies have helped create over 50,000 new jobs (Moore, 1988, p. 23). According to one report in

The Link, the Livewire scheme has created 8,000 jobs since its inception in 1982 (Livewire, 1992/93).

Recent academic studies of enterprise agencies suggest that a tempered appraisal of the job-creating potential of enterprise agencies is required. Moore (1988) examined the claims being made about enterprise agencies against trends in the local economy, focusing on Neath, St Helens and Tyne and Wear where enterprise agencies have been active for a number of years. The actual contribution of the enterprise agencies to local economic development was found to be marginal: the level of unemployment grew in the areas under investigation. Moore's research supports the findings of other studies that show how small firms are unable to overcome the structural and economic disparities between regions (Storey, 1985; Moore, 1988; Goss, 1991). Indeed, Storey (1982) claims that incentives to encourage the creation of small firms are regionally divisive. These support schemes end up reinforcing economic inequalities between deprived and prosperous areas (cited in Goss, 1991, p. 132).

The above evidence indicates that corporate engagement in the local economy through the enterprise agency network has not produced the sort of benefits depicted in copious publicity materials. Furthermore, the potential effectiveness of the enterprise agencies might be limited by the nature of corporate support, which lacks uniformity and is often biased towards the larger enterprises. Nevertheless, it should be remembered that enterprise agencies are intermediary organisations for channelling corporate resources into local economic and urban renewal. A fuller judgement about the capabilities of the private sector in urban renewal is required. This can only be made by considering direct corporate intervention in local economic development.

Direct intervention

While much corporate activity in the urban arena has been coordinated by organisations like BITC or local enterprise agencies, there are companies which operate autonomously in assisting the process of local and urban economic growth. The impetus may come from different divisions within the company but often these activities are placed under the control of community affairs divisions (Gibb and Durowse, 1987). These autonomous interventions are normally confined to leading players in the field. BAT Industries provides a useful example of such corporate activism. Since the early 1980s the company has participated in a variety of inner-city and economic renewal schemes.

BAT Industries' social and community programme was developed in the mid-1980s. Support for the small enterprise sector and participation in inner-city rejuvenation dominated the programme. One aspect of enterprise creation where BAT has made a distinctive contribution is in the provision of managed work spaces for small enterprises in urban areas. The original impetus for BAT's interest in this area came during the early 1980s from the company's then chairman, Peter Macadam. According to one former BAT manager, Macadam was influenced by the proclamations of government spokesmen and BITC officials. He was especially taken with the idea of private sector-led rejuvenation of inner-city areas (Fieldwork interview, Brixton Enterprise Centre, 15.9.92). Toxteth was identified as a possible area which could benefit from an enterprise centre (BAT already had long established links with the city of Liverpool through its Sandhills cigarette factory). The company eventually chose to renovate a derelict warehouse in Liverpool's south docks, allocating £1.1 million in 1982 to restore the warehouse into 120 separate units and offices for small businesses. The Merseyside Development Corporation, which was overseeing the redevelopment of the south docks, provided BAT with a £300,000 grant for the task. BAT obtained further tax concessions for the project by deliberately borrowing the £1.1 million needed for the restoration through a lending house (Fieldwork interview, Brunswick Enterprise Centre, 4.1.93).

By 1983 the Brunswick Small Business Centre was fully renovated and was offering services to local enterprises. At this point, BAT acquired a second derelict building — the abandoned *Bon Marché* department store in Brixton. The company intended to pay for the renovation whilst renting the premises, as it had done in Liverpool but, in this case, was forced to buy the freehold — at a cost of £1 million. Altogether the conversion cost BAT £2.2 million, and a further £800,000 was obtained from central government grants. The *Bon Marché* Centre (or the Brixton Enterprise Centre) was opened in 1984 with 100 unit spaces meant for small, light industrial enterprises. Both enterprise centres were founded to operate on a flexible tenancy-at-will basis. Tenants did not have to commit themselves to a contractual agreement for any length of time and thus run the risk of losing revenue. To support the enterprises, both centres housed business advisers and counsellors.

BAT placed substantial resources into both enterprise centres. These included human resources, with managers involved in the centres and senior officials sitting on the executive boards. However, subsequent events have demonstrated that Peter Macadam's original plans seemed to underestimate the potential range of difficulties that could emerge from such intervention.

One problem was that demand for units by small enterprises in both centres was considerably short of the actual supply: in 1990 Brixton had only 50 per cent of its units filled, while Brunswick had a better rate at 75 per cent (Fieldwork interview, Brixton Enterprise Centre, 15.9.92). Because take-up rates were lower than expected by 1992, BAT found itself subsidising losses of around £200,000 for each centre. This setback, however, can be put in perspective by the fact that the Brixton Centre is now worth £5 million; this could yield a considerable profit from the original investment of £2.2 million should the company wish to sell the property. At first, though, the realisation that both centres could not survive unless BAT provided ongoing support caused some consternation among senior managers. A former BAT manager involved with the centre commented:

> I think they were slightly upset originally because they had been led to believe that it was a piece of cake, that the projects were going to break even, no problem at all, within two or three years. In practice, that turned out to be completely optimistic if we wanted to continue to do it the way we had planned to do it. So, I think they were a bit upset initially. I think everybody accepted that it was a good cause to be in but I think they didn't want to see a perpetual, never ending expense. (Fieldwork interview, Brixton Enterprise Centre, 15.9.92)

BAT managers accepted the financial burden posed by the centres as part of the company's ongoing community programme. To deal with the financing and general monitoring of the two organisations, the Brunswick and Brixton Enterprise Centres were placed under the aegis of a specially created company — BAT Industries Small Businesses Ltd. The subsidiary reported to corporate headquarters and the main board of directors on a monthly basis. This was problematic as the directors were responsible for weighty financial decisions and were unlikely to place much emphasis on the relatively minor financial concerns of the enterprise centres. As one official from the Brixton Enterprise Centre commented:

> We're totally foreign fish in the corporate world. I think they find a certain amount of difficulty knowing exactly how to handle it. To be fair, most of them do, if they can spend the time, take quite a lot of interest. But I can't believe that it is something foremost in their minds. (Fieldwork interview, Brixton Enterprise Centre, 15.9.92)

The institution of a direct line of command between the Small Business subsidiary and the main BAT board is less a sign of the company keeping a tight rein over its finances than an index of its uncertainty.

The problems which BAT has faced in its contribution to local economic generation may be due to the fact that large firms are substantively different from small enterprises. Contrary to theoretical and empirical economics, company size is not part of a continuum, with large firms at one end and smaller companies at the other (Storey *et al.*, 1987). There are sharp differences between these organisations, covering a whole gamut of areas such as employment practices, market power, financial structure and performance. Corporate managers and executives are thus unlikely to fashion the type of support specifically required by small firms (see Chapter 7 for a further discussion of this point).

These difficulties might be compounded by geographical distance between sponsoring corporate partners and the small enterprises — some located in deprived areas — that are being supported. This is well exemplified by one scheme in which community affairs managers from BT established a venture capital fund. The Future Start Fund aimed to provide venture capital loans of between £50,000 and £250,000 to small enterprises wishing to expand. The fund was specifically targeted at enterprises within inner-city districts where medium-term finance is characteristically difficult to obtain. To manage the £3 million fund, BT brought in Top Technology, a venture capital company. This company was answerable to Future Start's executive board, comprising of senior BT community affairs managers and consultants. The fund was in operation by June 1991. The executive members from BT envisaged that, within three years, at least ten companies would be receiving support from Future Start. Since 1991, however, Future Start had invested in only five companies, two of which nearly collapsed (Fieldwork interview, BT, 30.4.93). These results deflated the original expectations surrounding the scheme. For the BT managers, the recession of the early 1990s was the main contributory factor to these difficulties.

Oakey's (1985) work on the role of financial infrastructures in small firm development suggests that other variables might account for the modest success of Future Start. The argument put forward by Oakey is as follows. To achieve economic growth in regions, there has to be a financial infrastructure capable of responding quickly and flexibly to local businesses. To provide this, financial organisations need to be operating in the indigenous economy, since provin-cially-based firms are reluctant to use external funding lest they relinquish internal control to outside interests (Oakey, 1985, p. 159). Thus, the limited success of Future Start may have been due to the lack of contact between those operating the scheme — Top Technology and the executive board — and inner-city firms. A solution to the problem might be to give local community affairs managers control over the scheme. But at BT, as with many other corporations, community interventions are tightly controlled from central departments. This means that the scope for devising local activities is limited by the necessity for prior approval from central departments and higher-level management (see Siegfried *et al.*, 1983). One local community affairs manager from BT articulated this very dilemma:

> What we're trying to get sorted is a share of the money which BT gives to the community so that less is doled out by London and more money is

available to the districts where the people are and the charities are working. (Fieldwork interview, BT North-East Regional Centre, 7.1.93)

From the preceding analysis, it is questionable whether corporate action in local economic rejuvenation has reversed urban decline — both economically and socially. The selective support given to enterprise agencies, the minimal impact of small firms on economic growth and the uncertainty over the ability of corporations to harness effectively the resources at their disposal for local economic development have all demonstrated how the expectations surrounding corporate social involvement have proven to be unrealistic. Advocates of corporate involvement have made exaggerated claims about private sector partnerships. There is no empirical evidence that private sector involvement can bring economic renewal or raise living standards for marginalised groups.

A concluding assessment

The involvement of the private sector in local economic development and urban policy-making has implications for local democracy. The private sector undoubtedly has an important part to play in any policy strategy for local economic recovery. However, there has to be accountability on the part of businesses towards the local communities they purport to serve. The determination of recent governments to involve the private sector in devising and implementing regeneration policies has marginalised town halls. During the 1980s, resources and policy-making powers for the local economy were transferred from local government to unelected agencies and central government (Colenutt, 1988, p. 121). Misgivings about the devolution of responsibility for urban policy to the private sector has not been the preserve of academics. Carley (1991) examined business involvement in the rejuvenation of Birmingham: a number of commercial participants in the study expressed doubts over the diminishing financial and political powers of Birmingham City Council to intervene in the local economy.

Private sector contributions to local economic regeneration must, ultimately, be judged according to whether this policy has reversed economic and social decline. Throughout the 1980s and early 1990s, extensive resources and political capital were invested in expanding the role of business in rejuvenation policy — a strategy which would be expected to have a modicum of success. Willmott and Hutchison (1992) in a survey of urban trends between 1977 and 1991, provide an empirical study of how urban areas have progressed under this policy regime. A significant index of socio-economic conditions studied by the authors concerned employment trends in 36 local authority districts. A number of the authorities were assisted by urban development corporations, Task Forces, and City Action Teams, all of which have strong business input. Their findings provide a certain amount of succour for policy-makers and business leaders:

It...looks as if the efforts of urban development corporations, City Action Teams and Task Forces have helped improve the relative employment position of some deprived areas. On some other indices, too, there have been relative improvements in some areas. (1992, p. 81)

All the London boroughs that experienced increased levels of employment between 1989 and 1991 were either covered by City Action Teams or Task Force schemes.

Much of this improvement could be put down to the general fall in unemployment throughout the country during the boom of the late 1980s. In fact, the share of new jobs in the most deprived areas of the country during these years was smaller than for the rest of the country: large conurbations, such as Manchester and Liverpool, did not enjoy a proportional share of increased employment. The pattern remains the same according to major trends in education, training, housing, poverty and welfare: despite general improvements, the economic and social conditions within underprivileged localities have not improved in relation to the rest of the country. Moreover, in times of recession, the quality of life for people living in these areas has shown a marked deterioration, especially when compared to other groups in society. Willmott and Hutchison note:

But in general the gap between conditions and opportunities in deprived areas and other kinds of place — the gap that the government's 1977 White Paper sought to narrow — remains as wide as it was a decade and a half ago. In some respects the gap has widened. (Willmott and Hutchison, 1992, p. 82)

In addition to national economic conditions, central government policies have contributed to economic decline in certain areas. For instance, the decrease in government money for local authorities in deprived areas, and the provision of special urban programme funding to unelected urban development corporations rather than needy authorities, have exacerbated difficulties for those areas already in decline (Willmott and Hutchison, 1992, p. 81). Hence, the considerable emphasis placed on the private sector has to be questioned. From Willmott and Hutchison's analysis, these policies, contrary to expectations, have not narrowed the gap between deprived and prosperous regions:

After 15 years, and many new initiatives, surprisingly little has been achieved. Given the record so far, it is difficult to have much confidence in more of the same or to feel at all hopeful about the future prospects for deprived urban areas. (Willmott and Hutchison, 1992, p. 82)

5 Befriending the Environment

Introduction

The development of environmentalism and environmental politics in Britain has been characteristically uneven. Even so, green issues now command a significant position in the public awareness and in mainstream politics. A concomitant of this has been a growing awareness of the environmental impact of industry and commercial activities. Pollution, overuse of natural resources, destruction of natural habitats are some of the environmental consequences resulting from the global activities of modern companies — especially large multinational corporations.

The aim of this chapter is to examine the relationship between business and environmentalism. The first part examines the way in which businesses have responded to the challenge posed by environmentalists. From here, the chapter considers the extent to which companies have improved their environmental performance. This part of the analysis is based on case studies of environmental programmes established by BT, Shell and Unilever. Again, these studies underline how the perceptions and views of a company's decision-makers help to shape its response to issues such as environmentalism. What is significant about all three companies is that they all regard environmental protection as part of their responsibility towards wider society.

Consideration here will also be given to whether market mechanisms or legislative regulations are better able to protect the environment. This is a particularly important question for businesses which have an impact on the environment. This part of the analysis delves into the possibility of whether the central motors of the market economy — the financial markets and consumer activity — can be harnessed for the purpose of improving the environmental performance of companies.

Capitalism and the environment

The consideration given to environmental issues within business cannot be separated from the general raising of environmental awareness in postwar Western societies, such as Britain. Environmental campaigners have operated since the nineteenth century, but it is only since the late 1960s and early 1970s that the environmental movement has raised awareness in the wider public. During this time, public awareness about green issues has been characteristically uneven, oscillating between periods of popularity and inertia (Lowe and Rudig, 1986, p. 513). Nevertheless, environmentalists have made important strides. Most notably in the late 1980s, British society, like much of the Western world, underwent a conspicuous greening of public opinion. The unprecedented success of the Green Party at the 1989 European elections, where it picked up 15 per cent of the vote, was a milestone for the movement. The polls indicated that the green message was winning over popular sentiment.

A number of opinion surveys, carried out initially in the United States and later in Britain, confirmed further that public awareness of environmental issues was gaining momentum (see Lowe and Goyder, 1983; Yearley, 1992, p. 79). A 1989 questionnaire survey by the Department of the Environment (DOE) provided a useful longitudinal view of the growing interest in green issues throughout the 1980s. The survey asked respondents, *inter alia*, which areas they believed that government should prioritise: of the sample interviewed, environmental pollution was regarded as second only to the health and social services. By contrast, a similar DOE survey carried out in 1986 showed that only 8 per cent of respondents thought the environment should be a priority concern for the government (Yearley, 1992, pp. 79—80).

This surge in green opinion was partly due to a series of spectacular environmental disasters that took place during the 1980s. The Chernobyl nuclear reactor explosion (1986), the Exxon Valdez oil spillage in Alaska (1989) and the Bhopal explosion in India (1984) all dramatically brought to public attention the problem of environmental degradation and the threat of pollution to human existence.

However, public perceptions over the external threat posed by the deterioration of the ecosystem were not sustained by these dramatic events alone. Kitsuse and Spector point out that a vital factor in sustaining public interest about social problems is the work of active social groups:

...we define social problems as *the activities of groups making assertions of grievances and claims with respect to some putative conditions*. The *emergence* of a social problem, then, is contingent on the organization of group activities with reference to defining some putative condition as a problem, and asserting the need for...changing the condition. (Kitsuse and Spector, 1989, pp. 203—4, original emphasis)

The authors are referring to the construction of social problems in general terms but their observations apply to green awareness. The rise of environmentalism during the 1980s displayed a dynamic relationship, as outlined by the authors above, between actual ecological conditions and the campaigning work of environmentalists.

Most of the agencies central to the raising of green awareness in the late 1980s were formed during an earlier period of green mobilisation in the late 1960s and early 1970s. In contrast to the 1980s, when environmental groups consolidated their position, the early 1970s saw the expansion of existing groups and the formation of many new green agencies. Researchers have found that, between 1966 and 1975, the growth of environmental groups was more prolific than at any time in British history (Lowe and Goyder, 1983; Robinson, 1992). Amongst the new organisations formed in this period were Friends of the Earth, the Ecology Party, Transport 2000, the Wildlife Advisory Group, the Tree Council, the Farming and Wildlife Advisory Group, Watch, and the Professional Institutions Council for Conservation (Lowe and Goyder, 1983, p. 17).

The raising of environmental awareness during the 1980s owed a great deal to the ability of these groups to promote the environment as a social problem. As part of this, ecology groups ran several high profile campaigns throughout the decade to emphasise specific environmental threats and problems. These campaigns managed to attract media, political and public attention. The most noteworthy of these was that spearheaded by Greenpeace in the late 1980s to raise awareness about the hole in the ozone layer. The purported defect was of particular concern because the ozone gases protect the earth against harmful ultraviolet radiation from the sun. According to Yearley (1992), the perceived threat to the ozone layer was a turning point in the political fortunes of the green movement. It contributed to the popularisation of the green cause and provoked protest campaigns. Most notably consumer campaigns were organised to ease the use of non-reactive CFC gases — the source of chemical threat to the ozone — in everyday consumer products like aerosols.

The work of both formal and informal organisations in making social problem claims about the environment resulted in the semblance of a 'comprehensive green ideology...which allowed ecological politics to continue in the absence of an immediate threat' (Yearley, 1992, p. 86). The ideology centres around the understanding that detrimental changes in the ecosystem are the result of human agency and decision-making in the economic, political and social spheres. According to the belief system, damage to the ecology constitutes an all-encompassing threat to immediate and future human existence.

Commercial organisations responsible for commodity production figure centrally in green ideology. Indeed, environmental groups have been particularly adept at remonstrating against the environmental damage caused by modern industry and corporations. Many green activists have successfully used acid rain as an example. This process is caused by emissions from power stations and factories. Harmful emissions cause moisture in the air to be polluted with various toxins, which in the advent of rainfall causes wastage to building structures. There is also the phenomenon of global warming. This is caused by the build-up of carbon dioxide in the atmosphere, which acts as an insulator and thus causes the sun's warmth to be retained, leading to a dramatic increase in the temperature of the earth's surface. Environmentalists have pointed out that industry is responsible for producing vast quantities of carbon dioxide. Moreover, CFCs, which were referred to above, contribute to this insulation process. This product again is extensively used within industry, especially in the production of certain commodities (Yearley, 1992, pp. 17—19).

It was no coincidence that, by the late 1980s, companies across a range of sectors were embracing green issues. A popular way in which companies drew attention to their support for the environment was to employ green symbolism to promote products. For instance, a Shell advert for unleaded petrol announced that its product was not only 'ecologically sound', but also 'economically sound'. The electronics company AEG, in its press advertising, claimed: 'People don't buy AEG just to care for their clothes. Our Lavamat automatic washing machines are also designed to look after something more delicate. The environment' (Myers, 1991, pp. 193—6). Research evidence has shown that interest in green issues was taking root at board level (Gillies et al., 1992, p. 5) and that environmental protection was preoccupying a growing band of companies (Lane and Saxon-Harrold, 1993, p. 31; Adams et al., 1991).

The endeavours of corporations to demonstrate their environmental credentials should be seen as a specific manifestation of the awareness generated by the environmental movement in the late 1980s. However, it should be noted that green awareness within the business sector was not just a reaction to counter environmental campaigners and activists. This would detract from the way in which some environmental groups and companies have formed active partnerships to develop green programmes. In fact, there are organisations — mainly voluntary groups engaged in practical conservation — that have taken a conciliatory approach towards the business community. As shall be demonstrated in the following, corporate support of the environmental sector forms a significant element in the greening of business and is an area imbued with broader political significance.

Business and the voluntary environment sector

Active partnerships between businesses and voluntary conservation groups is not a new phenomenon. In 1969, the Nature Conservancy Council and the petroleum company, Shell, jointly funded the Better Britain Campaign, an initiative supporting conservation groups working on local environmental projects. The Campaign is still active and is now supported by Shell and a variety of environmental organisations (Shell Better Britain Campaign, 1988).

During the 1980s, however, collaborations of this type grew significantly. Existing public agencies for the environment acted as interlocutors between firms and environmental organisations. The Nature Conservancy Council formed a specialist Partnership and Industry Liaison Unit as well as attempting to stimulate business sponsorship of environmental schemes by forming Industry and Nature Conservation Associations (Forrester, 1990, p. 23).

Apart from the growth of green awareness in society, these partnerships were able to expand because of emerging interest in corporate social responsibility during the early 1980s. As shown in previous chapters, one of the chief characteristics of corporate social responsibility was the emphasis on developing cooperative links between business and social groups. This extended to environmental and conservation agencies.

An integral part of this was the creation of organisations to promote social activism in the corporate sector. The most significant development in this respect was the creation of Business in the Community (BITC) in 1981 (Richardson, 1983). Formed out of a joint venture between ministers, civil servants and high-level executives, its central rationale was to encourage active business involvement in society through the brokering of collaborations between the private sector, public agencies and voluntary organisations. As shown in Chapter 4, BITC initially concentrated on engaging companies in the task of small firm creation and inner-city rejuvenation. This was done by harnessing corporate resources and expertise in the creation of the enterprise agency network, which was mainly concentrated in deprived inner-city areas (Moore, 1988).

Over time, BITC widened its scope to include other social causes. The environment was an important focus for these broader concerns and, as part of its widened remit, BITC formed the Business in the Environment Target Team in 1989. The members were exclusively drawn from the ranks of senior executives of major corporations and financial institutions, including the likes of ICI, TSB, Tesco, BT and IBM. The Target Team acted as a forum where members delineated the environmental priorities of the private sector. Discussions also centred on how the notion of sustainable development could be applied to commerce (Forrester, 1990, pp. 32—3).

Government departments also assumed a direct role in stimulating corporate support for environmental organisations. Forrester claims: 'Wherever possible governmental agencies try to defuse confrontation and encourage environmental understanding and good practice by business' (1990, p. 22). The DOE — historically at the forefront in promoting corporate social involvement — was instrumental in generating openings for corporate support of environmental schemes and organisations. The Conservation Foundation was one of its first initiatives of this sort. The body was launched by the DOE in 1982 to broker private business sponsorship of voluntary environmental groups. In a similar intervention later in the decade, the DOE, together with the Scottish and Welsh Offices, helped the World Wide Fund for Nature develop the Conservation and Business Sponsorship Scheme.

The DOE was also instrumental in forming independent environmental organisations to develop conservation networks, which were expected to draw on the resources and expertise of business. One such body was UK 2000, created by the DOE as a limited company with charitable status. The aims of this new body were twofold: firstly, it was to coordinate a number of national bodies with local networks; secondly, it was to distribute DOE grant aid for environmental causes. There was an added expectancy that this government money would be matched by private sector sponsorship. However, the aims of the organisation became confused: partnership organisations were expected to raise funds both as independent organisations and as part of the UK 2000 network. Consequently, eight years after its creation, UK 2000 announced that it would cease to allocate DOE funds but would continue to oversee an environmental network operated by six partners.

A more successful attempt to create an independent support agency for voluntary environmental associations was made with the Groundwork Foundation in 1985. This agency grew out of Operation Groundwork, an urban renewal scheme initiated by the Countryside Commission in areas around the north-west during the early 1980s. Since its inception, the Groundwork Foundation has attempted to bring together support from local authorities, government, businesses and voluntary organisations. The rationale has been to create a national network of autonomous trusts — cell-like voluntary groups — involved in rejuvenating the urban environment. Most of the financial support comes from the DOE, which has made funding available until 1995 to expand the present number of trusts from 31 to 50 (Fieldwork interview, Groundwork Foundation, 7.5.93).

The government Treasury secures the bulk of the Foundation's income. But, as an independent organisation, it was expected to attract private sector funding; and indeed it managed to attract wide-ranging business support. The Foundation's first major private sector collaboration was with Shell in the Brightsite

Campaign — a scheme that became axiomatic of the Foundation's work. Launched in 1988 by Shell in conjunction with the Countryside Commission and the European Community, the campaign essentially formed part of a practical conservation programme. Its central focus is to assist and encourage small enterprises to restore derelict land around their factory premises by offering free landscape design and low-cost maintenance services through a network of local Groundwork trusts. Once presented with these proposals for renovation, a company would then be left to decide whether it wanted to follow up the plans. In 1989, over 300 companies used the landscape design service, and around 40 per cent of these businesses accepted the improvement plans (Forrester, 1990, p. 31).

The Groundwork Foundation and its network of local trusts assume operational responsibility for implementing the renovation plans, but the private sector has also made a considerable input over the years since Brightsite's inception. The Foundation has generally used the financial resources at its disposal to undertake practical environmental projets that have definite, concrete results; contentious political issues are avoided. As such, several companies have patronised its work. As the main private sponsor, Shell has placed over £255,000 over a three-year period. In addition to Shell, British Gas agreed to a three-year sponsorship of Groundwork's training programme for environmental managers, while BT seconded staff to the Colne Valley Groundwork Trust (*Groundwork Today, 1992*).

It appears, then, that government intervention has helped promote business support of voluntary environmental organisations and practical conservation schemes. The liaison between the private sector and voluntary environmental groups has constituted a significant advance, engaging corporations in the area of environmental responsibility. However, surveys have shown that, despite government efforts in recent years, environmental bodies have been less successful than other voluntary and social causes in corporate giving schemes. The Charities Aid Foundation, in a 1991 survey of top corporate donors, found that the number of environmental organisations mentioned as beneficiaries of corporate funds stood at 419 compared to 2,718 in the medical and health field and 1,014 in education. A further survey of 213 companies for the 1991—92 period revealed that only 4.9 per cent of total corporate cash donations went to environmental causes (Woollett, 1993, p. 11).

Furthermore, there are questions over the extent to which these sponsorship activities do improve environmental protection. Campaigning bodies, such as Friends of the Earth and the World Wide Fund for Nature, have come to see environmental sponsorships as only 'light green' solutions to environmental problems. Forrester notes:

The new decade is opening with some important changes in the relationships between major environmental groups and companies. The current sponsorship approach of Friends of the Earth and World Wide Fund for Nature...now illustrates the creative recognition of a simple truth. That no matter how worthy and useful company sponsorships of environmental groups may be they are of negligible importance to or influence on the quality of our environment as a whole, that it is far more important, if not imperative, for companies themselves to develop coherent environmental policies, audited, monitored, staffed and reviewed regularly at board level. (1990, p. 143)

Below, consideration will be given to how companies have managed to embrace these recommendations for improving environmental performance.

Improving environmental performance

The main focus here is on how firms can assume responsibility for protecting and improving the quality of the environment. The most obvious way to achieve this objective is for companies to adhere strictly to environmental legislation. From 1831 to 1986 there have been over 80 Acts of Parliament, covering various aspects of the environment. Much of this legislation, in one way or another, has attempted to regulate the impact of industry on the environment (Cutrera, 1991, pp. 832—3).

In Britain, strict adherence to environmental legislation is not commonplace. Historically, relations between government and the most powerful sections of the business community have been conducted on the basis of cooperation. As such, environmental legislation has followed a flexible strategy, leaving considerable scope for administrative discretion and interpretation (Vogel, 1986, p. 70). Researching the enforcement of environmental regulations, Peacock (1984) found that officials were often sensitive to the specific circumstances of individual companies. These were taken into account when applying statutory requirements. Hence, in times of economic recession when profit margins are tighter, regulatory obligations tend to be less demanding than usual (Peacock, 1984, p. 104). Peacock concludes that the task of setting regulatory standards and their enforcement involves a constant process of bargaining and negotiation between company representatives and officials.

Symptomatic of such flexibility is the reluctance of enforcement agencies to prosecute businesses found infringing environmental regulations. Research has shown that the number of prosecutions as a ratio of actual environmental infringements is very small (Ogus, 1983, p. 62). In fact, officials and agencies often rely on informal mechanisms to secure compliance. One common ploy, according to Hawkins, is for field officers to reason with company representatives and appeal to their sense of social responsibility (1983, p. 51).

Under the deregulation banner peddled by successive Conservative administrations during the 1980s, the status quo was readily accepted. If anything, they augmented the flexible and informal approach to the enforcement of legislation by reducing the burden of environmental regulations. As part of this strategy, implementation procedures for legislation passed in earlier Parliaments were relaxed: many of the clauses contained in the Control of Pollution Act of 1974 and numerous EU directives for protecting the environment had their enforcement delayed (Goldsmith and Hildyard, 1986, pp. 18—19).

By the early 1990s although the government was expressing the need for rigorous enforcement of environmental standards, it favoured a voluntarist, quasi-market form of regulation. The White Paper on the environment, *This Common Inheritance* (DOE, 1990), indicated a distinct shift in policy emphasis towards the use of such a method. The document maintained that, while legislation would continue to provide the basis for pollution control, recourse to the state was not necessarily the most effective way of improving environmental standards among businesses: 'Regulation...does have limitations. It can be expensive to monitor and difficult to up-date quickly in response to scientific and technical advance' (DOE, 1990, p. 13). Instead, the document argued that environmental protection could be more efficiently and flexibly pursued by 'working with the grain of the market' (ibid., p. 14). The White Paper specifically considered how fiscal modifications, such as the introduction of carbon taxes, could be used to monitor the impact of industry on the environment. Representatives of major businesses have generally supported this position. For instance, the Advisory Committee on Business and the Environment — a DOE and DTI sponsored policy forum made up of executives from some of Britain's largest companies — endorsed the recommendations of the 1990 White Paper (Advisory Committee on Business and the Environment, 1993, p. 59).

Recent developments in the market economy have given a significant fillip to advocates of market forces for improving and monitoring the environmental performance of companies — a feature acknowledged by the 1990 DOE policy paper (DOE, 1990, p. 14). The most significant practices in this respect concern the emergence of green consumerism and ethical investment. The notion that these market forces can impose environmental responsibilities on businesses has achieved much prominence in recent years (Elkington and Hailes, 1988). Two of the ways in which companies have responded to these economic pressures is through the adoption of environmental reporting and product analysis. The extent to which companies have embraced such practices is examined below.

The greening of finance and environmental reporting

Serious environmental disasters in the 1980s alerted banks and insurance companies to the liabilities which they could be incurring by financing environmentally hazardous businesses. The American financial community has become particularly sensitive to such eventualities following the Exxon Valdez disaster and legislation covering financial liability over contaminated land. In Britain, the raising of green awareness within the financial sector has proven to be a gradual affair. In recent years, insurance companies and banks have insisted on carrying out environmental audits of potential borrowers (Peacock, 1984).

However, the greening of the financial sector was not entirely reactive. The emergence of ethical and environmental funds is of significance to the greening of finance in Britain. The United States led the way in the field of ethical investment with the establishment of one of the first such funds, the Dreyfus Third Century Fund, in 1972. Nowadays, the United States possesses several financial management houses solely devoted to this form of investment.

It was not until the early 1980s that similar funds began to operate on the British stock market. The initial signs of this form of financial activity came with inception of the Ethical Investment Research Service (EIRIS) in 1983. This was followed a year later by the first ethical investment fund, the Friend's Provident Stewardship Trust. Britain, though, is still waiting for a financial house devoted exclusively to ethical investment. Nevertheless, several financial institutions have established specialist divisions to plug the social and ethical market. For example, in 1988 Jupiter Tarbutt Merlin launched the first authorised unit trust fund with environmental credentials — the Ecology Fund (Simpson, 1991, p. 20). The actual number of ethical funds operating in the UK markets to date is encouraging: according to recent EIRIS (1993) estimates, there are around 26 ethical and environmental funds in operation.

The investment programmes of these funds are underpinned by both positive and negative criteria. In terms of the latter, funds will try to avoid placing investments in sectors deemed unethical — such as tobacco, alcohol and gambling. They would also refrain from investing in particular businesses with socially unacceptable interests, including the defence industry and nuclear power, and from placing investments in oppressive regimes. On the other hand, using positive investment criteria, funds tend to favour businesses with social attributes. For environmental funds, this may result in favouring recycling businesses and manufacturers of pollution abatement equipment.

For the American social theorist, Severyn T. Bruyn, ethically-oriented investment can potentially advance the well-being of society at several levels: employment policies, the urban community and Third World development. This is achieved through the financial pressures exerted on companies: 'The trend towards social investment may seem insignificant in the context of the larger forces of business today, but evidence is accumulating that it could become a significant movement in the near future' (Bruyn, 1987, p. 253). Even those on the left of the political spectrum have acknowledged that finance capital, such as pension funds, can be utilised for progressive social change (see Murray, 1983).

According to Bruyn's thesis, the expansion of ethical and environmental investment in Britain, though still in a development phase, has repercussions for corporate social responsibility. Ethical and environmental funds are most likely to have an impact in terms of improving the emerging practice of corporate social reporting. The reason for this, as Rockness and Williams (1988) have found, is that ethical investors are heavily reliant on company reports and publications to guide their investment decisions. A similar point is made by Miller, as he observes that social investment is 'dependent upon the availability of extensive and accurate information' (1992, p. 245).

As a distinct user group, ethical investors require, and need to demand, better disclosure of information on company performance across a range of areas: environmental protection, relations with repressive regimes, product quality and so on. In the process of divulging socially relevant information, a company should become accountable and sensitive to the needs of society. This chapter focuses specifically on environmental investment and its influence on the disclosure policies of companies.

Environmental reporting, like ethical investment funds, is a recent phenomenon. It is an activity which has taken root with the upsurge in green awareness. At present, there are a number of statutory provisions and EU directives requiring the disclosure of environmentally sensitive information. However, the business community and recent British governments have favoured flexible and voluntary reporting practices. Indeed, there are several mechanisms that can be adopted to make environmentally sensitive information freely available: the eco-audit, which is a variant of the social audit that gained popularity during the 1970s as a response to factory closures; eco-labelling, indicating the environmental properties of a commodity; the setting up of environmental management systems, such as BS7750; and the adoption of environmental charters such as the Valdez Principles. (Studies have shown, however, that these voluntary disclosures are mainly confined to larger institutions.)

In recent years, an increasing number of companies have provided environmental information through in-house and financial documents, although such practices are still far from being the norm among British and European corporations in general (Roberts, 1991). Nevertheless, a distinct expansion of environmental reporting has taken place. Harte and Owen, studying environmental disclosures in the annual reports of what are considered to be 30 of the top reporting companies in Britain, make this observation:

> Although we have concentrated on detailed reporting in the 1990 annual reports, we have observed on the basis of a comparison made with the previous year's annual report what we believe is a general increase in the level of environmental disclosure. (1991, p. 55)

Some notable exponents of environmental reporting have also recently emerged. The Norwegian industrial combine, Norsk Hydro, published a report on the emissions, discharges and hazardous substances produced by its UK businesses. The cosmetics company, Body Shop, produced an extensive 32-page environmental report. BT's *Environmental Performance Report*, the first in the company's history, examines BT's impact on the environment. As it illustrates the requirements and institutional changes that have to be implemented by this form of social reporting, the development of the BT report is worth detailed comment.

The telecommunications industry is generally regarded as environmentally benign. The sheer size of BT, though, means that it does have a significant impact on the environment. Towards the end of the 1980s, BT was alerted to the environmental implications emanating from its size as a commercial organisation and began to act accordingly. Prior to this, the company's environmental considerations were confined to a few isolated schemes, often part of cost-cutting exercises (Bowtell, 1991). By the late 1980s the Community Affairs Division had organised several environmental sponsorship schemes as a part of the company's expanding social programme at the time. However, BT's interest in environmental responsibility went beyond supporting environmental groups. At around the same time, the decision was made to provide information on the impact of BT's operations on the environment.

BT's adoption of a reporting strategy came after an environmental consultant made his recommendations to the main board in the late 1980s (Fieldwork interview, BT, 30.4.93). The role of the main board in this development was pivotal. In fact, from available research, the influence of environmentalism on corporate policies often depends on how senior personnel view its significance. As an example, Logsdon (1985) conducted a study of how American oil refining companies dealt with the issue of pollution. It was found that the attitudes of senior managers and executives, rather than financial or strategic considerations, were central in determining a company's sensitivity to environmental issues. Logsdon writes: 'While environmental problems and possible solutions occur at all levels in the hierarchy, top executives must acknowledge the existence of pollution problems and provide financial resources and encouragement before much will be done' (1985, p. 68).

Following the sanction of the main board, BT in 1989 commissioned the environmental consultancy group, SustainAbility [sic], to carry out a scoping study of the company. The final report recommended that BT should institute environmental functions within the management and board structure. Central to this would be the adoption of a formal, company-wide policy on the environment. In response, the specially appointed environmental liaison panel was to draft a policy statement, which was then approved by the main board and published in March 1991.

The policy detailed ten principal commitments which the company would make to minimise the impact of its operations on the environment: to meet and, where possible, exceed legislative requirements; to promote recycling; to design energy efficiency into new services; to reduce, where practicable, the level of harmful emissions; to minimise waste; to help suppliers minimise the impact of their operations; to protect visual amenity; to promote, through community programmes, environmental protection; to include environmental considerations in company training programmes; and to monitor progress and produce an environmental performance report on a yearly basis (BT, 1992).

In 1991 the company began to act on the last of its stated commitments: to publish an environmental performance report. Managers who eventually became part of the Environmental Issues Unit acknowledged that the company took a considerable risk. By producing a report containing environmentally sensitive information, the company could tarnish its reputation as an environmentally clean company (Tuppen, n.d.).

The information for the intended report was gathered by an independent consultant and then modified for publication by managers from the Environmental Issues Unit. In the process, BT did face certain difficulties in obtaining relevant statistical information, as it was not under statutory obligation to monitor waste and emissions. Consequently, most of the details for the 25-page report were derived from purchasing statistics, and disposal contracts (Tuppen, n.d.).

The final document — published in May 1992 — combined narrative and statistical data for 'a self-critical and open review of BT's operations and how they affect the environment' (BT, 1992, p. 2). It also included future target objectives for improving environmental performance. Indeed, the document could afford to be selectively candid because BT does not operate in environmentally contentious areas. The information in the report was deliberately presented to address each of the ten commitments made in the environmental policy statement. For instance, in terms of energy consumption, the report reveals how the company's use of electricity, oil and gas represents around 0.2

per cent of the UK's total energy use. As part of its pledge, the report maintains that BT will stabilise carbon dioxide emissions resulting from its heavy energy use to their 1990 levels by the year 2005. Regarding harmful emissions, the document discloses that BT's emission of 28 tons of ozone depleting chemicals represents around 0.25 per cent of the UK total. To reduce these harmful emissions, the company has pledged to use refrigerants with lower ozone depleting potential (BT, 1992, pp. 12—13).

To what extent have other companies made similar environmental disclosures? The growing body of work being carried out on disclosure practices shows that the actual standard and quality of environmental reporting is variable. From the viewpoint of prospective user groups such as environmental investors, the information provided is not characterised by the type of detailed assessment demonstrated by BT.

In one study, Harte and Owen (1991) examined 30 businesses, highly regarded by ethical investors for their consistent and open reporting of social and environmental information. According to the authors, the list includes the majority of the best reporters on the environment, such as the Body Shop, BT, Marks & Spencer, NFC and Unilever. Using annual reports as their source material, Harte and Owen considered the extent of financial and non-financial disclosure on the environment (1991, p. 53). The authors found a paucity of detailed information on environmental performance and innovations in this area. A great deal of the information presented included statements of good intent:

> Much of the disclosure appears to be linked to the development of an image, suggesting that it is good for both customers and shareholders that the company be environmentally aware, rather than representing a commitment to the concept of public accountability. (Harte and Owen, 1991, p. 55)

This point about the utility of company documents for ethical investment forms the basis of a study by Perks *et al.* (1992). The authors identified 17 companies, such as Body Shop, British Gas, the Argyll Group and Tesco, which regularly enjoyed investments from environmental funds. The authors focused on the environmental disclosures provided by these companies within their annual reports, analysing whether these reports were sufficiently detailed for environmental funds to make informed and considered judgements about their investment strategies. They concluded that there was only a modicum of information which could assist ethical investors in deciding whether or not environmental requirements are being satisfied. Indeed, although company reports are presented as meeting the information requirements of investors in general terms, they lack the specific information required by ethical investors who are concerned with environmental issues:

> But, in common with other information included in this part of the annual report, such information is selective, partial, unquantified and not subject to external verification...If annual reports are used as a basis for environmental investment decisions it seems that in many cases investors have little more to rely on than scattered references to environmental concerns. (Perks *et al.*, 1992, p. 55)

The findings from this research are reinforced and confirmed by other studies. Ullmann, in a review of the research literature on corporate social disclosure, concludes that studies generally show a weak link between social disclosure and social performance (1985, pp. 544—5). Furthermore, some researchers have found only a tenuous relation between the information disclosed and independent measures of environmental performance. Ingram and Frazier, from their research of environmental disclosure by American companies, argue that because 'management is free to use its own discretion in selecting information to be reported, it is possible for poorer performers to bias their selections in order to appear like the better performers' (1980, p. 620).

The three other case studies companies in this research illustrate the points made in these studies. For example, Unilever's *Annual Review* for 1992 contained a short section on environmental responsibility less than a page in length. The details included descriptions of the company's attempts to improve the environmental quality of products and packaging but little in the way of rigorous analysis or statistical information (Unilever, 1992b). BAT Industries community factfile included two short sections describing the support for environmental schemes provided by foreign subsidiaries in Brazil and Nigeria. More detailed information was made available by Shell in its 1992 business and social report. This included a detailed account of Shell's attempt to reduce emissions and discharges across a range of operations (Shell UK, 1992, pp. 12—21).

It appears that corporate procedures for disclosing information do not provide the level of transparency and detailed information required by ethical investors. Some practitioners argue that improvements in the flow of environmental and social information will depend largely on the mobilisation of ethical funds. Harte *et al.* write:

> Future developments in social and environmental reporting in Britain may arguably hinge upon the growth in both size and influence of the ethical

investment movement…and its consequent ability to lobby effectively on issues of accounting policy making. (1991, p. 245)

Although they have been operating for a relatively short period of time, ethical funds have grown significantly in recent years. Their performance in the financial markets, according to some business analysts, have not only equalled but surpassed the FT Ordinary Index (Dunham, 1988, p. 104). In future, these funds may come to exercise a decisive influence over business operations. However, such a conclusion must be tempered by this observation: there are certain structural factors which may limit the ability of these funds — contrary to Bruyn's (1987) assertion — to act as the harbingers of corporate accountability and social change.

The influence that ethical funds are able to wield is inversely proportional to their financial wherewithal. According to available statistics, ethical funds comprise only a small proportion of total equity investments: in 1989 ethical funds were valued at £200 million, but this constituted only 0.06 per cent of the total value of UK equity. Furthermore, the £6 billion invested according ethical and environmental principles (Dunham, 1990) still only amounts to 2 per cent of the total UK equity (Perks et al., 1992). The marginal economic status of ethical funds has confined them to a passive investment role: they either avoid companies which fail to meet social and environmental criteria or they invest in those that meet various ethical characteristics. Indeed, research shows that ethical funds do not tend pressurise companies into changing their commercial policies. In a study of 13 ethical funds by EIRIS (1989), it was found that only one of these funds had tried directly to influence company activities and only three of them had carried out a policy of informing companies from which they had disinvested of the reasons for withdrawing their funds (cited in Harte et al., 1991).

These structural constraints have been compounded by the limited number of enterprises that comply with ethical and social criteria. This may result in a situation where ethical funds are permanently locked into a vicious circle, where they are unable to amass the necessary resources because the range of possible investments at their disposal are limited. On the other hand, these funds may occasionally relax their ethical and social principles when making investment decisions. Investigations by EIRIS have revealed specific cases of ethical funds investing in areas that would ordinarily be excluded.

In view of the limitations faced by ethical funds, there might be considerable possibilities in mobilising institutional investors behind ethical and environmental causes. Despite the action taken by some pension funds belonging to local authorities and university investors, their demands for greater information, especially environmental data, have proven to be minimal. Most investment decisions made by institutions are the purview of technical specialists who aspire to financial, rather than social and environmental, goals (Perks *et al.*, 1992).

Further restrictions have been imposed by the demands of investment law on financial organisations. Under the Trustee Investment Act (1961) investors and trustees of a fund have to pursue maximum financial returns. It is illegal, as demonstrated by high profile court cases such as *Cowans v. Scargill* (1984), for trustees to forego a higher return on ethical grounds. Consequently, a significant proportion of possible environmental investments are closed off to major funds in the capital market because the profit yield would not be as high as mainstream investments (Ward, 1991; Gray *et al.*, 1993).

While the financial markets currently have only a minor influence over corporate procedures, the mobilisation of the green movement at the end of the 1980s witnessed the emergence of green consumerism. This phenomenon was seen as having the potential to make companies aware of their environmental responsibilities. The following section examines green consumerism and the impact that it has had on commerce.

The greening of consumerism

The postwar growth of the commodity market alerted social scientists to the importance of consumer behaviour in the overall functioning of the economic system. Gist writes:

> A fundamental tenet of our economic system is that scarce economic resources are ultimately allocated by the preference patterns of final consumers; that is, we as consumers vote, as it were, for particular types of institutions and for particular types of products and services. (1971, p. 33, quoted in Craig Smith, 1990, p. 93)

A notable development within the commodity purchasing market has been the recent expansion of ethical consumer behaviour. Here, consumer groups have organised product boycotts or disclosure campaigns against commercial organisations seen to be infringing ethical and social standards (Johnson, 1986). The rise to prominence of these campaigns has led some authors to argue that ethical consumerism can act as a force for making companies aware of their social responsibilities. While consumers will have divergent views over what constitutes socially responsible action, 'this is not a disadvantage to the notion of ethical purchase behaviour; it is simply indicative of the essence of consumer sovereignty and the right to choose' (Craig Smith, 1990, p. 96). Central to the mobilisation of consumer action, according to Craig Smith, is the work of pressure groups which provide information on ethical purchase issues and educate the public in ethical consumer strategies. Such action in turn alerts corporate managers and directors to the need to embrace more ethical and socially responsible practices.

In Britain, the issue of ethical consumerism has emerged in the past 20 years — brought to public attention largely on the back of the green movement. A number of campaigns organised by environmental groups have alerted the general public to the fact that certain products are damaging to the environment. Included in this category are aerosols, which produce ozone-depleting CFC gases and detergents which contain harmful phosphates and bleaches. Even if a product is inherently benign, its actual extraction and production can result in unintended harm to the ecosystem. The destruction of dolphin populations resulting from tuna fishing nets is a typical example. The proposition of those advocating green consumerism is that, by purchasing the right products, individuals can help protect the environment.

This form of consumer activism was initially popularised in the 1970s through campaigns by Friends of the Earth against wasteful packaging and the importation of products from baleen whales (Irvine, 1989, p. 6). The resurgence of environmentalism during the late 1980s gave significant impetus to green consumerism. One feature of this was the publication of consumer literature, such as Elkington and Hailes's (1988) seminal book, *The Green Consumer Guide*. In addition to these tomes, independent agencies — the Ethical Consumer and New Consumer — were founded specifically to mobilise the consumer market, estimated in 1990 to be worth a total of £290 billion, into purchasing environmentally safe commodities (Adams *et al.*, 1991).

The proliferation of green consumerism during the late 1980s saw advances being made in terms of the number of environmentally friendly commodities available on the market. Indeed, the prevailing view within business and government circles is that the introduction of environmental considerations into the production process can bolster profit margins (see Elkington *et al.*, 1991). MacKenzie (1989) argues that the consumer market for green products is expanding. This makes the production of environmentally sensitive commodities an attractive business prospect. There are instances where companies have been able to gain a competitive advantage over their rivals by producing such products. The battery manufacturers, Varta and Ever Ready, outwitted their rivals by launching mercury-free products in anticipation of EU legislation (Irvine, 1991, p. 22).

Before green products can be introduced into the consumer market, companies need to carry out environmental impact studies. This process requires investment for new research procedures and institutional facilities. The branded consumer multinational, Unilever, has responded to changes in the consumer market by introducing a number of provisions to monitor commodities at the research and development stage of the production process. The company's policy document, *Unilever and the Environment* (Unilever, n.d.(a)), notes: 'Environmental considerations are recognised as being of major importance to Unilever and are taken into account throughout the decision-making, development, manufacturing and marketing processes'.

Unilever's sensitivity to the consumer market is understandable: the company's commercial fortunes are intimately tied to the purchasing decisions of individual consumers. In fact, 75 per cent of its business is in branded and packaged consumer goods — mainly foods, drinks, detergents and personal cosmetics (Unilever, n.d.(b)). The production and use of some of these items has clear implications for the biosphere: detergents, constituting 21 per cent of the company's product turnover, emit phosphates responsible for eutrophication in waterways, and the company's involvement in food production, amounting to 49 per cent of its commodity production, is associated with the use of pesticides in plantations. As a result of both new consumer demands for environmental goods and EU legislation, Unilever has introduced new research procedures to scrutinise the environmental impact of its products.

The principal innovation is Unilever's new Environmental Division, which falls under the company's Safety and Environment Assurance Centre (SEAC). The Division was created as a result of restructuring within SEAC to engender a focused commitment to the environment. The organisational reshuffle consolidated and brought under SEAC's central direction those areas of research and product design relevant to the environment (Unilever, 1992b, pp. 18—19). One of the central responsibilities of the Environment Division is to supervise the range of interactions between manufactured products and the environment. It has done this through the adoption of life cycle analysis techniques, which evaluate the environmental qualities of a product through its entire life cycle.

Unilever adopted life cycle analysis for the purpose of examining fats and spreads in food products. The company's Environmental Division has also used this technique to minimise packaging waste. The foods, detergents and personal products units at Unilever now use life cycle analysis databases to monitor the use of packaging and to reduce the impact of these materials on the environment (Skelly, 1993, p. 20). The company's 1992 *Annual Report* announced that, as a result of using these databases, the incorporation of recycled materials into non-food contact packaging has increased by about 60 per cent, and that particularly high percentages were achieved with glass and metal packaging (Unilever, 1992a). The Ecotoxicology Section of the Environmental Division has also applied this life cycle analysis to pathways followed by chemicals in the environment. For example, work has been carried out on sucrose polyester in food products, and on biodegradation and toxicity (Unilever, 1992b, p. 18).

The life cycle analysis process, however, does not guarantee automatic environmental improvements because it is a highly complex process; identifying a product's journey from cradle to grave requires information for measuring impacts that are often beyond the reach of scientists. This means that the results obtained are highly equivocal rather than definite. But as Gray *et al.* (1993) observe, the main benefit of the technique lies in the process of undertaking the exercise rather than the final results.

Unilever, on the whole, remains taciturn about disclosing research findings generated by the Environmental Division, whether from life cycle or waste analysis. The company tends to provide general pronouncements on its environmental performance, rather than detailed disclosures from the Environmental Division's ongoing research of products (Fieldwork interview, Unilever, 30.6.93). The company's 1992 *Annual Report* included a section on 'environmental responsibility', which included various positive statements about the company's commitment to environmental responsibility in terms of product analysis and the reduction of packaging. But, as shown above, there was a lack of concrete information concerning Unilever's overall environmental performance.

The lack of detailed information on environmental performance is very much a consequence of the fact that environmental reporting is largely a voluntary matter for businesses. This suggests that producing for an ethically motivated consumer market, as Unilever has endeavoured to do, might not lead to fundamental changes or improvements in the environmental performance of businesses. Like ethical investment, environmentally motivated purchasing behaviour is thwarted by the lack of detailed information emanating from enterprises. Irvine writes:

> The green consumer is...hindered by commercial and government secrecy over the results of testing, ingredients and much other information that is necessary to make a wise choice...Time after time, the cosy relationship between big business and government compounds the problem of 'commercial confidentiality'. (1989, pp. 11—12)

Further problems emerge when companies exploit the general lack of environmental data to manipulate consumers. Green consumerism is susceptible to accepting the promotion of commodities as environmentally friendly, when their actual environmental properties may be merely superficial. The 'super unleaded' petrol launched by BP, Esso and Mobil has faced charges of being overpriced and generally negligible in terms of environmental improvements (Irvine, 1989). In fact, producers normally charge higher prices for environmental commodities, even when such products cost less to make. This, as a result, excludes many low-income groups from ethical consumerism and considerably blunts the capacity of ethically-oriented purchasing to act as a market mechanism which can press for social change (Irvine, 1991, p. 24).

Radical environmentalists point out that green consumerism ultimately falters as a tool for reforming capitalist organisations, chiefly because the practice takes place within a dominant framework dictated by economic growth and profit orientation, leading to only superficial and limited changes in business strategies. However, many of the causes of environmental damage are the result of the developed world's unyielding use of finite natural resources and the systematic exploitation of the Third World in pursuit of economic expansion (Harte *et al.*, 1991). Hence, the point is not to change the style of purchasing behaviour or what is consumed, but to reduce the level of consumption in the capitalist world. This structural, global appreciation of environmentalism will require distinct reductions in economic growth and, therefore, business performance (Gray and Morrison, 1992). As Plant and Albert argue:

...the production of environmentally friendly goods doesn't address the major structural and institutional obstacles in the way of an authentic greening of industrial society. It doesn't deal with the problem of infinite growth being the mainspring of industry on a finite planet. (1991, p. 4)

The complexity of the environmental problem means that market solutions such as green consumerism, and ethical investment for that matter, can offer only local and uncoordinated pressures for change. Some commentators suggest, in contrast to Bruyn (1987), that the markets are not the conduits of social change. The mechanisms and the institutions that promote them must be challenged if the problems of environmental degradation are to be overcome (Owen, 1990). Thus, we must conclude that the greening of business and the willingness of companies to adopt a responsible approach to the environment during the 1980s is a welcome development. However, as it has taken place within clearly defined parameters which have been acceptable to the private sector, these improvements have proven to be of only marginal significance in dealing with the environment as a social problem.

Part Three
Corporate Philanthropy in Italy

6 Civic Activism and the Origins of Industrial Philanthropy in Italy

The concern now is to explore the nature of business philanthropy and corporate responsibility in the context of Italian society. To this end, the dominant social preoccupations and interventions of socially active Italian enterprises are examined. It is also important that comparison is made with the situation in Britain, where in the past 20 years social activism in the business community has undergone considerable expansion. The objective of this comparative analysis is to analyse, more fully, the political and social factors that shape corporate responsibility in capitalist economies.

The focus on Italy begins, in this chapter, by tracing the history of commercial philanthropy. The analysis is separated into two epochs. The first part focuses on the social activities of commercial institutions and tradesmen in the pre-industrial period. In this era, economic activities and commercial institutions were inextricably linked to social and religious objectives. Indeed, from the early years of medieval society up until the Renaissance a distinctive tradition of civic activism emerged. This exercised an influence over many facets of Italian society, including the participation of commercial agencies in society. For the second part, the analysis turns to the social role of business during, and after, the industrialisation of Italy in the late nineteenth century. The intention here is to understand how the distinctive course of modernisation followed in Italy helped shape the nature of business-led social action in contemporary society.

Civic activism in the pre-industrial age: guilds in the city-republics of medieval Italy

Following the demise of the Dark Ages, much of early medieval Europe was embroiled in destructive internecine warfare between various monarchal dynasties. Events in Italy proved equally tumultuous. The south of Italy continued to remain under monarchal rule for much of the medieval epoch. In contrast, the imperial system of government in northern and central areas, during the eleventh and twelfth centuries, began to lose its influence. This transition, unlike in the rest of Europe, was relatively temperate and devoid of tyranny, largely due to the fact that monarchal rule in these regions was replaced by self-governing city-republics and city-states. These governing entities were based around the political organisation known as the 'commune' which relied on horizontal forms of collaboration. The communes shared a number of features: they operated as secular authorities, with many of their ruling officers chosen by rudimentary electoral methods. Even though the communes were under nominal monarchal or papal rule, they possessed *de facto* republican independence (Hearder, 1990).

The communes originally emerged in newly urbanised city locations. Members of the landowning aristocracy, rather than city merchants, assumed the initiative to create these political institutions. This class group joined forces with rural migrants to collaborate on economic matters and provide mutual assistance. It is noteworthy that commune members placed their allegiance to the commune as opposed to archaic feudal political powers (Lane, 1966).

The twin attractions of liberalised governmental rule and economic prosperity brought ever increasing migrant flows from agricultural areas to the city-republics. One estimate maintains that Padua's population grew from 15,000 in 1175 to 35,000 by 1320 (Waley, 1969, pp. 21—2). The expanding urban population brought with it a number of new social classes that clamoured for representation in the communes. Thus, by the twelfth century, the cities of Florence, Bologna, Genoa, Milan and most other prominent locations in the central and northern regions of Italy had created some form of independent communal government. Initially, popular participation was limited and informal but, as the number of inhabitants grew, the administrative machinery of government became increasingly sophisticated to accommodate different interests (Tabacco, 1989, pp. 222—3). A medieval town like Siena, with an adult male population of around 5,000, created 860 part-time city council positions (Putnam, 1993). Similarly, thirteenth-century Bologna had 2,000 public servants, or notaries, who had responsibility for keeping records of business and legal transactions (Hearder, 1990). However, when it came to electing officials and administrators, the communes only practised a limited form of democracy. Effective political power was, more often than not, located in the hands of a small group of men who were members of the 'consul'. According to Martines (1979), by 1200 the small consul, characterised by limited representation, had become the basic means of governance in the communes.

Despite the limited nature of democracy, the city-republics were progressive in the art of collective rule, fostering a level of popular participation alien to most medieval societies. In fact, the communal political system was part of a manifest 'burgeoning of associative life' (Becker, 1981, p. 36) that gave rise to confraternities (religious charitable bodies), and *vicinanze* (neighbourhood associations).

They also facilitated the cultivation of highly innovative commercial operations based around cooperative networks. The communal republics provided the requisite social conditions for the invention of credit and banking facilities. The spirit of mutual cooperation and the integration of communal societies were imperative to the use of credit. Usher notes: 'The distinctive features of the primitive bank of deposit were largely derived from the predominant use of the verbal contract' (1934, p. 410). (In etymological terms, 'credit' derives from the Latin *credere*, meaning 'to believe'.) In addition to credit facilities, guild organisations, responsible for representing merchants and regulating trade, flourished in the communes. These organisations were sensitive to the needs of wider communal society and contributed extensively to its well-being.

The historical antecedents of the Italian guilds can be traced to the compulsory taxpaying trade associations, or *collegia*, of the late Roman Empire. The advance of Byzantine and Germanic rule in the late sixth century, together with the influence of Roman Catholic bureaucrats, brought about their demise. But some Byzantium protectorates — Naples, Amalfi and Venice — were administered and financed by merchants. Such was the success of these guild run cities that the Frankish Emperor, Lothar I, permitted seven areas located in the north of Italy — Bologna, Cremona, Ivrea, Florence, Milan, Padua, Turin and Venice — to establish independent associations of craftsmen and traders. This eventually culminated in a veritable proliferation of guild institutions in the tenth century (Staley, 1906).

By the twelfth century, guilds could be found regulating trade and securing monopoly interests for town merchants throughout the city-republics. As well as administering trade, these trade associations would collect taxes to fund the construction of defence fortifications and other public services (Hickson and Thompson, 1991). It was exigent for guildsmen to be integrated into the machinery of communal government. Inclusion gave them an opportunity to promote the interests of their own trades within the corridors of power. Hearder (1990) reports that artisans and shopkeepers could be found in Modena's town council by 1200.

Participation of the guilds in civic life extended to the provision of welfare services and mutual assistance to both members and non-members. The religious ancestry of many guilds helped sensitise members to the plight of the less fortunate, both within and outside the organisation. Sometimes membership of a guild required active participation in mutual assistance (Hyde, 1973). The guild statute of Verona of 1303, probably inherited from a much earlier statute, demanded the following:

> 'Fraternal assistance in necessity of whatever kind', 'hospitality towards strangers, when passing through the town, as thus information may be obtained about matters which one may like to learn', and 'obligation of offering comfort in case of debility' are among the obligations of the members. (Kropotkin, 1907, p. 174n.)

The nascent philanthropic impulse of these local trade associations can be partly explained by their religious and fraternal origins. Of equal significance was the proliferation of charitable activities in communal Italy, which were not without their influence on communal institutions and leaders. Using archival sources from medieval Tuscany, Becker (1981) records a marked increase in charitable activity after the eleventh century. In the diocese of Lucca between 824 and 1008, the cause against indigence received only four donations in total, compared with 22 registered gifts from 1008 to 1100. A similar pattern was recorded for Florence: in the ninth century, only three bequests were made for the establishment of pious foundations, and none at all in the tenth century before 978. For the next 30 years after this date, information exists on 19 new foundations — equalling the total for the previous 200 years.

Becker maintains that there is no straightforward explanation for this heightened interest in philanthropy. A likely scenario is that the demise of the feudal order and its replacement by a society predicated on cooperation and mutual responsibility between different orders proved ultimately conducive to charitable sensibilities. For instance, lay associations that were active in the Church demonstrated a profound concern with worldly matters as expressions of religious devotion. Becker notes: 'Empathy for the plight of the poor was matched by a vital concern for human suffering' (1981, p. 37). In feudal society, charity was rarely linked to collective ideals and was sporadic. In contrast to the communal age, charitable action in the Dark Ages was motivated more out of selfish, utilitarian needs than human compassion: individuals gave to the poor in order to gain God's favour and salvation after death.

Moreover, in feudal society charity was the preserve of leading families and was looked on as an expression of pietistic observance rather than pastoral concern. After the eleventh century, the world of benevolence in Tuscany was 'democratised': philanthropy became an occupation open to all those individuals who were genuinely moved by deprivation and poverty. Along with ordinary gentle folk, the emerging artisans, shopkeepers and craftsmen of Tuscany were similarly welcomed into the philanthropic world, previously reserved for the landowning elite and ecclesiastical leaders (Becker, 1981, p. 100). The guilds, as representative agencies of these new entrepreneurial classes, possessed the financial and human resources to undertake a prominent role in charitable work.

Florence was a major centre of guild activity. Apart from their importance to the communal economy, the Florentine guilds were noted for their charitable work. Following the example of the premier guild in Florence, the Calimala guild, various other trade associations patronised local monasteries. The guilds were attracted by the religious orientation of these centres, and by their functions as rest homes for the infirm (Staley, 1906).

The guilds often targeted medical centres in their benefactions. In Florence, it was commonplace for leper stations on the outskirts of the city to obtain donations from individual guild members. The propagation of hospital institutions in the northern and central regions of Italy, especially Florence, during the twelfth and thirteenth centuries was assisted by munificent donations from guild institutions. By 1338 there were 30 hospitals in Florence, including around 1,000 beds for the sick. The guilds of Florence helped to finance the establishment and maintenance of these hospitals (Staley, 1906, p. 538). In 1338 the Calimala guild built a hospital in the hamlet of Campoluccio, endowing it with food and medical treatments for patients. Unfortunately, the institution carried on its work only until 1529 when, during the siege of Florence, it was demolished to build fortifications.

The social relations that characterised communal society gave rise to civically minded commercial institutions like the guilds. Yet a spirit of egalitarianism and democracy was not all-pervasive in the city-republics, as factionalism was rife and the nobility remained an important part of communal life. Nonetheless, the cities of northern Italy maintained a distinct sense of social order and cooperation that was lacking in most other European societies at the time. However, the ability of communes to maintain social order and a vibrant associative life was manifestly threatened by a series of events in the fourteenth century.

The crisis of communal Italy

The pinnacle of republican rule came during the late thirteenth and early fourteenth centuries. Thereafter, the healthy associative life encouraged in the city-republics of central and northern Italy were besmirched by a series of catastrophes — famines, wars and epidemics (Lane, 1966).

One of the most injurious episodes in the history of communal Italy was the arrival of the Black Death in 1348. This plague struck when the resilience of the people was already at a low ebb due to a series of famines which began around 1339. The Black Death was probably brought to Italy by Genoese merchants coming from the Crimea. Once in Genoa, it spread to Pisa and then throughout central and northern Italy, with Florence being the worse affected republican city-state. From historical studies that have examined this tempestuous period in pre-Unification Italy, it would seem that around one-third of Italy's population died as a result of the epidemic (Hearder, 1990). The Black Death was not an isolated event: other, less severe, epidemics broke out at various times during the fourteenth century. This retarded the opportunities for economic recovery, and introduced a note of dislocation into the previously cohesive communal milieu. Even the number of available administrators and political leaders was severely curtailed by the plagues.

The destabilisation caused by successive plagues and famines saw the city-republics place their faith in seigniorial rule and hereditary succession. It was envisaged that these systems would be better able to restore stability than elected representatives and secular administrators. Martines argues that 'residual political feeling of a popular sort evaporated in the course of the fifteenth century. The political stability of republics came increasingly to be moored in fixed classes and a fixed patriciate' (1979, p. 139).

Not all was lost for communal Italy. A belt of cities running across Venice, Emilia, Tuscany and Genoa had managed to preserve communal rule and resisted subjugation to monarchal authority. Even so, for many areas, authoritarian pedagogy was fast subsuming civic republicanism as the dominant form of rule within the communal networks of Italy.

Under these new political conditions, many of the institutions, integral to city-republics, were systematically dismantled. In communal Italy, the merchant and craft guilds were noteworthy victims of this abrasive political culture. More specifically, it was the emergence of Hellenistic thought in fifteenth century northern Italy that helped erode the legitimacy and function of the guilds (Hickson and Thompson, 1991).

As a distinctly occidental school of thought, Hellenism could be traced to the writings of Socrates, Plato and Aristotle. It was popularised by Alexander the Great and the Caesars throughout the ancient world. Hickson and Thompson (1991) argue that the spread Hellenistic concerns during the fifteenth century inculcated a negative and cynical evaluation of popular democratic rule, epitomised by the city-republics. For the guilds, this meant a loss of autonomy and subjection to the 'oligarchies of centrally directed, Hellenized bureaucrats...' (Hickson and Thompson, 1991, p. 152). With these new seigniorial despots, the guilds were divested of their entry-restricting powers and bureaucratic administrative function in collecting taxes. The emaciation of the guilds had severe repercussions for many city-republics, such was their importance as commercial and tax collecting institutions. This could be seen by the way communes, such as Venice and Florence which had restored their guilds, economically outperformed despotic cities like Milan (Carpanetto and Ricuperati, 1987). Furthermore, because, in many cities, the guilds were responsible for collecting defence taxes on behalf of the local commune, the active dismissal of the guild system immediately extinguished a source of government revenue for defence spending.

These myopic policies, together with the politically volatile situation, rendered the peninsula susceptible to colonial domination. Inevitably, this is exactly what happened during the fifteenth and sixteenth centuries when France and Spain played out their imperial ambitions in Italy.

Spanish domination and the rise of the Christian loan banks

When Charles VIII invaded Italy in 1494, the Italian republics tried to undermine the French monarch by pitting other European powers, such as Spain, against him; this only ended up dividing rather than uniting Italy. A destructive phase of the Franco-Spanish War thus began in 1521: Charles V, Emperor of Spain, drove Francis I of France from Milan, resulting in a protracted confrontation between the two powers. In this war, Italy was the principal battlefield, and the city-states acted as satellites for French and Spanish interests. Spanish successes at Pavia and then Rome in 1527 proved decisive in the battle. In 1559 the war was concluded with the Treaty of Cateau-Cambresis. This marked the start of Spanish domination over Italy for nearly 150 years. And, with the exception of Turin, it also meant the end of French sovereignty over the area for some time.

For many commentators, the start of Spanish domination in the early decades of the sixteenth century signalled the demise of independence and republican rule for the northern city-states. As a result of these foreign invasions, the city-republics experienced a sharp economic and demographic decline. Some historians describe the years following the Renaissance — the Baroque period — as 'perhaps the dullest in Italian history' (Hearder and Waley, 1963, p. 98); others simply note that the republics were moving towards 're-feudalisation' (Putnam, 1993). The great philosophers and thinkers of the Risorgimento — Francesco De Sanctis and Benedetto Croce — argued that Spanish rule in Italy caused its vibrant cultural life to decay.

Modern historians have come up with findings at variance with orthodox formulations of the 'decadent' Baroque period. In seminal works on Florence and Tuscany, the historian Eric Cochrane found that the sixteenth and seventeenth centuries were not dreary historical interludes, but periods of intellectual, artistic and political vitality. Cochrane (1988) shows how the pan-Italian alliance established by Charles V of Spain led to a period of stability and relative peace; for Cochrane this was not the genesis of the Counter-Reformation, but the beginning of the 'age of consolidation'. During this period of political stability, Italy — especially the war torn areas of the north — witnessed demographic expansion and commercial recovery.

The ecclesiastical reforms introduced by the decrees of the Council of Trent (1545—62) produced a religiously devout and well instructed laity. By the same token, this emphasis on piety produced a zealousness for religious activism and charity. Even the *vita civile* — the impulse of mutual solidarity and cooperation fostered by the city-states — was not totally eradicated by the eclipse of communal government. The 'age of consolidation' saw the rise of religiously inspired institutional configurations that shared an affinity with the organisations and traditions of the city-republics. Foremost among these new associative formations were the *monti di pegno* (or *monti di pieta*) which were primarily formed as Christian banks to combat indigence and serve the poor. The Christian banks are significant to the present analysis, particularly as their influence is still evident in contemporary Italian society (see Chapter 8).

The banks were founded in the latter part of the fifteenth century by the Observant Franciscans. Their principle function was to relieve burden of poverty. This was achieved by supplying small loans, either gratuitously or at low rates of interest, to the genuinely poor or needful. Although similar Christian loan banks existed throughout Europe in the mid-fifteenth century, the Italian *monti di pieta* proved unique. They aimed to both relieve the distress caused by poverty and systematically replace Jewish moneylenders and banks with Christian-run operations. Having been marginalised from mainstream economic activities, moneylending, which was regarded as un-Christian, proved one of the few modes of work available to Jewish people.

Despite their aims, the anti-Semitic ecclesiastical authorities treated the idea of Christian loan banks with a certain amount of suspicion because of their perceived dalliance with 'usury' — a financial practice which, according to the Catholic Church, was a direct contravention of divine law. Nevertheless, the *monti di pieta* had the favour of the secularised judiciary; loans and interest payments were approved on the grounds of economic necessity. Even some religious representatives were apt not to dismiss interest payments out of hand: the Tuscan preacher, Bernardino of Siena, argued that interest payments could be used for charitable purposes (Pullan, 1971).

After the first *monte di pieta* was established in Perugia in 1463, a number of similar institutions were founded in the areas around central Italy, gradually gaining acceptance in the Papal states and thereby providing the movement with authority (Pullan, 1971). By the late fifteenth and early sixteenth century, the Christian banks could be found widely dispersed across Liguria, Lombardy and several territories in Veneto. In 1515 a Papal proclamation in support of the *monti di pieta* was finally granted by the Bull of Leo X. The Bull defended the use of interest payments on the basis that banks had to generate surplus income to employ full-time administrative officials.

Because of their charitable origins, the average rate of interest stood at 4—5 per cent — or in the case of smaller banks no interest charge was made. The level of income generated proved to be of nominal proportions. However, the early *monti di pieta* did not expand their capital reserves by participating in financial speculation or by providing private banking services. Instead, recourse was made to a variety of non-profit fund-raising methods. Favoured strategies included the charity sermon, religious festivals and the setting of special taxes, which were rarely used.

Eventually, it was inevitable in a society where financial practices were so advanced that, as Pullan notes, 'the Monti di Pieta began to raise capital for the use of the poor by acting as deposit or savings banks' (1971, p. 474). A number of institutions experienced marked growth during the sixteenth century because of their forays into deposit banking. To attract deposits, some organisations started to offer interest payments in return for investments. However, such displays of entrepreneurial ingenuity were in danger of being ruled *ultra vires* on the grounds of usury. The main note of justificatory support for interest payments on deposit payments was this: that an investor deliberately giving to charity was entitled to limited forms of compensation. Papal briefs granted to Modena (1542) and Vicenza (1555) stipulated that interest could be paid to depositors. Other cities, assuming that the Papal briefs given to Modena and Vicenza had a general applicability, copied their example. The ecclesiastical authorities, on this issue, proved less intransigent, for in most cases the ruling public institutions could guarantee the return of deposits.

Despite the inroads being made into deposit banking, the contribution to poverty relief was still an integral function of the Christian loan banks. Their main contribution in tackling indigence took the form of low-interest loans. When requests were made, officials from the *monti di pieta* would carry out meticulous investigations to discover the reasons behind the petition; this initial screening proved necessary in order to distinguish between those who were genuinely in need of loans. The cause against poverty went beyond munificence. Some *monti di pieta* produced large quantities of small currency for their claimants. Other banks made specific efforts to assist agricultural production in order to create jobs and promote economic self-sufficiency among the poor in their localities (Pullan, 1971).

The charitable work of the banks increasingly had to be balanced against their involvement in deposit banking. The embroilment of the Christian loan banks in such areas attracted a clientele other than the destitute or poor. Religious organisations which could not invest in land and capital used the facilities of the *monti di pieta*. Members of the middle class did the same. A number of

Christian banks followed Verona's example of having two separate banks. One, exclusively charitable, lent small sums to the poor; the other supplied personal loans of any amount to all individuals.

Throughout the sixteenth and seventeenth centuries, the nature of the *monte di pieta* continued to change gradually, as capital was increasingly generated by the banks through interest-bearing deposits. Although they still retained their charitable status, external financial demands forced them ever further into mainstream banking. Several private banking failures in the late sixteenth century had led to the *monti di pieta* being used as a public service banks. Larger cities utilised funds from these banks to construct defences or to purchase surplus grain supplies during periods of emergency. This embroilment in public banking threatened to dismantle the *monti di pieta* following a series of catastrophes in northern Italy during the early 1600s. Between 1630 and 1633, a serious epidemic to rival the Black Death struck Italy, causing some towns to lose 70 per cent of their inhabitants (Hearder, 1990). A second plague hit Italy in 1656, with the port cities of Genoa and Naples losing 50 per cent of their citizens. In addition, by 1627, the relative stability that had reigned over Italy came to a sudden end with the resumption of the struggle over Italian territory between France and Spain. In 1629, French and Spanish forces fought over Mantua and Monteferrat — a battle subsequently won by the French in 1631.

The arrival of wars, epidemics and economic instability brought many Christian banks, increasingly involved in public investment, to near ruin. The ruling body in Brescia was unable to pay back the loans to one of its *monti di pieta*, thus reducing the financial capacity of the bank. In the case of the large Christian bank of Verona, loans were made to the ruling house of Mantua during the war of the Mantuan succession in the late 1620s. Few conditions had been placed on the loan, and when the Duke of Mantua failed to redeem his pledges or pay interest on them, the bank lost around one-third of its capital.

This period of instability was compounded, as already mentioned, by the resumption of hostilities between France and Spain in 1627. During the final phase of this long colonial war in the early 1700s, the protagonists were joined by the Austrians who saw this as their opportunity to gain influence in Italy. The Peace of Utrecht, marking the end of the war in 1713, was significant; it established the Austrian Habsburgs as the dominant power in Italy. Under Austrian rule, Italy experienced relative tranquillity, especially in the period between 1748 and the invasion of Napoleon in 1796. Yet, it had all the hallmarks of a discordant society: the contrasts between rich and poor seemed to be more entrenched than anywhere else in Europe, and crime was on the upsurge (Hearder and Waley, 1963, p. 104).

The fragile position of Italian society was not helped by a series of free market reforms, implemented by the new Austrian rulers. The reforms disrupted local economies and disassembled surviving guild institutions. Tuscany's Austrian monarchal ruler, Leopold, was committed to private landholdings and the free market and his adherence to the private economy nearly obliterated the medieval guild system in the 1780s. This provoked an economic and social crisis as the number of commercial institutions offering stable employment opportunities was reduced considerably (Woolf, 1979, p. 131).

By the eighteenth century, the civic traditions and institutions of the peninsula were either eradicated or disrupted by despotic rule and the imposition of reforms. But the *vita civile* of the city communes, so resplendent throughout the Middle Ages and during brief interludes such as the baroque period, was not doomed. The former locations of the city-republics — the northern and central regions of the peninsula — would see the rise of new communitarian-based institutions during the nineteenth century.

The new wave of benevolent institutions

Our attention now turns to the early years of the nineteenth century. This was a period of momentous political change which saw the emergence of new civic associations, including socially oriented commercial institutions. The new decade marked the start of Napoleon's reign as Emperor of Italy — a mantle which he assumed after a prolonged war between revolutionary France and monarchal Austria over Italian territory. This war raged from 1792 to 1804 and saw Napoleon rise from director over colonial policies in Italy to dictator of France. In 1804, four years after capturing Italy's northern territories from the Austrians, Napoleon declared himself Emperor of the Kingdom of Italy.

From this omniscient position, Napoleon was able to impose his form of governmental authority throughout Italy. The ushering in of this new political order, according to Putnam (1993), involved officials in France and Italy keeping close scrutiny over, and sometimes actively suppressing, organised forms of sociability; even innocuous associations such as working men's clubs. In Napoleonic law, there was an in-built distrust of institutions that were not formally recognised by the state. Hodson observes: 'the development of law was profoundly influenced by the principle that the supremacy of the democratic State should not be impoverished by unregulated power given to private institutions' (1991, p. x). Despite Napoleon's undemocratic and imperialist tendencies, he installed an efficient administrative system and occasionally imposed enlightened monarchal rulers over Italian territories.

Once France's claims over Italy were secure, Napoleon began to pursue his imperial ambitions in Eastern Europe. Early successes were gained over the coalition powers of Austria, Prussia and Russia throughout the 1805—7 period, and later over Austria at the Battle of Wagram (1809). But then France took the ill-advised step of invading Russia, incurring significant losses for the French army in the ensuing battles. In March 1813 Prussia and Austria went to war against France, with Italy once again providing the battlefield location. Eventually, Napoleon's army was defeated at the four-day battle of Leipzig (Hearder, 1983).

The settlement of 1815 incorporated the treaties of Vienna and Paris. Metternich, the Austrian Foreign Minister, made no secret of his aspirations that Italy should come under Austria's sphere of influence. His wishes were largely fulfilled: the north-east and much of the remainder of Italy came under Austrian control; monarchal dynasties were installed at Genoa and Venice; and the Treaty of Vienna placed Lombardy, Tuscany and Modena under the Habsburg monarchies.

Once in power, the Austrians were loath to dismantle the effective administrative system brought in by Napoleon, or even sack appointed officials. Instead, they used this system to encourage economic development and mutual assistance throughout the peninsula. In fact, they helped revive the tradition of social banking — first seen in the *monti di pieta* — through the formation of savings banks (*casse di risparmio*) at the hands of Conte Franz von Saurau, the Interior Minister of the Austrian government. The first group of such banks was established between January and February 1822 in Venice, Padua, Udine, Treviso, and Rovigo. The *casse di risparmio* shared an affinity with the *monte di pieta*, functioning as quasi-public institutions that generated funds through the use of interest payments. However, they used more advanced methods and, on the whole, executed their administrative duties with greater proficiency (Senin, 1976, p. 910).

The *monti di pieta* continued to operate during this period, despite the economic set backs which they had faced in earlier centuries. However, they were soon numerically surpassed by the proliferation of the *casse di risparmio*: in 1823, the Milan-based Cassa di Risparmio delle Province Lombarde was established; the neighbouring region of Piedmont, in 1827, witnessed the establishment of the Cassa del Regno di Sardegna; and, soon after, cities in central Italy — Florence (1829) and Rome (1836) — formed their own casse di risparmio. By 1850 there were 70 such banks in the northern and central regions of Italy, with 20 of these located in Lombardy and Veneto. In the southern regions, where patterns of sociability had been repressed, it was only after the Unification of Italy that the first savings bank was formed in the Mezzogiorno (ACRI, n.d., p. 5).

The significant point about the *casse di risparmio* is that they continued the tradition of social and philanthropic banking (Magini, 1992). The aims of the original sponsors was for the banks to cultivate a system of welfare assistance, whereby funds would be distributed to the needy and indigent. For example, the funding of hospitals, recovery homes, schools, and art conservatories for the poor were among the social and philanthropic causes that occupied the Cassa di Risparmio di Roma. Indeed, when the regulation for instituting the bank was passed in 1836, much was made of the need for the bank to partake in social and charitable action (Varni *et al.*, 1991, p. 13).

In addition to these philanthropic interventions, the *casse di risparmio* contributed to the economic and commercial well-being of their localities: they gave didactic advice to depositors on the practice of saving and provided artisans and landed proprietors with loans to assist local economies. These commercial policies, however, left the *casse di risparmio* open to accusations that those benefiting most from their services were the comfortable classes (small capitalists, merchant landowners and public employees) rather than the underprivileged. Those who most required easy access to cheap loans did not possess the financial wherewithal to build up savings and, hence, deposits in the banks. Consequently, the banks lowered their rates of interest from 4 to 3 per cent in 1830 to attract less prosperous customers. With the lower rate of interest producing the desired effect six years later the maximum limit for a single account was reduced from 300 to 75 lire (Neufeld, 1961, p. 56).

The Austrian regime undoubtedly retained a semblance of administrative efficiency in its rule over Italy and proved instrumental in forming the *casse di risparmio*. There was nevertheless a strong undercurrent of dissatisfaction against Austrian occupation. Hearder observes that there was particular 'resentment against the Austrian imposition of a censorship of a kind far more rigorous than anything Napoleon's officials had imposed' (1983, p. 31). The grudging acquiescence of the Italians towards foreign occupation soon spilled over into active opposition. Disaffected troops and underground societies which had originally been formed to undermine the Napoleonic regime in Italy were at the forefront of this opposition. The Adelfi sect (later called 'Sublime Perfect Masters'), led by Filippo Buonarroti, and the later La Giovine Italia (Young Italy), formed by Giuseppe Mazzini, pursued republican objectives. These societies, amongst others, proved to be important precursors of the Risorgimento movement. Leaders of that movement, such as Mazzini, made vital contributions to the Unification of Italy in 1861 (Hearder, 1983).

These politically motivated societies, however, seemed more than the epiphenomena of the ground swell of opposition against the Austrian regime. They were manifestations of the surge of associative and civic behaviour at the turn of the century. Nineteenth-century associative life assumed diverse forms of sociability: civic, charitable and educational associations emerged in most cities and towns (see Putnam, 1993). This resurgence of associative life brought about new forms of charitable and associative action. As the traditional conduits of charity and welfare — the ecclesiastical authorities and the *monti di pieta* —

were in some disarray (Clark, 1984), mutual aid societies rose to prominence to promote new benevolent associations. Although these associations could be found in the fourteenth century, they only became widely established after the mid-1800s. Between 1800 and 1849, the number of mutual aid societies stood at 38, but this total increased to 174 between 1850 and 1859 (Neufeld, 1961). In terms of geographical dispersion, the north of Italy was the prime area for their operations. The Kingdom of Sardinia (incorporating the region of Piedmont), in the 1850—60 period, held over two-thirds of the mutual aid societies in Italy. This was facilitated by the Kingdom's adoption of a liberal constitution that guaranteed the freedom of association (Neufeld, 1961, p. 61).

The rehabilitation of associative life brought to the fore a number of new commercial organisations with benevolent leanings. These institutions gained prominent support from members of the middle class, who, due to a religiously inspired spirit of humanitarianism, found themselves moved to alleviate indigence (Neufeld, 1961, p. 56). Prominent among this new wave of socially inclined business institutions were the cooperatives. As commercial institutions, they acted more as benevolent associations for workers than orthodox profit-making enterprises. They grew out of the conservative principle — similar to that advocated by the mutual aid societies — of facilitating the process of self-help through mutual solidarity. The inspiration for the Italian cooperatives, and principal advocates of the movement, such as Mazzini, could be linked to the Equitable Pioneers of Rochdale, although the Italian movement lacked the commercial acumen and solidarity found in its English counterpart. But if the Italian movement had a distinctive feature, it was the sheer variety of industrial and commercial organisation that came under the cooperative umbrella.

The exact temporal appearance of the cooperatives can be traced to the post-revolutionary period of 1848. Here, groups of craftsmen and artisans, mainly in the north-west of Italy, collaborated to form small workshops. The creation of cooperatives was facilitated, in 1848, by a statute of King Charles Albert of Turin that permitted freedom of association. According to leading authorities, the first true producer cooperative was the Associazione Artistica Vetraria (Society of Artistic Glassware) of Altare, a village located in the Ligurian hills. The cooperative was formed in 1856 when the village doctor, Dr Giuseppe Cesio, in the wake of a cholera outbreak and a local economic recession, persuaded 84 labourers to form a glass-making association as a way of reviving the village economy (Earle, 1986, p. 12). The glass-makers marked their agreement with a ritual that revived the traditions of the guild of Altare, which had sustained successive attempts of repression by ruling monarchs. By the 1870s the Associazione Vetraria had doubled its membership.

Like the Associazione Vetraria, many of the formative producer cooperatives could be found in the north of Italy: the Printing House of Compositors founded in 1859 in Turin; the Stonemasons of Milan (1860); the Tailors of Genoa (1856); and the Wool-carders in Milan (1862) (Earle, 1986, p. 13). All these fledgling producer cooperatives drew on the most immediate cultural resources available: the tradition of civic responsibility and associative social action of the Middle Ages. This tradition was drawn upon principally as a pragmatic response to changing economic conditions in nineteenth-century Italy. Por observes: 'There is then, in Italy, a well-pronounced general tendency among the workers, originating perhaps in the traditions of medieval guilds, to fight against the sabotage of production by the present economic system' (1923, pp. 3—4).

The producer cooperatives performed the important social functions — mainly for their members — of providing secure employment and insurance services. On the other hand, the cooperative credit societies, emerging after the producer cooperatives, served a wider constituency within communities. The first cooperative banks or people's banks (*banche popolare*) were founded at Lodi near Milan in 1864 by the Venetian polymath, Luigi Luzzatti, who adapted them from the German model of the *Schulze-Delitzsch*. Using this model, members would buy shares, normally with a small deposit, and loans would be made in proportion to these deposits. Under Luzzatti's leadership, cooperative banks subsequently appeared in Milan and Brescia. The movement then extended beyond the northern cradle, and the number of credit societies grew from four to 64 between 1865 and 1871. By 1881, there were 171 cooperative banks, and the level of subscribed capital had nearly doubled within a ten-year period (Earle, 1986, pp. 14—18).

Many of the new benevolent institutions that were founded during the 1880s tended to converge around the centre and north of Italy. The south was still shackled to century-old, feudalised, authority structures which were responsible for economic underdevelopment and the rise of powerful crime syndicates (Gambetta, 1988). According to Caracciolo (1977), by the 1870s, the northern and central regions of Italy had already cultivated a wealth of new associations — savings banks, cooperatives, rural credit societies and people's banks.

The impact of modernising forces on these new civic and business institutions will dominate the second part of this historical chapter. Specific consideration will be given to the industrialisation of Italy and its repercussions for the wider social and philanthropic interests of business enterprises.

Commercial philanthropy in the age of modernisation

The modern period naturally begins with the industrialisation of Italy. This was a pivotal moment in the peninsula's history, for it brought about a fundamental transformation of a society based on agrarian production. The aim here is to examine the transition from traditional to modern forms of economic production. The analysis focuses on how this transition affected the social and philanthropic commitments of the new industrial class and of semi-public commercial entities, such as the savings banks and cooperatives.

Significantly, Italy delayed her entrance into the industrial age. It was not until the early 1890s that country's economic base made the leap from traditional to an industrial mode of production. The years between 1896 and 1908, as one commentator has described them, were those of 'the great push' towards industrialisation (Gerschenkron, 1962, p. 77). The reason why Italy lagged behind the rest of Europe can be partly attributed to the inability of the entrepreneurial class to build a hegemonic base. Instead, the emerging business class found itself tied to the pre-industrial landed elites, which hampered its attempts to transform Italy's agrarian economy.

There were small groups of businessmen, influenced by what was taking place in other European states, who advocated the adoption of industrial production methods. In response, societies and institutes were established to promote industrialisation, and schools for instructing workers in modern production methods emerged in Milan and Turin (Cafagna, 1973, pp. 284—5). These modest advances took place in a climate still dominated by agrarian production. Influential opinion, that of the Catholic Church and the landowning classes, was still pitted against industrialisation. Eventually, it was only through a heavy dependence on state intervention that the bourgeoisie was able to transform Italy's tardy economy.

Direct state intervention was integral to the industrialisation of many European nations. The level of government involvement in economic affairs tended to vary across societies. Different national configurations approached the process of industrialisation in their own distinctive manners. Prodi makes a telling statement with reference to Italy on this point:

> Italy's industrial development has been supported by the public sector to a degree that has few equals among the nations that operate on the basis of a market economy. Italian capitalism was born and developed through a continuous series of privileged relations with the state...In the history of all the European industrial systems, there have been periods of strong state intervention. But these have usually alternated with periods of pronounced 'laissez faire'. In Italy, on the other hand, the close tie between the public and private sectors developed permanent elements even though there were continuous institutional changes. (1974, p. 45)

From the late 1880s onwards, the economy began to take faltering steps towards industrialisation. It was at this point that the government capitulated to the demands of the pro-industrial lobby to intervene on behalf of the nascent industrial sector. From then on, the state used a whole panoply of political and economic instruments at its disposal — tax concessions, investment and tariffs — to prioritise industrial production, mainly in expanding areas such as shipbuilding, steel and cotton production. Government intervention proved equally significant when it came to modernising the infrastructure, such as the railways. As other European states had already demonstrated, a fully operating railway system was critical to economic and industrial growth (Toniolo, 1990).

By the late nineteenth century, Italy had achieved tangible growth and was beginning to industrialise. Such expansion was mainly the result of what Saraceno (1976) terms the guaranteed model of development, where banks and companies depended extensively on public sector support. Much of the growth was concentrated in cotton production, which had a limited market, and the high-cost steel production industry at the expense of developing potentially dynamic chemical and engineering industries (Toniolo, 1977). And even though Italy's economy grew considerably during the late 1890s, this was confined to the north, leaving the south underdeveloped (Eckaus, 1961). There is no doubt that the overall economic performance of the peninsula still lagged behind many of Europe's leading nations.

The weakness of the business class, and its concomitant dependence on the public sector, had significant repercussions for the social and philanthropic commitments of entrepreneurs and business institutions. Due to the late arrival of industrialisation, business owners were not in a position to emulate the level of social action demonstrated by commercial institutions like the guilds of the city-republics. Indeed, the extent of entrepreneurial support for voluntary and charitable agencies was limited, the main reason being that charities were brought under state control through Crispi's charity reform law of 1890. This law reflected state concern over the effectiveness of charity work and was also a general manifestation of distrust, emanating from the influence of Napoleonic law in Italy, displayed towards non-state agencies (Farrell-Vinay, 1989).

The centralisation of the Italian economy and society did not, altogether, prove a hindrance to business philanthropy. The ubiquitous presence of the state in Italian society helped to safeguard the communitarian business institutions that had emerged during the pre-industrial period — namely, the cooperatives and the public service banks. Special government regulations enabled these institutions to remain firmly within the public domain and to continue providing various services. For instance, the *casse di risparmio*, although mostly privately owned, were officially recognised as public service and charitable institutions by a series of regulations passed in 1888. In 1890, Law no. 6972 publicly confirmed the charitable and public service functions performed by the *monti di pieta* (Senin, 1976, p. 911). (The *monti di pieta* still existed during this period, albeit on a much reduced scale compared with their heyday in the 1500s and 1600s.)

As for the cooperative movement, it continued to proliferate and expand into new areas of the economy during the early twentieth century (see Costanzo, 1923). Giovanni Giolitti's Liberal government in the 1890s helped secure the position of the cooperatives by granting them access to public contracts and facilities for dealing with banks. In addition, in 1904 the government set up the Istituto Nazionale di Credito per la Cooperazione (State Bank for Cooperatives), as a common fund to invest in, and assist, the creation of cooperatives (Lloyd, 1925, pp. 25—4; Cohen, 1967).

While the period of industrialisation witnessed vital functions of the economy and society coming under state control, there were opportunities for private capital to be involved in social action. However, the most conspicuous social interventions by business owners and firms was the establishment of welfare facilities for the workplace. As the most fully industrialised sector of the economy, the textile industry demonstrated precocity in introducing paternalistic strategies as a response to the social consequences of industrialisation. The cotton manufacturing sector was largely owner-controlled, with only 18 of the 727 cotton factories operating in 1900 being owned by shareholders (Cafagna, 1973, p. 295). This meant that employers enjoyed a high degree of discretion in procuring a variety of social and welfare facilities for employees. One of the most notable paternalists in the textile industry was Alessandro Rossi who was reputed for his progressive ideas with regard to economic policy and the improvement of the factory environment (Baglioni, 1974). In the Milan area, employees at the Crespi textile firm benefited from social services, including a factory village which housed workers and a local police station.

The paternalism of these early textile factory owners has generated some interest among Italian socio-economic historians (see Merli, 1972; Guiotto, 1979). However, scholars who have studied the benevolent endeavours of early industrialists generally equate paternalism with an ebbing away of autonomy for labour groups. An underlying characteristic of paternalism is that social relationships in the workplace are based on vertical principles of patronage and deference to the owner's authority (Pollard, 1965; Joyce, 1982). Wilson notes:

Paternalist employers were basically benevolent dictators, providing facilities for their workers and in turn hoping for their loyalty and affection. Their employees benefited from their 'generosity' but remained entirely dependent on the goodwill of the management, for paternalism implied no rights to welfare. (1987, p. 190)

The main features of Italian industrialisation and business-led social action contrast markedly with those that prevailed in Britain during the same period. For a start, Britain was the first state to industrialise — an achievement that took place with limited direct state intervention. For Supple, the proximate causes of British industrialisation are to be found in the market rather than the government:

> Compared with the continental experience...the British Industrial Revolution was a triumph of individualism...because its mechanisms of supply and demand and resource allocation were geared to the decisions of individual economic agents. (1973, p. 314)

Furthermore, the economic position of industrialists was not undermined by the opposition to modern economic trends of pre-industrial interest groups. In fact, the industrial class augmented its political and social authority in the last third of the nineteenth century by fusing with already powerful landed and financial classes (Scott, 1985, p. 253). Thus, industrialists and entrepreneurs held sufficient levels of wealth and the necessary political autonomy to engage in generous acts of philanthropy.

Entrepreneurial and free market ideals were so prevalent in Britain that there was strong opinion against government intervention. This extended to state intervention in the amelioration of the social and physical impacts of industrialisation. Throughout the eighteenth and nineteenth centuries, private charities and business philanthropists were mainly engaged in poverty relief (see Chapter 2 and 3). In contrast to Italy, there was minimal interference with the private system of welfare. The main regulatory body for charities, the Charity Commission, had very few statutory powers at its disposal. Hence, it seems that the political and economic structures of nineteenth-century Britain were favourable to extensive philanthropic involvement on the part of business owners. Even when a consensus emerged over the necessity of state-organised welfare, sections of the business community contributed to the extension of social services provided by local government (see Frazer, 1979).

In contrast to Britain, Italian capital was in a position of relative weakness and was dependent on direct state intervention. This economic and political subservience of Italian entrepreneurs to the state curtailed the social role of the private sector. Such was the socio-economic standing of the Italian business class in this period that its social activities were confined mainly to the provision of social and welfare services for factory workers. It was only during the early years of the twentieth century, as the economic situation in the peninsula improved, that advances in commercial philanthropy and social action began to appear.

In the immediate years leading up to the First World War, the position of private capital changed markedly in several respects. Economically, private industry consolidated some of the limited gains of the late nineteenth century, as Italy embarked on a second phase of industrial development. Central to this later phase was the ready availability of hydroelectricity — an energy source that was integral to the growth of modern engineering industries. This enabled Italy to achieve a modicum of success in emerging consumer industries and new commercial ventures in the chemicals industry and typewriter manufacturing (Clark, 1984).

Private capital also started to organise political representation through the establishment of employers' associations, which emerged at a much later date in Italy than in other European countries (Martinelli and Treu, 1984). Industrialists were thus able to attain a degree of independence from the paternal tendencies of the state. As the industrial economy expanded during the first half of the twentieth century, business owners in Milan and Turin gained the confidence to establish the first representative associations for employers. This culminated in the foundation of the Italian Confederation of Industry in 1910. Coinciding with this growth in economic and political confidence, isolated, yet conspicuous, examples of business social activism began to surface.

Out of the new industries, the typewriter and office equipment manufacturer, Olivetti, was the most renowned for its social interventions. The company was founded in 1908 by Camillo Olivetti who chose the north-western town of Ivrea as the location for his firm. He followed the tradition of Italy's textile sector by providing a range of welfare and after-work facilities for his workforce (Olivetti, 1983). It was Camillo's son, Adriano, who acted as the main inspiration behind Olivetti's social policies after joining his father in the management of the firm in 1926.

Once Adriano Olivetti began to assume control over the company in the 1930s, he organised an ambitious plan to develop the infrastructure and services for Ivrea. Using the increased wherewithal generated by a threefold increase in production between 1929 and 1937, Olivetti, under Adriano's direction, built hospitals, roads, schools, libraries, housing and recreational facilities (Martin, 1991). This philanthropic programme affected many of the inhabitants of Ivrea, including those not directly involved with the Olivetti company. Adriano also engaged two young architects — Figini and Pollini — who designed company buildings following the progressive ideas of Le Corbusier. These buildings were in keeping with the natural beauty of the area, and also incorporated modern features to create a pleasant working environment for employees. Kicherer notes:

In contrast to other socially conscious companies like Zeiss or Bosch, Adriano did not restrict himself to the limits of his company. Starting from the narrow integration of industry and the surrounding regional social structure, he asked for an industrial development plan which took into consideration the effects on the social and cultural structure. (1990, p. 15)

These social interventions extended to areas outside Ivrea. The company contributed resources and ideas towards the development of the south, urban planning, and art (see Fabbri and Greco, 1988). Adriano Olivetti also launched a political and cultural think-tank and pressure group known as the Movimento Comunità — a vehicle for stimulating public and intellectual debate about a wide range of political-cultural issues such as architecture, the role of the firm in society, local politics and urban planning. As part of this movement, Adriano Olivetti gathered a coterie of artists, philosophers, psychologists, publishers, academics and politicians to examine how work and the quality of life could be improved in an industrial society. Many of these discussions found their way into articles, company periodicals and books by the Movimento Comunità's own publishing house, Edizioni di Comunità (Ronci, 1980, pp. 50—1).

The Fascist period and the dopolavoro

Adriano Olivetti was the most significant industrial philanthropist to emerge from the industrialisation and modernisation of Italy's economy. His company showed how the economic and political confidence attained by private capital enabled firms to engage more fully in communitarian action than in the late nineteenth century.

The political and social position of private capital was subject to further vicissitudes as the Fascists, led by Benito Mussolini, assumed control of the government in 1921. This was initially thought to be a fleeting phenomenon, but Mussolini remained in power for over 20 years. This period in Italy's history was relevant to dealings between private capital and the state, and the social expectations surrounding business enterprises.

During the Fascist period of rule, the direct interventionist approach to economic and civil life continued. In many ways, this strategy was the result of necessity: in the ensuing industrial crisis at the end of the First World War, the government was at hand to salvage industries and faltering credit institutions (Posner and Woolf, 1967). The Fascist regime continued along this vein, establishing the Istituto per la Ricostruzione Industriale (IRI) to operate as a financial investment body for industry. Initially, IRI was created as a temporary remedial measure, providing managerial and financial assistance to banks and joint-stock companies in danger of collapse. By 1937, it had become a permanent industrial holding company and was used to increase military production for the impending war effort.

The formation of IRI was symptomatic of the regime's control over considerable areas of the economy; even the savings banks and cooperatives were brought under state control. While this divested them of their autonomy, it ensured their survival throughout the Fascist period. The regime, despite these centralising tendencies, was generally supportive of the private sector. Major businesses and the Confindustria were granted a degree of autonomy from the state machinery. At the same time, the Fascists provided favourable conditions for intensive capital accumulation by suppressing the trade unions (Martinelli and Treu, 1984, p. 265).

The Fascist government was keen to fill the void left by the subjugation of the trade union movement. It therefore used its close ties with the business community to cajole industrialists into adopting enlightened practices in the workplace. The origins of this campaign can be traced back to the *dopolavoro* (after-work) scheme introduced by Mario Gianni, a former manager at the Westinghouse subsidiary in Vado Ligure. His original plan for the scheme was to improve work conditions by encouraging employers to provide welfare services and leisure facilities for after-work activities. These facilities, it was envisaged, would also be open to the wider community.

Being an opportunist, Mussolini seized upon the *dopolavoro* as an expedient measure to divert labour unrest and engender support for the regime among factory workers. The *Duce* made the following comment, during a series of strikes organised by metallurgical workers in 1925: 'Intelligent capitalists gain nothing from misery; that is why they concern themselves not only with wages, but also with housing, hospitals and sports fields for their workers' (quoted in De Grazia, 1981, p. 62). To expand the scheme, Mussolini created an umbrella organisation in 1923, the Opera Nazionale Dopolavoro (OND). The OND enjoyed relative independence as a charitable body. It had the power to confer on work-based institutions and committees various fiscal privileges in support of local initiatives. The organisation was given a modest grant of 1 million lire, which it was expected to supplement by organising sponsorship deals and attracting private donations.

The level of private sector support for the OND began to increase after 1925. Much of this was due to the fact that the economic depression had induced unemployment and labour unrest. Furthermore, employers were using welfare services to ease the introduction of rationalised production techniques. These production methods came into force after the mid-1920s because of the quadrupling of larger joint-stock companies between 1913 and 1928 (De Grazia, 1981). The clearest indicator of the scheme's popularity was the number of firms that joined the OND or the number providing *dopolavoro* programmes: according to De Grazia, between 1929 and 1931, the number of firms claiming to be *dopolavoro* subscribers rose from 1,660 to 2,938. A 1927 survey of firms in Milan showed that 40 companies provided industrial housing, a further 10 had dormitories for their staff and 13 supplied libraries (Wilson, 1987).

The Fascist regime expected firms to extend these services to the wider community because of the concessions that had been granted to businesses (De Grazia, 1981, p. 68). It began to use a mixture of outright threats and propaganda to ensure that business owners incorporated social schemes into their factories and into their local communities. This pressure helped elicit charitable donations from companies to finance services outside the commercial domain: the Ente Opera Assistenziali — a Fascist-operated welfare agency — benefited from these solicited donations, as did construction projects and holiday camps for children. Some employers raised the necessary funds for their benefactions by surreptitiously cutting workers' wages, especially when economic conditions were less favourable.

The *dopolavoro* scheme, although organised as a service for workers, also gave companies the opportunity to become involved in activities of a social nature. Much of this expansion resulted from the promotion of the *dopolavoro* by the Fascist regime. In fact, the campaign was so successful that the *dopolavoro* and the OND survived the demise of Fascism in 1945. By this time, the OND was mainly preoccupied with the organisation of after-work leisure pursuits. In a bid to divest itself of its Fascist origins, the body was renamed ENAL (the National Organisation for Worker Assistance) in 1945. What is relevant here is that, after the Second World War, ENAL and the *dopolavoro* did not place great emphasis on company involvement in society. Consequently, Chapter 7 examines how philanthropic activities fared in the postwar period, outlining the dominant expressions of business-led social action.

7 State-Private Enterprises and Social Action

The objective of this chapter is to examine the social role of enterprises in contemporary Italian society, defined here as spanning the immediate postwar period to the present. Italy has not experienced a general surge of interest in corporate social responsibility similar to that which took place in Britain throughout the 1980s. However, this is far from implying that commercial organisations have not been engaged in social functions: with the expansion of state control over the economy in the postwar period, commercial units under government ownership were used for social just as much as economic purposes. Indeed, over the years, the state enterprise sector has cultivated an important social ethos. An attempt is made below to detail how state enterprises have contributed to the well-being of society.

Growth of state ownership cannot be disassociated from attempts by the ruling political bloc to construct an alternative power base to that of the private sector. Hence, for much of the postwar period, the private sector was divided and marginalised from mainstream power. However, the dominant position of the state did not remain unrivalled. By the 1960s, some of the most powerful sections of corporate Italy endeavoured to gain more effective political representation. Although this certainly legitimated greater corporate involvement in social action, the examples of social involvement by Italian companies has proven to be limited when compared to Britain. On the other hand, the state holding sector, although rocked by scandal and criticised for its inefficiency, continues to perform a significant economic and social role in Italy.

This chapter aims to emphasise the following point: the political organisation of the state economy and relations between the public and private sector has shaped the parameters which define the social role of companies. The socio-political and economic context in Italy is quite distinct from that which has emerged in Britain. Thus, dominant modes and patterns of corporate social activity have tended to diverge as well. At the same time, case studies of Italian

126

companies underline an argument made in previous chapters: that these wider structures can both constrain and provide opportunities for agents in institutions to engage company's in a social role.

The enlightened state enterprises in the postwar period

Any examination of entrepreneurial social action in contemporary Italy is inextricably linked to the operations of state owned industries in the postwar years. The intervention of the public sector in Italy was, by its very nature, unique: such involvement during and after the period of industrialisation proved to be extensive, albeit lacking in proper administrative coordination. Extensive state intervention across the economy was also prominent during the Fascist period of rule. The collapse of Fascism at the end of the war might have brought about a decisive break with the economic and political configurations that existed under Mussolini. Indeed, the disbanding of the monarchy and the modernisation of political institutions, including a new constitution, suggested that postwar Italy was entering a new epoch. However, throughout the postwar period, the mechanisms of state intervention utilised by Mussolini were left intact, extended and were even fundamentally reorganised for the purpose of social and political reform. Much of this took place due to a mixture of economic necessity and political expediency.

Following the armistice, the economy was in turmoil: Italy's industrial capacity, much of it destroyed by Allied bombers during the war, was predominantly geared to military production, rather than the pressing needs of peacetime reconstruction. The Italian administrator for the American European Recovery Programme (ERP) recommended that the government should endeavour to coordinate public intervention and finance public works to reconstruct the socio-economic infrastructure (Castronovo, 1975).

The Italian authorities, however, failed to put forward a coherent policy for reconstruction. Italy was a bemusing case. Although the government controlled vital sectors of the economy through the Istituto per la Ricostruzione Industriale (IRI), it seemed reluctant to embark on a planned reconstruction of the economy. Contributing to this period of inertia was the emergence of distinct positions on state intervention in the Italian polity. Those in favour of central economic planning could be found on the left of the Christian Democrat Party (for example, Ezio Vanoni and Amintore Fanfani) and the Republican Party. The bulk of the Christian Democrat Party, the employers' confederation (Confindustria) and powerful industrialists represented by Fiat, and the leading wool producer, Gaetano Marzotto, rallied against interventionism (see Amato, 1972).

These divergent views were articulated in a number of public inquiries conducted on state planning and the future of IRI. The conclusions of the Economic Commission to the Constituent Assembly provided the pro-interventionist lobby with a significant boost. The Commission ruled out the return of IRI to the private sector. The postwar markets, it was argued, could not absorb this huge industrial conglomerate, and many of its companies were simply too unprofitable. With high levels of unemployment (19 per cent), the break-up of IRI would have exacerbated the acute economic crisis of the postwar years (Sassoon, 1986, p. 21). In the end, the prospect of disbanding IRI was fraught with such dangers that there was a bipartisan agreement for the company to be kept under state ownership. Thus in 1948, IRI gained a number of new statutes, securing its position. Subsequently, despite the infrastructural problems of Italy's economy, it managed to recover its pre-war capacity by 1948 (Allen and Stevenson, 1974, pp. 222—3).

It seems, then, that Italy's political leaders found convincing economic and social arguments for not dismantling the state economic sector. However, the prospects of expanding the state sector still elicited stern opposition, much of it vanquished by political developments following the demise of the anti-Fascist coalition.

The anti-Fascist coalition government, comprising Communists and Christian Democrats, proved untenable at the end of the Second World War. Pressures from the powerful southern gentry, business leaders, the Catholic Church and even the US government forced the hand of De Gasperi, leader of the Christian Democrats. Consequently, in May 1947, De Gasperi excluded the Communists and their Socialist allies from the coalition government. This eventually forced an election in 1948, where the Christian Democrats won an outright majority (48 per cent of the vote).

The Christian Democrats were formed in 1942 by members of Catholic Action and leaders of the old Catholic Popular Party to organise Catholic opposition against the Fascist regime. The party gained support from the Catholic Church, big business and the southern gentry to win the election. These groups regarded the Christian Democrats as the political force best able to contain the Communist Party. However, events show that the party of government did not implement the sort of reform programme expected by the Italian establishment.

The Christian Democrat Party was not a typical liberal-bourgeois configuration: it maintained a strong popular sentiment, and did not strictly represent the aspirations of a single class. The Catholic origins of the party made it appeal to wide sections of society (Maraffi, 1980). The party's stated aim, as revealed in numerous party documents in the 1940s and 1950s, was to create a broad alliance of workers, peasants and middle classes. This was to be achieved by breaking down antagonism between capital and labour, landowner and peasant. This populist strategy spilled over into parliament where the Christian Democratic Prime Minister, De Gasperi, permitted alliances with the three centre parties. These went ahead even though his party had an absolute majority in the Chamber between 1948 and 1953 (Webster, 1961, p. 181).

Economically, the new government, particularly its left-wing elements, was positively disposed towards planning and state intervention to create employment. But this caused some consternation among such interest groups as big business. The steel industry is a pertinent example. The IRI owned company, Finsider, set a postwar strategy to expand steel production and to lower steel prices by adopting new production techniques. The proposals encountered stern opposition from the Confindustria and Giorgio Falck, a leading private sector steel producer (Villari, 1975). After gaining aid from the ERP, the plan was eventually carried and, by 1950, it helped Finsider reach pre-war levels of steel production of 1 million tons.

Although the Finsider plan was eventually implemented, the opposition that it provoked highlighted the government's difficulties in trying to carry through democratic and populist reforms. Indeed, Christian Democrat proposals for expanding welfare services and progressive reforms for industrial relations were similarly obfuscated by private industrialists. From 1950 onwards, the Christian Democrats introduced a range of welfare reforms and new spending schemes. Included was the extension of health insurance funds and monies for old age pensions to selective occupational categories. In addition, local and national welfare agencies were brought under government control. The Confindustria criticised these measures and insisted on the formation of a strong right-wing government, prepared to eschew popular measures (Weiss, 1988, pp. 142—3).

The inter-class strategy of the Christian Democrats was also threatened by the emergence of militant trade unionism during the early postwar years. Such militancy was organised under the auspices of the Communist-affiliated CGIL union. With the Communist Party absent from government, CGIL became the organisational vanguard for protests against both the government and deteriorating work conditions. The preponderance of strike action between 1947 and 1954 was denounced, even leading some politicians to consider ways of curtailing the ability to strike (Sabel, 1981, p. 237).

However, the Christian Democrat government was equally quick to single out industrialists and private employers in general as being partly responsible for the spread of worker militancy. Demands for a responsible and progressive approach to industrial relations were generally ignored by Italian employers. The Confindustria relinquished nothing on employee rights and on greater industrial democracy. Few concessions were given on wage increases (Weiss, 1988).

Such intransigence led to bitter acrimony between the business community and Christian Democrat leaders, thus undermining the close relations that had existed between both sectors in the immediate aftermath of the war. In the 1950s the government began to subject employers' industrial relations practices to critical scrutiny. As several documents emanating from central party organs reveal, references were made 'to the disorder provoked by the "antisocial selfishness of certain capitalist strata", and employers were criticized for attempting to escape their social responsibilities' (Weiss, 1988, p. 132). Prominent Christian Democrat members associated with the centre-left faction and members of the Christian Democrat-affiliated CISL union reverted to direct action: campaigns were organised in the provincial press throughout the country, attacking employers over their evasion of statutory obligations and for placing oppressive regimes within factories (Abrate, 1981). The campaign was so successful that the Confindustria pleaded with the Vatican to intervene on behalf of the business community.

These events produced a widening chasm between the Christian Democrats and the Italian business class. The Christian Democrat government was thus left with a perplexing decision: 'either to abandon its "interclass" objectives or to acquire greater organizational and financial independence' (Weiss, 1988, p. 141). Clearly, the government was unable to implement popular social reforms while aligned to dominant class interests, so it embarked on a policy of *sottogoverno* (subterranean government). This policy involved a systematic effort to place key areas of society under public control through government spending, political appointments and the establishment of ersatz government agencies (Clark, 1984). The expansion of the state economy was a vital element in the *sottogoverno* stratagem. Crucially, it provided the necessary financial independence from external interest groups to realise social democratic reforms (Cottino, 1978). These political developments partly explain why the state economic sector came to be guided by a strong social ethos.

Christian Democrat disposition in favour of state intervention in the economy was reinforced when the party's seasoned leader, Alcide De Gasperi, died. In his place, Amintore Fanfani was elected to the position of Secretary General in 1954. As a candidate from the left, Fanfani, in line with other like-minded colleagues, wanted to reduce the economic power of private capital. The concomitant of such a policy was an increase in the level of public planning to fulfil a variety of political and social goals. Pasquino writes:

Realising that financial independence is an important prerequisite of an independent policy, Fanfani, in the late 1950s, decided it was preferable to disengage the party from an excessive reliance on the Confindustria...through access to funds to be provided by the public sector of the economy. (1979, p. 100)

New state holding corporations were formed and existing state holding firms, namely IRI, were maintained to bolster the public sector economy.

Of the new state holding businesses, the formation of ENI (Ente Nazionale Idrocarburi) was a pivotal event, as it came to rival IRI in significance and economic dimensions. ENI was created by an Act of Parliament in February 1953, and its responsibilities centred on the exploration and supply of natural gas and petroleum for Italy's economy. Prior to the creation of ENI, a number of companies — both private and public-owned — jostled for a place in the energy market after successful gas and oil explorations in the peninsula. Under ENI, the bulk of energy production was brought under government control.

State intervention in the energy market under ENI was not guided by economic considerations alone: the Christian Democrat Finance Minister, Vanoni, in his speech to the Senate in 1953, stated that ENI was established to circumscribe private sector control over vital areas of energy production. Moreover, ENI's president, Enrico Mattei, envisaged that it would allow the benefits of economic growth to be spread throughout the peninsula (Frankel, 1966).

ENI expanded into areas of strategic interest to private capital (Sassoon, 1986, p. 40). Under Mattei's astute presidency, it achieved a vital *coup d'état* over the private sector when it gained control over oil exploration in the Po Valley. This gave ENI the financial wherewithal to obtain dominant stakes in several energy companies and achieve rapid growth. Fixed investment between 1954 and 1962 rose eightfold, sales by 170 per cent and employment by 250 per cent (Allen and Stevenson, 1974, pp. 233—4). Following Mattei's untimely death in 1962, the company began to overstretch its resources as a result of ambitious investments made in the early 1960s. But the energy holding company gained extra government endowments, bringing a general recovery during the mid-1960s.

According to Sassoon, the expansion of ENI forced its older state holding counterpart, IRI, 'to adopt a more dynamic posture' (1986, p. 40). In practice, this meant higher investment to increase employment and growth levels. Although IRI had dominant interests in iron and steel production, public banks and the engineering sector, the company diversified into new sectors of the economy: in 1957 it purchased the Italian airline company, Alitalia. It also moved generally into transport and took control of Italian radio broadcasting (1952) and the telephone service companies (1958).

These postwar developments in the state holding sector saw many significant areas of the economy placed under government ownership. The figures bear this out: a sample of some of the largest manufacturing firms found that, in the 1963—72 period, public sector output increased from 19 per cent to 24 per cent, while investment capital went up from 28 per cent to 35 per cent (Weiss, 1988, p. 139). During the same period, public sector firms accounted for 30 per cent of all workers employed in large industrial companies (Sasso, 1978, cited in Weiss, 1988).

The enlargement of the state holding sector enabled the government to undermine the employers representative organisation, the Confindustria. In 1953, the left wing of the Christian Democrat Party advocated that the state holding sector should withdraw from the employers' association (La Palombara, 1966, p. 28). It was not until necessary legislation was passed in 1956 that the state holding entities were removed from the Confindustria and placed under newly created employers' organisations. Consequently, Intersind was established as the employers' organisation for IRI and EFIM, and ASAP for ENI. Both bodies were given the responsibility of bargaining with relevant trade unions. This endowed the labour movement, after a period of militant activism, with a degree of legitimacy. The government was able to outmanoeuvre the private sector because of its political weakness at this historical juncture (Martinelli *et al.*, 1981).

In addition to undermining the Confindustria, the government gained further influence in the economy. The impetus behind intervention was provided by the centre-left coalition between the Christian Democrats and the Socialist Party (PSI) in 1963. One of the most notable reforms to emerge during the course of this alliance was the nationalisation of the electricity industry through the creation of ENEL. The government's interventionist strategy was also reinforced by the rejuvenation of Italy's economy and the general success of the state holding sector (Weiss, 1988, p. 151). Between 1959 and 1963, the economy grew at a faster rate than at any point in Italy's history.

The Christian Democrats, however, did not build up the state sector just to obstruct the operations of the private sector. The party had an important social agenda when it came to power, but it was often scuppered by business and other interest groups. Hence, the state economy was not only a source of finance and an organisational platform for undermining the private sector; state companies were also used to spearhead social reforms as evidenced by the managerial appointments made by the government to the state holding sector. The new managerial class was, like the Christian Democrats, committed to free enterprise, economic efficiency and growth. At the same time, state managers sympathised with the Christian Democratic emphasis on managed capitalism and state planning (Petrilli, 1967). As Prodi notes, the managers recruited by the government were radically different from their private sector counterparts: 'This new public manager, while a match for private industry in his entrepreneurial instincts, has had a more highly developed social conscience as well as stronger ties with the political structure of the country' (1974, p. 56).

Cultivating a managerially enlightened class and placing the state sector under political control were integral to the Christian Democrat reform agenda. These developments ensured that the public firms brought social considerations both to their own operations and to commerce generally. In particular, these holding companies were used to overcome the social deficiencies of the free market system. Significantly, the state holding sector helped alleviate plant closures and mass redundancies by supplying financial and managerial assistance to ailing firms (King, 1985).

Because its commercial interests are located in the heavy industrial sector, IRI dominated the task of rescuing firms on the brink of collapse. In 1956 it gave various forms of managerial and financial assistance to the largest cotton establishment in the south (see Lutz, 1962) and, three years later, it assumed control of the Taranto shipyard. Sometimes, IRI built up some of the firms on its casualty list into profitable concerns: ATES (electronics) and Costruzioni Metalliche Finsider (steel structures) were two success stories (Allen and Stevenson, 1974, p. 256). ENI, on the other hand, was less involved in rescue operations because it had few interests in the heavy industrial sector. Nevertheless, it did take over one of Italy's major textile concerns, Lanerossi, and the engineering firm Pignone.

The social contribution of the state holding sector included the long-term redevelopment of southern Italy. The Mezzogiorno refers to all the regions — Abruzzi, Molise, Campania, Apulia, Calabria, Sicily, Sardinia, Basilicata — found south of Rome. These regions, according to such indicators as employment, income, industrialisation, literacy and poverty, did not thrive and prosper to the same extent as northern and central areas of the peninsula. To eradicate this dualism, the state holding sector was required, following a 1957 law, to locate 60 per cent of its investments in new industrial plants and 40 per cent of its aggregate investments in the regions of the south. Prior to the law, the state holding sector was disproportionately concentrated in the north of Italy, with only 17 per cent of its total investments located in the south. Consequently, between 1958 and 1971, 49 per cent of this sector's manufacturing investment was placed in the south (Allen and Stevenson, 1974, p. 259). The IRI holding company went beyond the spirit of the law as it placed nearly all of its new industrial plants, after 1957, in the Mezzogiorno.

This detailed historical background underlines an important point: that, in terms of the communitarian functions of enterprises in contemporary Italian society, the state sector emerges as a key player. This reflects the magnitude of the state holding sector and the political control to which public companies have been subjected. Throughout the postwar years to the present day, the state sector has both expanded and colonised key areas of the economy, enabling it to implement social reforms.

Our analysis now turns to contemporary social interventions and programmes undertaken by the state holding companies that form part of Italy's labyrinthine public economy.

The state holding sector and social action

The postwar expansion of the state holding sector is central to understanding the nature of contemporary corporate social action in Italy. In recent years, the state sector has incurred considerable losses, resulting in attempts to privatise state holding companies. However, the systematic dismantling of the public sector through privatisation has been opposed by parties and government interest groups in government. Their main concern has been to avoid the transfer of state companies to the three main private corporations — Fiat, Olivetti, and Fininvest — which dominate the Milan Stock Exchange (Gianni and Giuliani, 1990). According to Prodi and De Giovanni (1993), until the early 1990s, privatisation measures were largely intermittent and superficial. Instead of resorting to wholesale privatisation, the likes of IRI and ENI have been restructured to restore profitability. The former head of IRI in 1986, Romano Prodi, managed to overturn the company's considerable losses into a modest profit while keeping it under state control (Ward, 1990). Hence, the state holding companies under political control have retained a certain social ethos.

To ensure that state firms comply with political and social requirements, the state holding sector is structured according to a descending hierarchy of control. At the top of this pyramid are the Interministerial Economic Planning Committee (CIPE) and the Ministry of State Holdings. Below this political tier, and answerable to it, there are five state holding entities. This group of holding companies is dominated, in terms of size and importance to the economy, by ENI and IRI. In turn, these companies have controlling stakes in private, as well as state-owned, subsidiaries. The state holding firms, however, are financially speaking, wholly owned by the government, as the government provides all the necessary equity capital.

The maintenance of political control has given state companies considerable latitude in pursuing social goals. In some cases, the companies have specifically invested funds according to social, rather than commercial, criteria, the development of the southern economy being one example. Thus, because of its ownership structure, the state sector has played possibly the most influential role in bringing social considerations into the commercial sphere. This in turn has provided a model for business intervention in wider society. This is particularly evident in the specialist subsidiaries under the ownership of holding companies.

State subsidiary and specialist enterprises

The state-owned economy has a number of specialist enterprises, normally the subsidiaries of larger holding companies, that perform socially relevant functions or public services on behalf of the state holding sector. These agencies, often structured like commercial enterprises or financial institutions, have reinforced the social objectives of the state sector. The activities of these specialist agencies can range across a variety of areas. A prominent example of this type of state company is GEPI, which was established in 1971 to assume from IRI and ENI certain responsibilities for rescuing ailing firms. Another example is ENEA which was formed as a subsidiary of the national electricity company ENEL in 1991. The general remit given to ENEA was to research and develop new energy-saving and environmentally clean technologies, with a view to transferring the results to Italian industry. The socially useful role that such specialist enterprises can perform will be examined through a detailed case study below. The study specifically focuses on the contribution made by the IRI-owned SPI company in promoting the small firm sector.

The small, artisan-based enterprise has figured, and continues to figure, prominently in the Italian economy. The micro-sector, as a geographical phenomenon, is concentrated in the north-east and central regions of the peninsula. In the Terza Italia (the Third Italy), as this distinctive geographical configuration is known, centres around the regions of Emilia-Romagna, Tuscany, Umbria, Veneto and Trentino. Around 80 per cent of the working population in these regions work in commercial units which employ fewer than 200 people (Bamford, 1987, p. 15).

The small firm sector gained an important boost from the state in the immediate postwar period. At that time, it seemed rather anachronistic that the government should choose to enlarge the micro-sector when major capitalist economies were centralising and concentrating the means of production. Nevertheless, a vibrant network of small enterprise units made some economic sense for Italy's beleaguered postwar economy: such firms required only small quantities of investment capital, they would bolster export potential, and they would help stimulate internal demand for goods.

Significantly, the small firm sector was an integral part of the Christian Democrat Party's inter-class strategy and reform programme. The small enterprise fitted in with the party's solidaire conception of dispersing property ownership to all classes (Weiss, 1984, p. 235). Extensive and generous provisions were thus made available to effect dramatic increases in the number of small business units. The cornerstone of this legislative support was the Artisan Statute of 1956. This provided various benefits to establishments with less than 20 employees: cheap loans, lower taxes, exemptions from keeping accounts and reduced premiums. The favourable legal and financial position of artisans produced a significant expansion in the small workshop economy throughout the 1950s and the 1960s (Barberis, 1980). In the years from 1951 to 1971, the number of units with under 100 employees increased by 16 per cent from 636,500 to 737,700; and of the 744,725 industrial enterprises censured in 1971, 99.5 per cent had fewer than 100 employees (Weiss, 1984, p. 216).

To assist the distribution of financial support for the small firm sector, a number of specialist credit institutions were formed, such as the Cassa per il Credito alle Impresse Artigiane (1947) and GEPI (1971). In recent years, one company that has operated as a conduit of state support for the small business sector is SPI (Promozione e Sviluppo Imprenditoriale). The company was originally established in 1955 as an industrial credit institution under the control of IRI. In the mid-1980s SPI was transformed into a small credit company (IRI, 1992).

The company's objectives are social as well economic: it has promoted small firm development, predominantly in areas that have undergone industrial or general economic decline. This is reflected by the geographical locations of its 19 local offices. They are, in the main, based in the north-west, which has been affected by de-industrialisation, and the underdeveloped south (SPI, n.d.). SPI has also redressed the imbalance in government funding for the small firm sector. Weiss calculated from official statistics of funding bodies, such as the Artigiancassa, that artisans from the Third Italy absorbed over nine-tenths of the loans and investment funds available between 1953 and 1976 (1988, p. 63).

Within the said regions, SPI has mainly assisted small enterprises in the industrial manufacturing and high tech sectors. These financial subsidies and investments are based on the provision of mixed forms of risk capital: acquiring minority holdings; setting up joint ventures; and subscribing to ordinary bonds. In addition, SPI has obtained shares in various firms. In 1992 it held stakes in 55 enterprises, such as the Genoa-based textile company SLAM and the information technology company, Spectrum Umbria, in which it had a 30 per cent stake (IRI, 1992). Loans have also been made available but interest repayments are below the prime rate, as the company does not seek to make a profit from its loans.

In addition to its role as a conduit for financial subsidies, a range of non-financial support services to small firms have been made available. Most notably, assistance is provided in drawing up business plans and in locating external sources of investment and finance. As part of these support services, the company established specialised workshop units known as Business Innovation Centres (BICs) and CISI (Centre Integrati per lo Sviluppo dell'Imprenditorialita). The BICs are located in various locations of interest, such as the industrial crisis areas in the north and centre of Italy (Trieste, Genoa, Massa Carrara, Terni and Teramo) and cities in the south (Naples, Taranto, Cosenza and Catania).

Small enterprises are able to draw upon a number of services provided directly by the BICs. Each BIC has a specialist department that performs various functions on behalf of small enterprises. These direct services include a range of support functions, from marketing to legal assistance. In 1993, the Genoa-located BIC Liguria, for example, had 20 companies housed in its workshops. A further 67 companies located around the city formed part of the BIC support network (*le aziende del network*). All these enterprises enjoyed access to personalised tutorial assistance in devising business plans, as well as professional assistance in forming and maintaining commercial links (BIC Liguria, n.d.). One of the most important functions performed by the BIC agencies is that of tracing new market outlets for small entrepreneurs. During the late 1980s BIC Liguria helped small supplier firms, affected by the downturn in steel production, find alternative market outlets in Europe (Fieldwork interview, BIC Liguria, 21.2.93).

Enterprises attached to BIC Liguria, whether in the workshops or in the network, may also contract out various administrative functions. A special services department attached to the BIC takes care of such functions as tax accounting, PAYE tax declarations and legal affairs, at a nominal cost.

In a similar fashion to BIC Liguria, the BIC based at Trieste offered administrative and management services, including budget control, tax and fiscal assistance, consultancy in marketing and patents, and a range of secretarial functions (BIC Trieste, n.d.). A senior official of BIC Trieste observed:

In February 1989 we opened our workshops to the first companies. We also offered services — telephone, fax and so on. In the second year we began to offer accounting services, wages, salary and so on. Now we can operate like an internal department of the companies themselves. (Fieldwork interview, BIC Trieste, 8.6.93)

According to Jones and Saren (1990), this form of direct assistance is not just confined to SPI, but is prevalent throughout Italy, especially in areas where there is a high concentration of small firms. The artisan association, Confederazione Nazionale dell'Artigianto (CNA) provides a range of key services, bookkeeping and advice on export finance. Moreover, provincial and regional governments have made available finances for support services. Small firms are able to entrust significant functions to external organisations such as the CNA or regional authorities. The reason for this is that such bodies closely represent the interests of small enterprises and are, according to Jones and Saren (1990), politically accountable to the artisans. The BICs, for instance, have involved other public bodies or local institutions — regional government, public banks, the state sector and chambers of commerce — in the support process.

The small firm sector and the role of external support functions provides a useful point of comparison with regard to corporate social involvement in Britain and Italy. In Britain a whole panoply of support agencies — local enterprise agencies, Technical and Enterprise Councils, and urban development corporations — has emerged to assist the creation and growth of small firms. These external support agencies, argue Jones and Saren (1990), primarily provide advice, information and training for small business owners. In contrast to Italy, there is less emphasis on direct forms of assistance. Furthermore, as discussed in Chapter 4, many of these support agencies were established to harness the private sector in small firm development. The private sector was viewed as best able to improve the competence and abilities of owner-managers to perform business functions. For Jones and Saren, such involvement may prove to be detrimental rather than beneficial to the small firm sector: 'In Britain the relationships are often dependent rather than representative through direct ownership or contractual ties with larger companies; or, indirectly, through various forms of patronage on the part of larger companies' (1990, p. 289).

The preponderance of corporate support for the small micro-sector in Britain may be symptomatic of the dependency of small firms on their larger counterparts (see Shutt and Whittington, 1987). For example, in the metal engineering sector, larger firms have practical control over their smaller subcontractors. This is particularly true in the vehicle component industry of the west Midlands (see Jones and Saren, 1990). In Italy, on the other hand, small businesses have attained relative autonomy from larger companies. This was evident during the early 1970s when many large northern firms responded to the economic crisis of that time by subcontracting to small firms. The small firms achieved a degree of independence from their larger contractors by recourse to 'flexible specialisation' (Brusco, 1982). The ability of the small firm sector to assert its autonomy has also been facilitated by the fact that large corporations do not feature prominently in the small business support network which, in Italy, is dominated by small business associations, regional government and public companies, such as SPI. Such bodies are rendered accountable to small firms and are thus in a better position to provide assistance that is closely shaped to the needs of the micro-sector.

The mobilisation of private capital

The previous sections have shown how, since the early 1950s, the state holding sector has made an important contribution to the economic, political and social life of Italian society. However, the early confidence placed in the state holding sector as the harbinger of industrial democracy and social reform was unsettled by economic and political circumstances. This did not lead to the dismantling of the state sector but, in fact, transformed relations between private corporations and the government. Such developments held repercussions for the social function of private capital.

The immediate threat to the state sector came as Italy's economic fortunes began to falter. The 'economic miracle' of the years 1950 to 1963 had provided the state companies with an important boost. However, indicators revealed that, by the mid-1960s, the economy was entering a period of recession: GNP fell, and productive investment dropped, while the level of unemployment and unit wage costs in manufacturing rose dramatically. According to Podbielski (1974), the economy moved into a situation in which high inflation and low demand emerged as near permanent features. In response, the Christian Democrats, who at this point were the dominant partners in a centre-left coalition government, were forced to deflate the economy. Thus, in September 1963 the neo-liberal personnel in the Bank of Italy imposed a harsh credit squeeze. Central to the deflationary strategy were curbs on public expenditure which, overall, limited the government's intended social policies. For instance, in its agricultural policy, the coalition government concentrated on existing entrepreneurs in rural areas rather than impoverished agricultural labourers (Sassoon, 1986). The credit squeeze imposed by the Bank of Italy had a detrimental social impact. Most notably, it led to reductions in investment, leading to a 2.5 per cent fall in employment by 1965. In addition, the government was unable to implement the Pieraccini Plan, approved by parliament in 1967, with its provisions for state intervention to achieve full employment.

There was some respite when the semblance of a recovery emerged after 1966. The profits generated were exported abroad and public spending was increased through higher levels of taxation, which proved detrimental to lower income groups. However, this upturn in the economy was also a short lived affair. The historical achievements of the labour movement in gaining significant wage concessions during the 'hot autumn' of 1969 precipitated another economic crisis. After 1969, wages increased at a higher rate than productivity; inflation increased in line with other developed countries; and growth decreased from an average of 6.56 per cent in the 1959—63 period to 3.36 per cent between 1970 and 1974 (Sassoon, 1986, p. 73).

Although it still maintained an important presence in the economy, the state sector was not immune from these economic crises. The achievements of the state holding companies in this period were mediocre: in the late 1960s, IRI's net profits averaged 0.1 per cent, while ENI's reached 0.2 per cent (Allen and Stevenson, 1974, p. 252). IRI managed stable profit levels in 1973, but the company's losses after 1975 — particularly in the steel, shipping and telecommunications sectors — spiralled upwards, reaching 900 billion lire (around £2 billion) in 1977. Typifying the fall in profitability was IRI's Alfa Romeo plant near Naples, which experienced a fall in profit that was greater than any other car plant in the world (Clark, 1984, p. 380).

These economic difficulties were compounded by allegations of corruption surrounding the state enterprises. A major contributory factor was the dominance of the Christian Democrats in most postwar coalitions up to the late 1980s. Thus, the Ministry of State Holdings, in Christian Democrat hands, functioned as a source of patronage, whereby party supporters and activists were rewarded with lucrative jobs and careers. Indeed, there have been public pronouncements alluding to such practices by a former Christian Democrat Minister for the state holding sector, Ciriaco De Mita, and Marcello Colitti, a manager from the public sector (Pasquino, 1979).

Martinelli argues that the crisis of the public sector 'reversed the situation of the late fifties and early sixties, when public firms represented innovation and industrial democracy' (1979, p. 84). In contrast, a number of the largest private sector companies — Fiat, Pirelli and Italcementi — responded to the economic crisis by attempting to consolidate their respective positions in the economy. These enterprises embarked on mergers and buy-outs that led to industrial concentration. Hence by 1967, 29 private firms owned 34 per cent of all shares, while the top ten firms (out of a total 60,000 firms in manufacturing industry) controlled 40 per cent of all exports (Castronovo, 1981, cited in Weiss, 1988).

This, in turn, created favourable conditions for the Confindustria to reassert its position. Up to that point the organisation had been undermined by factional infighting and the government's decision to form separate employers' organisations for the state holding companies. The industrial action of the 'hot autumn' of 1969 catalysed a coalition of private sector representatives. The coalition sponsored Gianni Agnelli, the head of Fiat, as a presidential candidate for the Confindustria — a move that was unopposed. Under Agnelli's presidency, the organisation assumed an explicit political stance in representing the interests of private capital. Crucially, the employers' association began to challenge the Christian Democratic-dominated government. The main elements of Agnelli's strategy involved transforming the Confindustria into an autonomous political force, modernising its internal structures and entering into a dialogue with trade unions. Martinelli and Treu argue that, with Agnelli at the helm, the Confindustria sought to unite the private sector and regain a key political and bargaining role (1984, p. 286).

The enhanced political stature of the Confindustria, under Agnelli's leadership, was helped by set-backs experienced by the Christian Democrat government. The Christian Democrats suffered significant defeats in the referendum on divorce in 1974 and the general election of 1975, resulting in key positional changes within the party. Benigno Zaccagnini was made the new party Secretary and Giulio Andreotti returned to head the government. The difficulties of the state holding sector, together with the growing power of big business, forced the Christian Democrats to modify their relations with the private sector. In contrast to their strategy of containment during the 1950s, the party used the economic and political levers at its disposal to mediate on behalf of private capital. For example, the Cassa Integrazione Guadagni was formed as a state insurance fund designed to cover the costs of redundant workers for a period of time. Politically, the scheme allowed companies, such as Fiat, to gain the upper hand in industrial relations disputes (Chiesi and Martinelli, 1989).

These developments had certain repercussions on the social operations of the state sector. Throughout the 1950s and early 1960s, the state holding sector engaged in socio-economic reform and reconstruction, one of the most sustained and important social interventions made by public firms being the industrialisation of the south. As will be outlined in the next section, it was symptomatic of the changing balance of power and realities of the new economic situation that the private sector gradually began to contribute to this area of social policy.

The Mezzogiorno and private industry

The state holding sector was deliberately harnessed to bring about economic prosperity in the south. Much of this was to be achieved through investment in new plants, infrastructure and services. The rise in investment from public companies proved to be impressive: southern manufacturing investment rose ninefold in the 1958—61 period and sevenfold between 1968 and 1971. Such financial backing had a considerable impact on the structural arrangement and growth rates of the southern economy, most notably by helping restructure it from agricultural to industrial production. Thus, in the 1951—71 period, the contribution made by agricultural production to the GDP of the southern economy went down from 34 per cent to 18 per cent, against an increase from 24 per cent to 39 per cent for industry (Allen and Stevenson, 1974).

These figures tend to belie the difficulties faced by state holding businesses in addressing the deep-seated structural problems of the Mezzogiorno. The state holding companies were still unable to bridge the age-old disparities between the north and south of Italy. Although the region's economic structure had become weighted towards industry, levels of agricultural production and employment in the south have, on the whole, been far higher than the north. By the early 1970s agriculture represented 30 per cent of employment in the south compared to around 13 per cent in the north (Allen and Stevenson, 1974, p. 34). However, the converse was true for industry. Moreover, the relocation of firms to the south did not absorb the unemployment created by the gradual reduction of agricultural production and the growth in population. For example, construction and public works had created 350,000 extra jobs in 1975, but these could not compensate for the 2.1 million who had given up agricultural work (Clark, 1984, p. 359).

It was evident, by the early 1970s, that the endeavours of the state holding firms had not brought about the intended economic rejuvenation of the south. In response, the government introduced tax and credit concessions, in a 1971 law, to attract private sector investments and factory relocations to the south (Graziani, 1972). Legislation in 1965 had already furnished loans to large businesses investing in the south, but the actual fiscal incentives were limited, as the government was wary of relinquishing political control over this policy area. The continued spectre of underdevelopment — together with the fundamental shifts in the political and economic standing of the private sector mentioned above — influenced a change in policy in the form of a generous array of loans to attract private sector investment in the south. The 1971 legislation meant that large firms were now eligible to receive grants worth between 7 per cent and 12 per cent of their investment expenditure in plants, buildings and equipment. However, the law also added the proviso that firms would have to obtain authorisation from CIPE (Interministerial Committee for Economic Planning) for investment programmes worth upwards of 7 billion lire (£1.5 million). This indicated that government officials intended to maintain a semblance of political control over southern policy (Amato, 1976).

The process of providing fiscal incentives to attract capital investment in underdeveloped economies is common to most Western states. The inclusion of the private sector, as a partner in southern economic expansion, has marked an important shift in the direction of policy; up to the mid-1960s, these interventions were mainly the preserve of the state holding sector. There are distinct commercial advantages in relocating plants because of the subsidies involved and the new markets which are opened up. At the same time, the private sector emerged as an important partner with government in this area of social policy. Consequently, for companies involved, this form of engagement can be perceived as an important contribution to the overall vitality of the local and national economy.

A notable example of this joint approach in southern investment was Fiat's decision to construct a high-tech, Japanese-style car plant (Fabbrica Integrata) at Amalfi near Naples in the early 1990s (Fiat, n.d.(a)). Consideration was given to other locations, such as Portugal and Eire. The company eventually decided it would be favourable to Italy's national interest and socially responsible to locate the plant in the south, where it already had considerable interests (Fieldwork interview, Fiat, 2.2.93). Consequently, Fiat negotiated with both central government and local authorities to obtain subsidies and services towards the construction of the plant. As part of the agreement reached between various parties, Fiat committed itself to creating over 7,000 jobs over a five-year period. The company also agreed that 80 per cent of the workforce would be hired and trained from the locality of Amalfi.

These efforts to involve the private sector in southern development are based on the idea of servicing capital. Financial incentives and institutional support is provided by government to attract private sector investment in the south. However, such endeavours to harness the private sector have contained, rather than solved, the problem of southern underdevelopment. By 1973 industrialisation was mainly confined to the coastal areas of Apulia, Sardinia and Sicily. According to Clark (1984), this created around 150,000 jobs in modern industries such as engineering. But these were secondary jobs in branch factories, and the operational sites did not produce the ancillary production in the surrounding localities. Indeed, between 1951 and 1975 the actual number of jobs in the south went down by over 500,000, and unemployment by the mid-1970s was three times the northern rate (Clark, 1984, p. 359).

There are political objections levelled at the strategy of servicing of capital. Governments and local authorities, in their determination to attract inward investment for deprived local areas, render the local polity, economy and trade unions subordinate to the dictates of the private firms which they are trying to attract (Crowther and Garrahan, 1988). For example, Fiat's investment at the Amalfi plant was agreed by the company on the understanding that competitive and flexible working arrangements would be in place. This included such arrangements as a six day week, 24-hour operations and the just-in-time system.

Despite these shortcomings, the government still uses fiscal incentives to attract investments from northern firms. Nevertheless, one legislative initiative — Law no. 44 of 1986 — has undergone a conspicuous change in emphasis. The legislation has endeavoured to harness private sector resources for the purpose of promoting small firm development in the south. What is interesting is that this scheme has involved companies in the more socially active capacity of providing advice and managerial training for entrepreneurs indigenous to the south.

The main purpose of Law no. 44 has been to create long-term growth and employment in the south. It has tried to achieve this through a small business development scheme specifically for young entrepreneurs between the ages of 18 and 35. The Comitato per lo Sviluppo di Nuova Imprenditorialita Giovanile (Committee for the Development of Young Enterprise — hereafter, the Comitato) was formed to implement and monitor the progress of this legislation. The distribution of funds is highly selective, restricted to only those young entrepreneurs or owners with feasible business plans. Recipients also have to comply with demographic and age requirements — that is, they have to reside in the south and be within the age range mentioned above (Comitato, 1988). If selected, the Comitato provides grants for initial capital outlays and subsidies for running costs. Up to 1993, 826 business proposals out of the 3,707 submitted obtained assistance (Comitato, 1993).

Those accepted for funding enter a period of training, organised and administered by the Comitato. Following this initial phase, and for a period of two years, the Comitato assigns a team of consultant tutors to the entrepreneurs being supported. Here, private and public sector businesses, such as Elea-Olivetti, Agnesi, Isvor-Fiat, Comerint, Snamprogetti and Bonifica, feature prominently as suppliers of tutorial services in the scheme (Comitato, 1991, pp. 38—9).

Once assigned to a particular entrepreneur, tutors perform three principal functions. Firstly, they provide specialist advice on production and managerial issues to enhance the capabilities of young entrepreneurs. The Olivetti managerial consultancy company, Elea, has tutored around 15 enterprises for the Comitato. Since becoming involved with the Comitato in 1987, the company has provided entrepreneurs under its tutelage with general instruction on business management and specialist advice on artificial intelligence, information systems and the location of foreign markets. For this specialist training, Elea has recourse to various experts from Olivetti (Fieldwork interview, Elea, 20.5.93).

The company tutors, as part of their work, are enlisted to help cultivate relations within and outside the commercial establishment. The tutor can act as an external arbiter during conflicts between the personnel of new firms. The relational function of the tutor extends to establishing contacts with markets, potential partners and other enterprises. Those providing tutorial services are expected to monitor closely the progress of the young entrepreneurs under their tutelage. According to one tutor from the Isvor-Fiat company, over a two-year period this will involve regular visits by the tutoring company, with the aggregate consultancy time totalling between 70 to 100 days (Fieldwork interview, Isvor-Fiat, 14.5.93). In fact the tutors, by working closely with the young entrepreneurs, are in a position to feed back information on the progress of the enterprises to the Comitato (Comitato, n.d.).

Although those contributing to the tutorial service are reimbursed by the Comitato, the nature of this pedagogic service — the level of monitoring, training and advice required by new businesses — means that the companies provide a social service. Indeed, the social dimension of the scheme is further underlined by the fact that tutoring companies are promoting the southern small firm economy which has been diminishing since the early 1960s. One senior member of the Elea consultancy team notes:

> You...become part of the [company]. Consultancy is a matter of providing advice and then leaving those who require assistance in the first place to act upon it themselves. Tutoring involves integrating with the young entrepreneur, doing it in partnership...I don't tell the entrepreneurs what to do, but I perform the task with them. (Fieldwork interview, Elea, 20.5.93)

The service is monitored by the Comitato, ensuring that the companies involved are providing effective assistance. This careful scrutiny, together with the screening of applicants, has contributed towards a considerable success rate for the scheme. Of the 826 new enterprises supported between 1987 and 1993, only 15 enterprises — 1.8 per cent of successful applicants — have been disbanded or dropped out from the scheme (Comitato, 1993).

While the scheme has a low failure rate, it would be another issue to presume that it could help the south reproduce the dynamic network of small enterprises found in the central and northern regions. For this to happen, the government would have to systematically address the decline of the small business sector in the south. This is a situation partly resulting from the disproportionately high level of government subsidies received by companies in the Third Italy in comparison to those in the south. In certain respects, Law no. 44 has attempted to redress this imbalance.

It appears, then, that the private sector has come to play an important role alongside the state holding companies in trying to deal with the endemic dualism between the north and south. It must be noted that the growing involvement of the private sector in the southern issue since the early 1970s has not diminished the importance of the state holding sector in this area of social policy. The IRI-owned SPI company, as shown above, has extensive interests in the small business sector. Moreover, the number of state-owned firms involved in the tutoring service of the Comitato far outweighs private sector firms participating in the scheme (Comitato, 1991). Nevertheless, the private sector involvement in an area of social policy previously dominated by the state holding companies is significant. The issue now is whether the private sector has adopted responsible policies in other areas of society.

145

A more expansive social role for business?

Official information — statistical or narrative — on corporate social action in Italy is very thin on the ground. There is evidence, though, of private sector firms making active, non-profit contributions towards the improvement of social life. The car manufacturer, Fiat, is a notable example. Fiat does not have a central department for organising social interventions, unlike British companies such as BT and Shell which have community affairs departments. There are, nevertheless, various functions spread across the company structure that administer and manage community-based interventions on the company's behalf. For instance, the Fiat per i Giovani (Fiat for the Young) programme forms part of the company's vocational education facility that has been operating since 1922 (see International Labour Office, 1932, pp. 53—8). The Fiat per i Giovani scheme was unveiled in 1986 to inform schools in the Turin area about the company's activities, and, at the same time, recruit school-leavers for the company. With the company reducing its intake of new employees from local schools in recent years, this recruiting function has become less important. The Fiat per i Giovani is now mainly involved in organising seminars and work-experience placements for pupils (Fieldwork interview, Fiat, 2.2.93). Another significant social initiative has been stimulated by Fiat's interest in environmental protection. In 1989 the company appointed an environmental officer, based at the Fiat headquarters in Turin, to coordinate and improve environmental performance across different sectors of the company. In 1990, to ensure uniformity in different sectors, Fiat launched an environmental policy statement. The policy committed the company to an assortment of environmentally friendly practices, such as waste management and the recycling of disused cars (Fiat, 1992a).

These social interventions are not the sole preserve of Italy's larger corporations. There is still a preponderance of medium-sized, family-owned businesses in Italy. Some of these companies, through the work of their owners, have built up significant philanthropic reputations. For example, the family-owned pharmaceutical company, Angelini, has a charitable giving scheme that generates funds through direct contributions from employees. The funds accumulated by these contributions are matched by the Angelini family and then distributed to chosen causes. Senior managers within the company have also helped a local charity for handicapped children, Lega del Filo D'Oro, to raise funds by organising local and national campaigns (Fieldwork interview, Angelini Pharmaceuticals, 12.2.93).

Fratelli Dioguardi, the Bari construction company, has gained a notable reputation for its social and philanthropic work. The director and owner of the company, Gianfranco Dioguardi has pursued certain socially responsible causes through his business. The most significant action to date has been Dioguardi's adoption of a local secondary school in Bari — Scuola Media Statale Lombardi. The school is located in the notorious San Paolo district which has all the problems associated with inner-city areas. The company has donated computers, videos, televisions and telecommunications equipment to establish a multimedia learning centre in the school. For Gianfranco Dioguardi, who brokered this link in the first place, the rationale for helping the school has been twofold: to steer pupils away from criminal activities and to demonstrate the rewards and potential of education (Villa, 1991). Dioguardi's involvement with the school has generated a great deal of curiosity throughout Italy, as testified by the number of articles which have appeared in both local and national newspapers. However, the government has made no attempt to coordinate or engage private sector participation in the education system; statutory education largely remains under strong centralised administration (Monasta, 1994).

These cases show that, in addition to participating in southern development, private sector companies have cultivated interests across a range of modern social problems and issues. Whilst these instances of corporate social action are significant in their own right, they do not form part of a comprehensive movement for private sector involvement in society. General evidence suggests that socially active businesses operate in isolation, with little support from external agencies or coordination by the government. There has been no surge of general interest in corporate social responsibility among private operators, as there was in the United States from the mid-1950s onwards, and in Britain during the 1970s and 1980s. Certainly, in contrast to Britain, no government-led support infrastructure for corporate social action has developed. The government has generally failed to provide coordinating agencies, information sources and fiscal mechanisms to consolidate the isolated instances of social involvement that prevail in Italy.

To this should be added some further remarks on the nature of corporate social activism in Italy. Throughout the postwar period, the state holding companies, rather than the private sector, were at the forefront of pursuing socially responsible practices. In fact, many of the innovations in progressive work methods and socially responsible action in wider society tended to derive from state holding firms. The expectations surrounding the state companies have been deflated by poor economic performances and accusations of corruption. Despite these problems, the state sector still remains largely intact and features prominently in the economy. Moreover, sections of the state sector have continued to fulfil the social expectations that surrounded the expansion of the state holding companies in the postwar period. The other point is this: although corporate social interventions have been ad hoc, Italian businesses have begun to assume an active part in supporting the cultural sphere of society. This will form the subject of the next chapter.

8 The Aesthetic Motive: Corporate Patronage of Cultural Heritage in Italy

Article 9 of the Italian Constitution of 1948 committed the Republic to protecting the nation's artistic heritage. In the main, it has been the state's responsibility to safeguard this Article of the Constitution; much of Italy's cultural and artistic assets are legally under the auspices of the government. Since the mid-1960s, however, there has been increasing public speculation over the condition of Italy's vast cultural patrimony to which both central and local government have responded by making systematic and considered interventions. At the same time, the cultural sphere is not the sole preserve of the public sector. The 1980s witnessed a general surge of cultural sponsorship and donations of support from corporations and public service banks. One of the distinctive features of such involvement is that a number of companies have become active patrons of the arts. Therefore it seems that the task of preserving Italy's cultural heritage has mobilised corporate engagement in social action, albeit of a highly specialised nature. Such activism shares certain similarities with the development of corporate responsibility in Britain during the 1980s. This chapter examines the factors behind such developments. The objective is to elucidate the nature of corporate philanthropy and social action in contemporary Italian society.

The state and the preservation of cultural heritage

In Italy cultural activities can either form part of a profit-making industry or part of publicly financed services for the collective well-being and education of society. The actual balance between public and private sector involvement will fluctuate according to specific areas of the arts: cinema, popular music, television and publishing are mainly funded by private means of advertising and consumer expenditure. The 'traditional' features of cultural life — museums, libraries, art galleries, archaeological sites and historical archives — are, on the whole, financed and administered by the public sector. In Italy, the state bears over 80 per cent of the expenditure incurred by the traditional cultural sector. This expenditure is used to oversee nearly 36 million pieces of artistic and cultural heritage, many representing the most important and prestigious cultural treasures in the world (Antonini, 1991, p. 50). The concentration of cultural heritage in Italy has come about as a consequence of the renowned art movements and the different civilisations that have influenced society since antiquity.

The performance of successive governments in safeguarding and promoting cultural heritage in the peninsula has been variable. In terms of legislative provisions, it was over 40 years after Unification before the Italian state passed its first law for the maintenance of the nation's cultural heritage. Law No. 185 of June 1902 was soon superseded by a more comprehensive piece of legislation, Law No. 364 of 1909. The 1909 Law was very much the legal standard-bearer, establishing definitive guidelines for protecting cultural heritage: all objects of historical, artistic and archaeological value under state ownership were declared inalienable. Law no. 364 also empowered the government to issue compulsory purchase orders for valuable objects on the private collectors' market and also ruled that the export of moveable cultural treasures was permitted only on condition that such transactions did not constitute a serious loss to the collection of national cultural treasures. On the whole, such provisions reinforced declarations about protecting the status of cultural assets under public ownership.

Major public inquiries conducted during the 1960s questioned the effectiveness of the legislative provisions made earlier in the century. These measures, it was argued, were failing to provide sufficient protection for cultural and artistic heritage. The Franceschini Commission (1966) and the Papaldo Commission (1968) pointed out, in their final reports, that, despite the efforts of governments over the years, Italy's cultural and artistic heritage had been neglected and left to decay (Palma and Clemente, 1987). Both Commissions recommended a coherent policy of government intervention through the establishment of a specialised government department for culture. This function at the time was integrated within the Ministry of Public Education (Ministero della Pubblica Istruzione).

It was not until 1975, however, that these recommendations were implemented with the creation of the Ministry of Cultural and Environmental Heritage (Ministero per i Beni Culturali e Ambientali). The Ministry was made solely responsible for maintaining heritage and art treasures. To fulfil these responsibilities, the new department had financial resources, a vast administrative network of specialist offices and advisory councils at its behest. In addition, several local supervisory offices (Soprintendenze per i Beni Artistici e Storici) were formed to oversee maintenance and restoration programmes (Antonini, 1991).

This specialist government department was a welcome and much needed innovation. Yet the geographical dispersal of artistic treasures across several Italian cities — Florence, Rome, Milan, Bologna and Venice — meant that the systematic upkeep and protection of cultural artifacts was logistically a very difficult task. The establishment of a system of regional government in 1972, however, added a vital new agent into the heritage process. Initially, the cultural responsibilities of regional governments were restricted to managing local museums and libraries. From the mid-1970s onwards, a number of regional authorities overstepped this limited remit and began contributing to the preservation of heritage in their own locality. Consequently, from 1976 to 1981, regional authority spending on culture quadrupled, with 50 per cent of this new expenditure being allocated to conservation projets (Bodo, 1984). In qualitative terms, the cultural budgets have been subject to greater democratic control: in many cases, the discretionary powers of regional governments to fund restoration works were regulated by regional councils. Strategies and decisions were made with the assistance of representative bodies (*consulte per la cultura*).

The establishment of public machinery for culture by central and local government helped to redirect financial resources towards the preservation of heritage. In the decade prior to the formation of the Ministry of Cultural and Environmental Heritage, most of the state's cultural expenditure had been directed towards the performing arts (Campa and Bises, 1980, cited in Palma and Clemente, 1987). Since then, resources have shifted dramatically in favour of maintaining cultural heritage. Figures from the Ministry of Culture and Environmental Heritage for 1989 show that nearly 98 per cent of its budget went on restoration and maintenance work (see Brosio and Santagata, 1992, p. 232).

The emphasis on placing resources into preserving Italy's vast cultural patrimony was sustained by the mobilisation of the environmental lobby during the 1980s. (This, as shown in Chapter 5, was a common feature in many societies during this period.) The green movement initially comprised those disaffected with traditional politics and former left-wing activists (Biorcio, 1988). By the mid-1980s, however, popular opinion had shifted towards green awareness. Between 1983 and 1986, the League for the Environment doubled its membership from 15,000 to 30,000; between 1983 and 1989 the membership of the World Wide Fund for Nature went up from 30,000 to around 200,000 (Diani, 1990, p. 162). As the green movement mobilised popular support, the message about environmental pollution was equated, by commentators, with the degradation of cultural and historical patrimony (see Alibrandi *et al.*, 1983;

Moratto, 1986). For Lumley, 'there was increasing awareness that threats to natural life were also threats to cultural artifacts, so the idea of conservation was broadened...' (1990, p. 125).

The generic appeal of conservation influenced the business and industrial community to take ameliorative action. The energy company, ENEA, developed technologies to be used as diagnostic tools for safeguarding artistic and cultural artifacts. The company has made techniques, such as neutronic activation, gammagraphy, and various chemical processes, available to the Central Institute for Restoration. The Istituto Bancario San Paolo of Turin has funded research by the Consiglio Nazionale delle Ricerche (National Research Council) into new methods for protecting monuments damaged by pollutants in the atmosphere (Fondazione Sanpaolo di Torino, 1991). In another significant intervention, the municipal electricity company for Milan, Azienda Energetica Municipale Milano (AEM), has made available specialist technology to protect exhibited art works in galleries (Fieldwork interview, AEM, 29.1.93).

The green movement has undoubtedly helped sustain and broaden interest in the preservation of cultural heritage. Yet the percentage of total government spending on this area has remained low. In 1955 expenditure on the arts rose to 0.74 per cent of total government spending. However, available statistics show a marked decrease, from 0.75 per cent to 0.62 per cent of total government spending, for the years between 1976 and 1981 (Bodo, 1984, p. 43). Research has also shown that, due to the lack of administrative efficiency, government bodies have problems in actually utilising the funds available to them. According to Palma and Clemente, from 1945 and 1982, between 43 per cent and 66 per cent of available funds for culture and the arts were expended (1987, p. 95).

The lack of administrative planning over the disbursement of funds is exemplified by the fact that the dispensing of available funds tends to vary from year to year (Palma and Clemente, 1987). This situation is not helped by the frequent changes in government which have bedevilled the Italian polity. This feature of political life often results in specialist ministries, such as the Ministry of Cultural and Environmental Heritage, being assigned to coalition partners from minority parties that have little technical competence in this field (Bodo, 1989).

At the beginning of the 1980s, public concerns over the condition of cultural patrimony heightened. The government at this point seemed to accept the need to generate extra funding and resources from outside the public sector.

The willingness of the Ministry of Cultural and Environmental Heritage to open up the cultural sphere to new partners was made evident by its attempts to involve the private sector. Principally, efforts were made to harness corporate support through the introduction of fiscal incentives. Law No. 512, approved in 1982, gave unlimited tax concessions for expenses incurred in the maintenance of specific cultural treasures and for donations made towards the restoration of cultural artifacts (Casiccia, 1989, p. 294). A further change in the fiscal system in 1985 allowed tax deductions of up to 2 per cent of income for gifts made to musical, film and theatrical productions. Although VAT deductions had been in place since 1978, these two laws constituted the first attempts by the Italian legislature to attract new patrons, especially private enterprise, in an area of social policy which had traditionally been the terrain of state agencies. The government introduced further provisions in 1988: businesses making contributions to the arts would receive deductions of up to 20 per cent of taxable income, but this would be available for only three years.

The legislation seemed to successfully fulfil its intended objectives: during the 1980s corporate involvement in the arts and culture surged. Significantly, according to a report commissioned by the EEC in 1986, the contributions by Italian corporations towards the support of culture and the arts surpassed corresponding totals for France and Britain. The report concluded that private sector contributions in Italy were amongst the highest in the European Community (De Chalander and De Brebisson, 1987). However, it is questionable whether adjustments to the fiscal system were directly responsible for the augmentation of corporate endowments for preserving cultural heritage. As Bodo (1989) observes, these fiscal provisions were seldom made available due to the lack of enforcement regulations. In addition, the incentives made available proved to be uneven, as heritage donations enjoyed more tax relief than those made to the performing arts. Even if the tax deductions had been more generous and efficiently distributed, it is doubtful whether these indirect mechanisms would have been able to attract external funding.

O'Hagan and Duffy (1989) found that indirect fiscal measures were commonly used measures among European governments. But, the authors maintained, these failed to attract the level of private sector investment for the arts envisaged by policy-makers. For example, British governments in recent years have provided numerous incentives to attract private sector involvement in supporting the arts, including a matching grant scheme launched in 1984. The overall results in terms of actual increases in business support have proven to be fairly modest (see Allen and Ward, 1990; Arthur Andersen, 1991, p. 5). A survey by the Association for Business Sponsorship of the Arts found a 13 per cent decrease in real terms of corporate donations to the arts between 1991 and 1993, despite the many fiscal provisions implemented throughout the 1980s in Britain, (ABSA, 1993, p. 3). Davidson Schuster, writing about private arts sponsorship in Europe, notes that tax incentives on their own cannot guarantee consistent and lucrative benefactions from the private sector:

A charitable deduction or a deed of covenant alone is not sufficient to ensure a healthy stream of private support for the arts, even if the financial incentives are generous and the field of application broad...Although technical adjustments may be of primary interest in establishing a fair and efficient system of tax incentives, these adjustments will have little effect in a system with little precedent for private support. Many of the Western European countries are currently struggling with the problem of how to increase private support for the arts...For them, the key does not lie in the implementation of tax incentives; most of them already have tax incentives for charitable contributions in their national tax laws. The key lies ultimately in a changing view of the relative roles of the private and public sectors, a much more difficult problem to address. (1986, p. 331)

It seems that, in Italy, this perception began to change with regard to cultural heritage. Certainly, throughout the 1980s and 1990s, there emerged a growing belief in the potential of businesses in respect of cultural heritage. There was a growing appreciation, certainly among larger firms, that the private sector could assume a significant role in two principal ways: firstly as benefactors to the arts; secondly, as proactive patrons of cultural and artistic heritage. As suggested earlier, the involvement of the corporate sector in the cultural sphere cannot be solely attributed to adjustments in the fiscal system. There has to be, as suggested by Davidson Schuster above, a shift in the balance of responsibilities for the traditional arts between the public and private sectors. In Italy, one of the major factors behind this shift can be located to contemporary advancements of the media industry.

The advertising industry and cultural heritage

In the mid-1970s there was a gradual concentration of ownership within various sectors of the media industry. Significant advances in the market were particularly made by advertising companies. This reflected, as shown in Chapter 7, a general improvement in the political and economic position of the private sector during this period. These are important considerations in attempting to account for the general boom in corporate support for the arts.

Prior to this period, most of Italy's private television stations were locally based and funded by small-scale advertising. The state broadcasting company, RAI, dominated the national networks. Through a special accord with the newspaper and publishers association, FIEG, it vigorously regulated broadcast advertising in terms of form and quantity. Private media companies lobbied vigorously for deregulating the air-waves in the early 1970s when RAI's exclusive concession came up for renewal. In 1976 the Constitutional Court ruled RAI's monopoly of local networks to be unlawful, but its monopoly at national level was upheld (Forgacs, 1990, pp. 143—4). For those seeking privatisation, this was a significant step towards launching national advertising through the television networks. The local stations, however, did not possess a high level of technical and commercial competence in selling advertising space. This gap in the market was seized upon by specialist advertising concessionaries, many of them under the ownership of publishing houses (Forgacs, 1990). These agencies plugged the gap in the market by sending out ready-made video packages with programmes and advertising space to television channels. As national advertising allowed private television to develop on an industrial scale, the obvious move was for local stations to form into a national network (Forgacs, 1990). By the early 1980s two television stations constituted the network: Canale 5, composed of 27 local stations, and Italia 1 made up of 18 stations.

As pointed out, advertising agencies, which distributed programme-advertisement packages, made a significant contribution to this general expansion of the television industry. Powerful figures emerged in the sphere of private television and advertising. The building tycoon and media mogul (and former Prime Minister of Italy) Silvio Berlusconi, through his Fininvest company, became the pre-eminent operator. Berlusconi opened new viewing slots and increased audience figures. His greatest skills were reserved for the sale of advertising. Initially, Berlusconi created Publitalia in 1979 for the acquisition and sale of advertising slots, and introduced smaller firms to television advertising on his Canale 5 (Forgacs, 1990, pp. 182—3). Once these programmes increased their audience figures, Berlusconi involved a number of large corporations, attracting the likes of Procter & Gamble, Unilever, Fiat and Nestle. The success of this strategy is demonstrated by the profit margins: Publitalia's revenues grew from $9 million in 1980 to $630 million in 1984 (Caraman, 1993, p. 7). From this position of power, Fininvest proceeded to acquire controlling stakes in other channels, such as Italia 1. In Machiavellian fashion, Berlusconi pressurised the government into passing relevant laws that would legitimate his commercial operations, particularly the concentration of media ownership under Fininvest.

The wealth and power attained by Berlusconi's Fininvest group in the broadcast media world had important repercussions on cultural heritage. From 1986, the media entrepreneur used his three national channels to promote cultural exhibitions through the medium of popular television advertising. Several events benefited from television exposure: the 1988 Van Gogh exhibition in Rome; Miro at the Rivoli Castle in the same year; and the Caravaggio and Michelangelo exhibitions of 1992 in Florence and Rome.

From promoting exhibitions, it was a logical step for Fininvest to promote cultural sponsorships as a new advertising forum for business. Publitalia, Fininvest's advertising company, began to advise businesses on how to run cultural sponsorships. The company made available advertising space on television and in publications to promote such campaigns. The Fininvest company also created the specialist Grande Eventi department within Publitalia to organise cultural sponsorships on behalf of companies, and to liaise between cultural institutions and possible commercial benefactors. For instance, the Grande Eventi department was commissioned by Cremona City Council to find sponsors and organise a series of events to celebrate the work of musician Claudio Monteverdi (Fieldwork interview, AMI, 11.5.93). These examples demonstrate that Fininvest has helped raise cultural awareness in the business community, principally by pioneering a form of support for cultural heritage guided by the commercial dictates of corporate advertising.

Given Fininvest's unique contribution, it was no coincidence that Berlusconi's media group sought to extend private sector involvement in promoting Italian art. In 1991, the company co-founded, together with Italy's Foreign Minister and the director of the Italian Association of Banks, the first association for commercial patrons of art and culture. The organisation, known as Associazione Mecenati Italiani (Italian Association of Patrons, hereafter, AMI), was founded to orchestrate and encourage private sector participation in supporting the arts. Its significance does not pertain only to the arts world: it is the first modern associative forum for socially active corporations in Italy.

In different ways, AMI and Fininvest subsidiaries, such as Publitalia, have attempted to coordinate and organise corporate involvement in the arts. Certainly, this process has been partly assisted by the growth and deregulation of television advertising. But one of the features of corporate involvement in cultural preservation is the tendency for companies, and key individuals in these businesses, to act autonomously as cultural patrons in their own right. According to Bodo, 'major corporations now aspire to produce culture on their own and often prefer to take their own autonomous decisions with the least interaction with public authorities' (1989, p. 146). This may partly explain why, between 1991 and 1993, only 14 organisations joined AMI (Fieldwork interview, AMI, 18.5.93). The following sections examine this trend in detail by referring to the current cultural interventions of prominent Italian enterprises. Two factors stand out: firstly, an important feature of this trend is the influential role played by the Olivetti company; secondly, publicly owned banks, such as the *casse di risparmio*, have emerged as generous benefactors to, and supporters of, the preservation of cultural heritage.

Commercial enterprises as the new cultural patrons

In the past 12 years, major Italian corporations have aspired to engage proactively in the maintenance of traditional cultural patrimony on their own autonomous terms. The main influence behind this trend is the Olivetti company, the typewriter and office equipment manufacturer turned information technology multinational. Since the late 1960s Olivetti has developed a thorough and more systematic form of intervention in the traditional arts. Even before this time, the original owners of Olivetti demonstrated a sensitivity to the cultural world around them. Camillo Olivetti helped to restore a series of frescoes at the Church of San Bernardino, located in the vicinity of the company's first factory site in Ivrea. Camillo's son Adriano, as seen in Chapter 6, took a pronounced interest in industrial architecture, and was influenced by the ideas of Le Corbusier. The special emphasis placed on industrial design infused Olivetti's products with a certain degree of cultural significance in their own right. During the 1950s the company was occasionally approached to provide information and exhibits for museum collections (Olivetti, 1983).

It was during a critical period of transition in the 1960s that Olivetti's modern cultural policies took shape. Adriano Olivetti's untimely death in 1960 plunged the company into a financial crisis, caused by Adriano's earlier acquisition of the American typewriter company, Underwood, which at the time of purchase was a liability. The decline in Olivetti's fortunes were not helped by the general economic depression that overwhelmed the Italian economy after the boom years of the 1950s. After four years of ineffectual control under Adriano's son, Roberto Olivetti, the company found itself submerged in debts. It was subsequently bailed out by a syndicate of state-owned industries and private enterprises and effective control of the company passed from the Olivetti family to the board of directors. The syndicate take-over was not entirely successful in that it failed to diversify into the fledgling electronic equipment market. However, it succeeded in overhauling the company's organisational structure from a centralised system, as it had been under Adriano, to a devolved structure of separate autonomous divisions (Kicherer, 1990, p. 51).

During this transition period, the main board gave a key company figure, Renzo Zorzi, a free hand to reorganise Olivetti's external relations policy. Zorzi had been a close associate of Adriano Olivetti since 1948 and was the editor of the company's newspaper, *Comunità*. Zorzi's main organisational contribution to the business involved the establishment of a Corporate Image Department. The department was responsible for conveying specific ideas about the company and its philosophy through products, sales, advertising and cultural activities (Kicherer, 1990). In the transition from owner to board management, the Corporate Image Department provided a certain amount of continuity between the old and new regimes. More importantly, the board and its chairman, Bruno Visentini, gave the Corporate Image Department autonomous status within the Olivetti organisation structure (ibid.).

Following the establishment of the Corporate Image Department, the company, under new management, made its first purposeful incursion into the cultural field. This intervention was precipitated by a serious flood of the river Arno in Florence during the mid-1960s. The flood threatened to destroy much of the city's vast collection of artistic treasures, especially the world famous frescoes that adorned the Florentine churches. The flood led to a major relief operation, involving volunteers, technicians and specialists worldwide. Once the restoration had been completed, it was initially planned that the frescoes should be returned to their original sites. Instead, following an intervention made by Olivetti representatives, a travelling exhibition of the restored artifacts was planned as an expression of Italy's gratitude for the international assistance. In 1967 Olivetti helped organise an exhibition of Florentine Frescoes Saved from the Flood. The travelling exhibition opened at the Metropolitan Museum in New York and then went on to the capital cities of Europe. Subsequently, between the late 1960s and early 1990s, the company's Cultural Activities Division has organised around 52 exhibitions worldwide in collaboration with institutions such as the Metropolitan Museum, British Museum and Royal Academy. Thirty-three of these exhibitions have been organised since 1980. This coincided with the general expansion of cultural interventions by the private sector.

Olivetti has now diversified into new areas of cultural interest under an enlarged Cultural Activities Division. The most conspicuous recent advancement has been Olivetti's involvement in the restoration of artistic patrimony. This has led the company to collaborate with the Ministry of Cultural and Environmental Heritage, local supervisory offices and cultural institutes. A number of illustrious cultural artifacts in need of restoration have benefited from Olivetti's interventions: the frescoes of Masaccio, Masolino and Lippi at the Brancacci Chapel of Florence; the Baroni room at the Castle of Manta, Piedmont; and frescoes by Masolino at the Castiglione Chapel in Rome. Since 1982 Olivetti has financed the ongoing restoration work being done on Leonardo Da Vinci's *The Last Supper* under the direction of the Central Art Restoration Institute (Olivetti, n.d.). In these projects, the company has gone beyond mere financial contributions: it has placed computer-operated electrophotographic equipment at the disposal of restorers and scientists. For Leonardo's masterpiece, X-ray and specialist microscopic technology was made available to recover the original surface of the painting. In addition, the Cultural Activities Division is co-publisher with the Ministry of Cultural and Environmental Heritage of an academic journal, *Quaderni del Restauro*, established to examine the progress made in restoring cultural monuments and works of art.

Most of these cultural interventions have taken place under the auspices of Renzo Zorzi, one of the principal influences behind the company's modern aesthetic policy. Under his direction, Olivetti's participation in the cultural sphere has not been one of a distant and passive sponsor: the Cultural Activities Division, now a sub-unit of the External Relations Department, is actively involved in exhibitions and heritage restorations supported by Olivetti. One senior manager of the division noted the following: 'The aim of supporting art exhibitions is not to provide sponsorship: we are directly involved with the project and the museum, but without any other agency' (Fieldwork interview, Olivetti, 9.2.93).

As part of this collaborative approach, the Cultural Activities Division has drawn upon various in-house resources. Staff responsible for corporate design materials have occasionally contributed equipment for exhibitions. In a similar vein, the Graphic Design Department has worked on catalogue designs for Olivetti-sponsored art events. The renowned Olivetti designers, Ettore Sottsass and Mario Bellini, have contributed their own work to exhibitions or have designed the layouts for conferences and museum displays (Fieldwork interview, Olivetti, 28.5.93). The former director of the Corporate Image Department, Renzo Zorzi, maintains that this comprehensive system of in-house support is the distinguishing feature of Olivetti's cultural policy:

Today, a very great many companies and organisations from every area of business promote the arts, but, in my opinion, providing financial support or sponsoring an event from the outside is one thing; 'doing' is quite another, by which I mean having ideas, planning, organising, directing studies and special projects, coordinating research, in a word, being an active part of an event. If anything distinguishes us, it is not the quantity of resources employed but this propulsive, non-passive involvement, which has made Olivetti a significant and recognisable participant in this field. (*Olivetti News*, 1992, p. 34)

Zorzi retired from his position as director of the Corporate Image Department in 1987, but Olivetti continued to employ him as a freelance consultant. The company also gave him special responsibilities for cultural publications. Subsequent directors of the Corporate Image Department have not deviated from Zorzi's vision of a distinctive and all-embracing cultural strategy to promote Olivetti as a commercial entity. In so doing, the aim has partly been to bolster its reputation for social responsibility.

It would be fair to argue that Zorzi's lengthy involvement with Olivetti not only had a formative influence on the company's cultural interventions. His presence also helped safeguard the cultural programme, even during the 1970s

159

when Olivetti faced financial ruin in the face of foreign competition. In 1978 the entrepreneur, Carlo De Benedetti, bought a controlling stake in Olivetti, injecting much needed capital into the company. In addition, De Benedetti streamlined the corporate organisation, restored profitability and overhauled its corporate image. Olivetti was forced to abandon its relaxed and friendly style. Instead, the company prioritised the twin objectives of efficiency and profit — a contrast with the company philosophy fostered by Adriano Olivetti (Martin, 1991, p. 145). Indeed, many of the company's traditional social commitments have receded under De Benedetti's reign.

Nevertheless, Olivetti, partly through Zorzi's influence, has continued to be one of the most influential corporate patrons of the arts. This may also be attributed to the fact that patronage of the arts is considered by corporate executives as an effective way of reaching a wider and influential audience (Useem, 1984). There is no tangible evidence that corporate patronage of the arts can produce a positive company image or bolster sales. According to Useem (1987), cultural policies are more likely to gain kudos amongst other company executives. The example of Olivetti is a case in point: Olivetti's active and formative involvement in this area has set an influential precedent. It is an example followed by a number of corporations during the 1980s — Fiat among them.

At this juncture, when there was considerable growth in corporate support generally, Fiat emerged as one of the most prolific corporate patrons of the arts. The company dedicated extensive financial and technical resources to cultural activities. These were portrayed not only as a contribution to the protection of Italian culture, but also as an outward demonstration of the company's sensitivity to the needs of society:

Its [Fiat's] involvement in this area stems from the awareness that a corporation's mission in modern times must not be limited to its basic economic responsibilities. It is imperative, in fact, that corporations help to promote the general progress of society and try to meet the ever increasing needs of a community which ascribes greater importance to culture. (Fiat, 1992b, p. 4)

These cultural activities have ranged across a number of areas — exhibitions, architectural restoration, and urban rejuvenation. Echoing Olivetti, Fiat's cultural policy is characterised by the same independent determination to make a purposeful and active contribution towards the preservation of artistic heritage. Fiat, though, has also participated in joint cultural ventures with government departments, specialist bodies and private companies. In 1985, the company, together with the Tuscan regional government and the public bank, Monte dei

Paschi di Siena, became involved in the Etruscan Project, an event composed of a series of exhibitions on the various aspects of Etruscan civilisation (Bodo, 1989). In addition, the Group construction subsidiary Fiatengineering [*sic*] joined IBM in 1987 in the Neapolis Consortium. This was a project to catalogue the information on the artistic and archaeological resources around the Vesuvius area.

More typical of the cultural projects embraced by Fiat throughout the 1980s was its restoration of the Palazzo Grassi in Venice. In 1984 the Fiat Group purchased the neglected palace — a renowned creation of the eighteenth-century architect Giorgio Massari — for $6 million. Fiat used its own engineering and electronics subsidiaries to renovate and transform the former aristocratic residency into a modern museum and exhibition centre. After 14 months, the restoration of the palace was completed at a total cost, according to Fiat reports, of $12 million (Fiat, n.d.(b)). Since 1986 the Grassi Palace has housed eight travelling international exhibitions from Futurism to the Futurists to a celebration of the work of Andy Warhol. It has also formed links with august cultural institutions such as the Museum of Modern Art in New York, the State Museum of Berlin and Spain's Museum of Contemporary Art.

The company has made a point of restoring cultural monuments and historical architecture in the area around Turin where Fiat has its central headquarters. In accordance with the pattern established by the Palazzo Grassi project, the company financed the refurbishment of a number of famous buildings in Turin, chosen because of their social and historical importance to the city. For instance, in 1986 the company employed architectural specialists Roberto Gabetti and Aimaro Isola to improve and extend visiting facilities for the public at the Royal Palace of Turin. At the same time, plans were initiated to transform the disused Fiat Lingotto factory into an exhibition centre. At the start of 1991 Renzo Piano, the renowned Italian architect, was commissioned to oversee the planned reconstruction of the Lingotto factory. In fact, the project was seen by Fiat as an opportunity to revitalise the surrounding urban zone.

From this, it is clear that Fiat has strived, like Olivetti, to be an influential and autonomous cultural agent in its own right. Significantly, in recent years, a plethora of companies — Benetton, Parmalat, Galileo Industrie Ottiche, Generali, and ENI — have adopted similar cultural policies. This has resulted in a prominent role for the private sector in maintaining cultural heritage. However, despite such growing interest, there are important additional observations that should be made.

The private sector may have become a more significant player in the cultural world but the task of preserving Italy's cultural patrimony is still dominated by government finances and by public institutions. Furthermore, much of this increased support for culture is directed towards particular causes. According

161

to Bodo (1989), corporate patronage of cultural heritage has focused on prestigious cultural events and monuments that are best able to generate kudos for those involved. Examining the field of corporate patronage, Useem maintains that: '...company giving in culture and the arts is strongly skewed toward the most prestigious organisations in the region. Corporate patronage of the arts is undertaken with discretion, but it is a discretion exceedingly well placed' (1987, p. 349).

This may be a legitimate claim to make for larger corporations. The analysis so far has not taken into account the participation of the public sector banks in the cultural sphere. One of the most conspicuous features surrounding the expansion in business support of the traditional arts is the contribution made by Italy's public banks, particularly the socially oriented savings and cooperative banks. These financial institutions have retained a strong social ethos which can be traced back historically to their founding statutes (see Chapter 6). As such, it is worth assessing the extent to which the cultural interventions of these institutions are guided by the needs of preserving heritage, regardless of how illustrious the cause.

The public banks and their cultural responsibilities

Italian banks have played a central part in the general increase in commercial support for the traditional arts and heritage during the 1980s. A 1991 survey of the level of private sector endowments to the arts in Piedmont found that 86 per cent of the aggregate total given by companies to cultural endeavours originated from banking institutions based in the region (IRES, 1992). Although the situation in Piedmont may not be entirely representative of all Italian regions, the banking sector is now widely regarded by cultural practitioners and commentators as a major commercial benefactor of the traditional arts. This situation has come about because several banking institutions — around 80 per cent of which are under public ownership — are obliged, for various historical and legal reasons, to give part of their profits to social and charitable causes. In recent years public banks have used the *erogazione sociale* (social donations) to help maintain Italy's cultural and artistic heritage.

Over the years the Bank of Italy has classified the myriad Italian banking institutions into five main categories. Out of these five categories, it is the *casse di risparmio* (savings banks) that have gained a considerable reputation for funding the traditional arts. The communications company Gruppo Prospettive carried out a cursory examination of 210 culturally active enterprises. Of those enterprises included in the survey, 45 per cent came from the banking sector, while just under half of this number were savings banks (Gruppo Prospettive,

162

1992). As recounted in Chapter 6, the savings banks came to be formed as philanthropic institutions, following the tradition of the *monti di pieta*, in the early nineteenth-century. This was a feature subsequently safeguarded by a number of government regulations. Most noteworthy was the Fascist Banking Law of 1936 that regulated the ability of deposit banks to provide long-term industrial credit (Ceriani, 1962). This law simultaneously placed the savings banks under public control, thereby confirming the philanthropic status of these institutions and entailing a legal obligation to divide their operating profits between reserves and gifts to charity organisations.

The government still had effective control of the financial sector after the Second World War — a legacy from the Fascist period. Under state control, banks were able to open up new branches only with government approval. During the immediate postwar years the government sought to extend banks into areas with limited financial services, mainly rural localities. It was also concerned that credit should be made more available to small banking institutions. To this end, the government tended to grant authorisation for expansion to such institutions as the savings banks, for they often served single localities and generally dealt in small credit loans. Thus, 83 per cent of the new bank offices and branches opened between 1948 and 1960 belonged to the smaller categories of savings, cooperative and credit banks (Ceriani, 1962).

The distinctive nature of the savings banks, over time, has become less pronounced; they have exploited the opportunities for commercial growth and now operate throughout the peninsula and the economy. Despite modernisation, they continue to operate as public corporations, possessing constitutional and legal obligations to donate part of their profits to causes of a social nature.

The savings banks, though, are not the only financial institutions that operate as public corporations. Of the five main banking categories operating in Italy, the public law banks and cooperative people's banks are, in legal terms, essentially philanthropic commercial institutions or foundations, as they are known. For example, the public law banks — the Banca Nazionale del Lavoro, Banco di Napoli, Banco di Sicilia, Monte dei Paschi di Siena and the Istituto San Paolo di Torino — mainly deal with small business operations, but also engage in long-term credit operations. All these institutions, in addition to their ordinary commercial activities, finance local public bodies, charitable and social organisations.

Since the mid-1980s, these socially-oriented public banks have been increasingly subject to modernising forces. To begin with, the centralised control over commercial outlets was scrapped by a special regulation. The most radical break with past orthodoxies was encompassed in Law no. 218 of 1990, otherwise known as the Amato-Carli Law. It was passed to authorise the privatisation of all public banks, including the savings banks and the public law banks. The Amato-Carli privatisation is not so much a doctrinaire response to current neo-liberal economic fads but more of a pragmatic response to the Single European Market and the competitive pressures that this creates for Italy's indigenous banks. Those who framed Law no. 218 envisaged that the rationalisation and commercial efficiency afforded by privatisation would better equip financial institutions to meet the competition from their powerful European neighbours. The Amato-Carli Law also aimed to remove various restraints from banks in order to facilitate their commercial expansion. Hence, these banks have easier access to capital markets; they have gained the opportunity to forge strong strategic alliances with other banks; and the philanthropic banks have been encouraged to establish organisational provisions that concentrate on commercial activities.

The framers of the new legislation were careful to ensure that these former public banks would be able to retain their philanthropic and social characteristics. The Amato-Carli Law decreed that the newly privatised institutions would have to place 51 per cent of their shares into the ownership of specially created foundations within the corporate organisation or under the control of external public institutions. In effect, it attempted to create a dual structure within these public corporations: the privatised section of the banks would control all banking and commercial activities, while the foundations would distribute part of the profits to social causes on behalf of the bank.

Since this law, a superficial form of privatisation has taken place; most of the newly privatised banks have reverted simply to being controlled by their own internal foundation organisations. In one notable instance, Cariplo (Cassa di Risparmio delle Provincie Lombarde), Italy's largest savings bank, placed all the shares from its newly privatised banking company under the ownership of a specially created social foundation (Fieldwork interview, Cariplo, 2.6.93). The Istituto Bancario San Paolo di Torino managed to privatise 20 per cent of its capital, dispersing it between 65,000 investors, which allowed the bank to increase its equity base. However, the Compagnia di San Paolo, which has inherited the function of the ancient charitable institution, holds the remainder of the shares contained in the holding Sanpaolo banking group (Sanpaolo, n.d.). Although the Banca di Roma was one of the few joint ventures to result from the privatisation law, all of the bank's shares are equally divided between two public institutions: Ente Cassa di Risparmio di Roma and IRI (Banca di Roma, 1992).

Hence, at present, there has only been a nominal privatisation of the banking system. The public-dominated status quo of the banking system has, for all the efforts made by Law no. 218, remained. The limited privatisation of the public banking sector reflects the general reluctance of the state to sell public industries. Although privatisation would produce receipts worth $10—15 billion

(Davidson and Roche, 1993), many politicians have been unwilling to carry out extensive privatisations, to prevent new investors in the public sector being dominated by a handful of undercapitalised, family-owned firms. This includes the likes of Olivetti (De Benedetti), Fiat (Agnelli) and Fininvest (Berlusconi) which hold a pre-eminent position in Italy's private sector and stock market (*The Economist*, 1993).

The moribund privatisation of the banking sector has meant that many public banks can be legitimately categorised as non-profit institutions. Hence, savings and cooperative banks are obliged by their legal statutes and articles of association to distribute a proportion of their yearly profits to charitable works or social initiatives promoting the wider public good. This would include charity work and the preservation of cultural heritage.

The actual amount donated against the level of profits retained for reinvesting in banking and commercial activities tends to vary from year to year. Some banks have definite percentages that they are obliged to use as social benefactions, but even here some flexibility is employed. The statute of the Monte dei Paschi di Siena, reputed to be the oldest bank in the world, stipulates that the bank must give up to 50 per cent of its yearly pre-tax profits to social causes, but its yearly endowments never reach this exacting level (Monte dei Paschi di Siena, n.d.). However, in 1992 the bank gave 20 per cent of its profits to social causes (Fieldwork interview, Monte dei Paschi di Siena, 4.6.93). The cooperative bank, Banca Popolare di Milano, was committed to giving up to 6 per cent of its profits, but when the bank's statute was modified in April 1990, this was reduced to 2 per cent (Banca Popolare di Milano, 1990). For many of these socially-oriented banks, the arts and cultural heritage present varied and worthwhile outlets for their community donations. The savings banks, often regional or provincial in character, use their contributions to support the maintenance of cultural and historic patrimony. These are regarded as distinctive contributions to the communities in which they are located.

The limited number of studies on the cultural policies of the public banks (see Confindustria, 1988; Gruppo Prospettive, 1992) show that banking institutions tend to favour the traditional arts, particularly the maintenance of historically significant artifacts. The statutes of certain banks prescribe that cultural endowments must be directed at traditional areas. Cariplo's (Cassa di Risparmio delle Provincie Lombarde) cultural policy is mainly concerned with the maintenance of antiquarian forms of art and excludes the possibility of supporting the work of living artists (Fieldwork interview, Cariplo, 2.6.93). The Cassa di Risparmio di Firenze (Savings Bank of Florence) has an unwritten code that precludes it from sponsoring exhibitions or acquiring paintings by contemporary artists (Fieldwork interview, Cassa Risparmio di Firenze, 1.6.93). However, there are some exceptions regarding the emphasis placed on supporting the traditional arts and cultural heritage. The Banca Popolare di Milano has organised art exhibitions of contemporary artists, photographers and sculptors (Banca Popolare di Milano, n.d.). The Cassa di Risparmio di Reggio Emilia has financed exhibitions of the contemporary local artist Gino Gandini (Fieldwork interview, Cassa di Risparmio di Reggio Emilia, 3.6.93).

The sums dedicated to supporting Italian culture and the types of project adopted tend to vary between banking institutions. Generally, the level and quality of support for the cultural sphere is determined by the size, geographical location and internal milieu of the bank. A notable development among the larger public banks is their tendency to emulate the active cultural interventions made by large private corporations such as Olivetti and Fiat.

Since the mid-1980s the public law bank, Istituto Bancario San Paolo di Torino, has gained a reputation for organising a number of prominent and long-term restoration projects. Originally, the bank was established in 1563 in Turin by seven local notaries to perform charitable acts and it is now one of Italy's largest domestic banks: in the early 1990s the bank had assets worth 200,000 billion lire, a presence across all principal financial areas and 782 branches in all 20 regions, including 200 operations abroad (Sanpaolo, n.d.). Although the Istituto Bancario San Paolo underwent restructuring and selective privatisations during the 1980s, the bank still remains a public institution. Istituto San Paolo shares are wholly owned by the Compagnia di San Paolo, which is a public foundation that has inherited the social obligations of the original institution and administers the bank's cultural and public policies. To this end, it operates through the Fondazione dell'Istituto Bancario San Paolo di Torino per la Cultura, la Scienza, e l'Arte (the Sanpaolo Foundation for the Promotion of Culture, Science and Art). The Foundation was established in 1985 by the bank's president, Gianni Zandano, in order to create a clear demarcation within the organisation between those areas responsible for banking and those involved in social operations. The central objective of the Sanpaolo Foundation 'is to engage in major projects...supervising all the stages from the planning to actual completion, not limiting its role to that of mere provider of funds' (Fondazione Sanpaolo di Torino, n.d.). The Foundation has 15 to 20 full-time staff. With these organisational resources, it is able to organise major cultural projects on behalf of the bank and develop its reputation as a cultural patron of the arts.

The Foundation's first intervention turned out to be its largest: in 1985 it signed an agreement with the Ministry of Cultural and Environmental Heritage to restore the Schiaparelli Wing of the Egyptian Museum in Turin. In accordance with its proactive strategy, the Foundation used its own organisational facilities to employ construction firms and technical experts for the project. Plans for its restoration were made in 1985, but work on the museum did not begin until 1988 and was eventually completed in August 1990 at a cost of £5 million (Fondazione Sanpaolo di Torino, 1991). The hiatus between signing the actual agreement and completing the restoration was mainly due to the inertia of the public bureaucracy. However, the Istituto San Paolo and other sponsors of restoration projects have no choice but to collaborate with the Ministry of Cultural and Environmental Heritage; most of the cultural treasures in the peninsula are administered by this governmental department. The bank's involvement in the Egyptian Museum, according to some of the bank's personnel, was an opportunity to bring commercial values into the arena of government:

> In practical terms we intervened with the intention of bringing private experience into the public sector. In Italy, there are great problems in the sense that state interventions are always very long. Instead, we want to be characterised as having a timed agenda that we can keep to. In our cultural interventions, we set out a particular time schedule, which we make public and try earnestly to keep. (Fieldwork interview, Fondazione Sanpaolo di Torino, 20.5.93)

In addition to its work with the Egyptian Museum, the Turin based bank has, since 1986, organised the restoration of the Abbey of San Fruttuoso and its village houses at Camogli, near Genoa (Fondazione Sanpaolo di Torino, 1991). The project lasted three years — from 1986 to 1989 — and cost £1.5 million.

The Cassa di Risparmio delle Provincie Lombarde (Cariplo), like the Istituto San Paolo, is one of Italy's largest public savings banks, with 711 branches across ten regions. This is a unique feature, as the savings banks normally operate in single regions or provinces. Like the Istituto Bancario San Paolo, Cariplo, after the Amato-Carli Law, created a separate foundation which owned the newly created joint-stock banking company, Cariplo Spa. The foundation created a specialist department responsible for organising cultural activities. With financial resources at its disposal, Cariplo has funded the restoration of 35 different artifacts of historical and cultural significance, mainly in the Lombardy region (Gruppo Prospettive, 1992, pp. 98—100). One of the most ambitious schemes adopted by the bank was its support of the restoration of Milan's prestigious library, the Biblioteca Ambrosiana. The bank donated £6.5 million, spread over a four-year period, for a structural refurbishment programme to preserve the library's building structure, which at the time was being threatened by humidity.

The vast financial resources for cultural projects in the hands of the larger public banks is exemplified by the Banca di Roma. This bank agreed to sponsor restoration work on the Colosseum in Rome, following direct intervention by the Ministry of Cultural and Environmental Heritage and the former Prime

Minister, the now disgraced Giulio Andreotti. Work on the Colosseum began in September 1992 and was projected to take four years. By the time the project is completed, the Banca di Roma will have donated around £16 million towards the restoration. According to the bank's president, Pellegrino Capaldo, the request for support could not be refused because it would act as an important reminder of the bank's humanitarian origins (Banca di Roma, 1992).

The above cases detail the interventions of the largest public banks. As has been shown, they closely emulate the high-profile cultural programmes found in the corporate sector. However, many of the public banks in Italy operate on a provincial or regional basis, and thus have only limited funds at their disposal. For instance, there are over 100 separate *casse di risparmio*, which, being small, do not possess the organisational and financial wherewithal to finance prestigious cultural programmes. Nevertheless, because of their confinement to single provinces or regions, they are well placed to support the preservation of less prominent monuments or artifacts that are often overlooked by larger institutions. The Cassa di Risparmio di Prato has, for example, contributed finance towards the restoration of local monuments, including unspectacular, though practical, tasks such as renewing the electrical circuiting of the local Duomo (cathedral). The Cassa di Risparmio di Reggio Emilia has funded restoration work on the Battistero di Reggio Emilia, helping to remove the humidity that had built up in its foundations (Cassa di Risparmio di Reggio Emilia, 1991). Although these interventions are generally more parochial and less noteworthy than those of some of the metropolitan-based public banks, this should not diminish their importance. As one senior executive from the Cassa di Risparmio di Prato observed:

> The large companies involve themselves in great restoration programmes, which gives them publicity returns. The *casse di risparmio* are involved in smaller interventions in the local community where they are based...It is important to restore these larger monuments, but it is probably more important to restore all the smaller monuments in a city or town because this would render the city more habitable. This is one of the merits of the casse di risparmio. (Fieldwork interview, Cassa di Risparmio di Prato, 1.6.93)

From this analysis, it seems that the public banks have made a range of contributions towards supporting the preservation of cultural heritage. Large banks, such as the Istituto San Paolo, have been able to replicate the type of proactive cultural interventions demonstrated by such conglomerates as Fiat and Olivetti. The banks in general have come to treat culture as an integral part of their contributions to the community. However, most of the public savings banks do not have the same organisational or financial wherewithal to sustain the type of cultural programmes adopted by their larger counterparts. Be that as it may, the smaller public banks, like many of the *casse di risparmio*, have made unspectacular, though important, contributions in supporting cultural heritage.

Conclusion

The traditional arts and the cause of preserving cultural heritage has attracted wide-ranging support from Italy's commercial over the past 14 years. Indeed, the cause of supporting cultural patrimony has witnessed a general and active mobilisation of commercial enterprises behind voluntary social action. This has come about with little systematic government coordination; and where the government has attempted to coax and encourage corporate intervention through fiscal incentives, the provisions made have had little effect. Of greater import has been the growth of the advertising industry and the cultural activities of prominent corporations such as Olivetti. Moreover, the social banks — *casse di risparmio, monti di pieta* and *banche popolari* — have emerged as generous patrons of the arts. Because such banks are largely under public ownership and have retained their charitable statutes, these institutions have made extensive and active contributions towards the support of cultural heritage in recent years. Governments have passed measures to sanction the privatisation of these institutions. Yet, the social banks have resisted these measures and have retained their philanthropic functions. This not only reflects the pervasiveness of the Italian public sector economy, it also highlights the importance of the public sector in sustaining the social ethos of commercial institutions that predate industrialisation.

9 Conclusion

The preceding chapters have analysed the social role of commercial enterprises. They have also examined the contribution that they can make to the well-being of society, especially in tackling social problems. Within the context of a capitalist economic system, this has involved companies, executives and business owners going beyond narrow commercial objectives to pursue wider communitarian, social goals.

This analysis has focused specifically on the incidence of business social action in the context of Britain and Italy. There are, in both societies, notable historical and contemporary demonstrations of business philanthropy and social action. It was found that historically the dominant expressions of industrial and commercial philanthropy proved to be distinct in both societal contexts — a feature linked to the development and organisation of modern society.

Analysis of this development begins in the Middle Ages. During the Middle Ages in Europe, commerce was organised, on the whole, within self-contained provincial and regional locations. The guilds, which were essentially organisations that provided collective representation on behalf of traders and craftsmen, were responsible for administering commercial transactions. However, regulating trade was not the only responsibility of these organisations. As the guilds of medieval Britain and Italy demonstrated, they also functioned as benevolent institutions. Hence, the guilds subjected economic activities to moral scrutiny, becoming actively engaged in the organisation of welfare provision and poverty relief for town inhabitants. Eventually, the advance of modernising forces in the economy after the sixteenth century, together with the emergence of new socio-economic interest groups, led to the abrogation of the guild system in Britain and Italy. But from this point on, the progress of both societies towards economic modernisation assumed distinct courses. This had a bearing over the communitarian role of business owners and dominant expressions of commercial philanthropy.

The development of corporate philanthropy

Central to Britain's economic advancement from the fifteenth to the seventeenth century were the small band of urban-based merchants. Despite the size of this new socio-economic grouping, it actively contributed to the dismantling guild regulations and expanding trade. Historical evidence shows that the merchant class also gained prominence in the social sphere. Merchants assumed much of the responsibility for supporting private welfare services and poverty relief. Here, commercial philanthropy, in contrast to the communitarian impulse of the Middle Ages, was predominantly shaped by the beliefs, whims and interests of individual merchants. These were increasingly influenced by Protestant doctrines.

By the eighteenth century, Britain was preparing for further economic growth, principally as a result of industrialisation. There are several factors that account for the process of industrialisation. Significant contributions were made by individual economic agents — business owners, entrepreneurs and traders — operating through the free market. Although government assistance was a vital factor in the move towards industrialisation, the role of the public sector was indirect, as it established a framework for entrepreneurial action. From this position of economic power, the business and industrial class augmented its status in wider society by fusing with already powerful landed and financial classes. Early industrialisation of Britain gave business owners the wealth and standing in society to undertake major acts of philanthropy. Business involvement in wider society was facilitated by the fact that the system of poverty relief and social care was dominated by private charity, to which industrialists were munificent contributors. At the same time, the prevailing influence of Liberal thought, and the proliferation of Nonconformist humanitarian religious denominations provided moral and political sanction for business philanthropy.

As shown in Chapter 2, the inexorable advance of industry brought with it a whole panoply of social problems. These problems could not be contained by private philanthropy and the selective largesse of business owners. There was a growing awareness of the deficiencies surrounding private charity from the late nineteenth century onwards. Public authorities, mainly at municipal level, responded by assuming greater responsibility for the provision of welfare and social services. The intervention of the public sector into the area of welfare provision began to gain decisive momentum during the twentieth century. The interwar period, characterised by high levels of unemployment and economic turbulence, witnessed major strides in state services, such as unemployment benefit and health insurance.

The welfare reforms after the Second World War established a system of universal provision across many crucial areas. The state came to assume control over essential welfare services previously administered by private institutions. However, after the Second World War, the voluntary sector continued to flourish, diversifying into new areas and pioneering modern charitable techniques. As Prochaska (1988) argues, even public institutions such as the National Health Service, in its formative years, relied on voluntary effort. This meant that industrialists still had opportunities to be involved in social action during the early and mid-twentieth century.

In Chapter 3, it was argued that the extent of business involvement in society throughout the twentieth century was influenced by the dominant structure of ownership that was emerging during its early years. What proved most significant at that time was the gradual replacement of the small family-owned business unit by the oligopolistic commercial organisation.

The concentration and expansion of commercial institutions meant that philanthropic action and charitable giving became increasingly problematic. Legally, those running enterprises could not easily expend resources for purposes which were not directly related to their shareholders interests. Indeed, there were isolated instances of shareholders attempting to bring injunctions against their companies for making charitable donations. The *Evans v. Brunner Mond* case (1921) mentioned in Chapter 3 is one example. Nevertheless, some outlets for industrial philanthropy remained, such as the cause of higher education which seemed to combine self-interest with charitable motives. Increased concentration of industrial ownership meant that directors and managers had less autonomy when it came to organising support for philanthropic activities. Thus, throughout the early postwar years, corporate involvement was mainly characterised by companies making formal donations to the subscription lists of large charitable and voluntary organisations. This situation began to change in Britain during the early 1970s.

It was then that the political and economic situation started to alter dramatically. This affected the social expectations surrounding the business community. Central to all this was the economic recession during the second half of the 1970s, which undermined the social democratic consensus of the postwar period. This, in its turn, helped create the institutional and political conditions for the type of corporate social activities which had been prevalent in the United States since the 1950s. Out of the economic recession came discussions about the limits of state intervention in society. Some argued for greater non-governmental involvement, especially the private sector, in forming policies and tackling social problems. Thus, there was a conspicuous increase regarding the interlocution between government and business in response to escalating economic difficulties. The links between both sectors created the necessary institutional opportunities for business involvement in areas of social policy. This included inner-city rejuvenation, the promotion of small firms and environmental protection.

Further momentum was given to corporate social involvement in the 1980s by the changing nature of British politics. The electorally dominant Conservative Party, in its pursuit of a New Right political agenda and a monetarist economic strategy, created a political climate in which corporate social involvement became an objective in its own right and an important part of the policy-making process. The emphasis on private sector engagement was deemed to be necessary in order to compensate for the perceived deficiencies and limitations of state intervention. For instance, it was shown in Chapter 4 how the private sector contributed to inner-city and local economic policies through such initiatives as City Challenge and the urban development corporations. The growth of corporate social responsibility in Britain throughout the 1980s was exemplified by the expansion of organisations — like Business in the Community — that coordinated corporate social involvement.

These political and economic developments established the context from which general interest in corporate social responsibility emerged. The wider context, whilst important, only forms part of the analytical terrain that should be covered. Explanations should take into account, at the same time, how purposeful agents within companies perceive and respond to these wider developments. Case studies of the social programmes organised by the likes of Shell, BAT Industries, Unilever, and BT highlight the significance of these considerations. The studies also underline how the close interface between private sector and government during these years provided a conduit in which political developments influenced the ideas and concerns of company personnel.

Presented above are the principal arguments relevant to corporate philanthropy in Britain. Certainly, it would seem that the involvement of companies in activities of a communitarian nature is linked at a societal level to two factors: firstly, the specific route assumed by society towards economic and social modernity; secondly, the vicissitudes surrounding state-business relations. The importance of these processes became further evident when examining business philanthropy in Italy. The new social and institutional arrangements brought about by Italy's transformation into a modern economic entity shaped the dominant expressions of commercial engagement in social action. The transformation of Italy into a modern industrial was assisted by the growth of public institutions and state enterprises.

When compared to other major European states, the industrialisation of Italy's economy was relatively late, coming in the latter stages of the nineteenth century. It was shown in Chapter 6 that the comparatively slow rate of modernisation can be located in the weakness of the Italian entrepreneurial class. This class was shackled by the landowning classes and the Catholic Church which opposed industrial development. Consequently, Italy's business class could only transform a predominantly agrarian economy into an industrial power through an extensive reliance on state intervention. Italian business owners did not emulate the philanthropy of the British industrial and business classes, and generally based their social interventions around parochial and paternalistic welfare schemes within the workplace.

These features of Italian industrialisation, however, did allow certain opportunities for philanthropic action on the part of commercial entities. The far-reaching intervention of the state in the economy and society helped preserve the communitarian institutions that had emerged during the mid-nineteenth century, prior to industrialisation. Regulations and laws were passed, helping maintain the essential social and philanthropic status of the savings banks and cooperatives.

By the beginning of the twentieth century, as Italy underwent a second phase of industrialisation, private capital was able to advance its position in both commercial and political terms. This phase of economic growth, which brought with it new commercial and industrial innovations, witnessed some notable instances of business-led social action. The most significant social achievements in this period were those of the typewriter company, Olivetti. The owners of Olivetti implemented and administered a number of significant social programmes in Ivrea where the firm was located. These interventions shared an affinity with the civic achievements of nineteenth-century industrial and entrepreneurial philanthropists in Britain.

The expansion of private industry and the philanthropic endeavours of the Olivetti family were of historical import for the peninsula. Nevertheless, the spectre of the state continued to have a profound influence over society — a fact that was compounded by the Fascist *coup d'état* in 1922. Throughout the Fascist period, there was a continuation of the far-reaching interventionist measures that had typified Italian society since the late nineteenth century. Crucially, the regime intervened on behalf of private industry to secure the necessary conditions for capital accumulation. However, Mussolini's Fascists were keen to build a mass support base through all sections of society, including the working class. As a result, Mussolini and a variety of Fascist *apparatchiks* became involved in the *dopolavoro* campaign. Here, employers and industrialists were advised to adopt enlightened practices in the workplace and to assume social responsibilities. The *dopolavoro* scheme was very symptomatic of the way in which the private sector had become subservient to the government's centralising tendencies.

It might have been expected that, with the demise of the Fascist government, a radical break with past institutional arrangements and policy orthodoxies would ensue. The Christian Democrat Party was relied upon by the Italian establishment, as well as business interests and Western powers, to safeguard the interests of private business and the Church against the perceived threat of

Communism. However, as shown in Chapter 7, the Christian Democrats cultivated a strong inter-class and social reform agenda in government. Being tied to interest groups such as the private sector, landowners and the Catholic Church meant it was unable initially to implement this reform agenda, involving new landholding schemes and welfare provision. Gradually, the Party attempted to distance itself from its original support base in order to carry out its policy of social reform, beginning a campaign, from the early 1950s, against the poor employment practices of private sector employers. In addition, it assumed control — against the wishes of business owners — over vital areas of the economy through the expansion of the state holding system. For companies such as ENI and IRI, the government established separate employers' organisations so that trade unions could enjoy an equitable bargaining position.

The enlargement of the state holding sector enabled the Christian Democrats to undermine the capability of private capital to monopolise areas of the economy. At the same time, the government used the state sector to spearhead enlightened reforms in the workplace and society. During the 1950s and early 1960s, the state holding companies — mainly ENI and IRI — were used to rescue ailing firms in order to avoid mass redundancies and redevelop deprived regions of the south. The state sector, and its expansion in the postwar period, proved central to the social contribution of businesses in contemporary Italian society. Indeed, the major state holding companies preside over specialist subsidiaries which perform essentially social functions. For example, some firms such as SPI are involved in promoting small business growth. The ENEA company, a subsidiary of the nationalised electricity company, ENEL, specialises in creating environmentally sensitive technologies for industry.

The colonisation of vital areas of the economy by the state holding sector did not rule out the possibility of private sector involvement in socially useful programmes. A key factor was the faltering of the economy and the performance of the state holding sector during the 1970s. One area where the state sector had not succeeded was in bridging the economic gap between north and south. This led to efforts to involve the private sector which, by this time, had began to reorganise itself politically and economically in redeveloping the south. Throughout the 1950s and 1960s, the policy issue of modernising the south was dominated by the state — namely ENI and IRI. The fact that, by the 1970s, the government was beginning to provide various fiscal and structural incentives to involve private capital in the south demonstrated how greatly relations between the state and business community had changed.

As the private sector began to assert its position throughout the 1970s and 1980s, there were signs of business-led social activity. But, on the whole, the private sector operated in isolation, in a limited range of fields, and in an institutional context with little coordination by either business or government agencies. Overall, it has been the state holding institutions which have assumed a leading position in bringing social considerations into commerce. However, the recent surge of active involvement by both private sector and state firms in supporting the maintenance of Italy's cultural heritage has proven significant. This is one instance where the Italian business sector has come to assume some of the features that have characterised corporate responsibility in Britain.

The above has outlined some of the main features, both historically and contemporary, of corporate social involvement in Britain and Italy. The whole rationale behind this analysis has been this: to identify general factors at a socio-political level responsible for creating awareness about corporate social action. Key individuals in companies do not respond mechanically to such external events. They make choices and have a vital role to play in shaping a company's involvement in wider society.

External developments in the political and social sphere which influence key agents in companies are often mediated through government links with the business sector. The relationship between the state and business across capitalist societies is not constant but subject to political, economic and social vicissitudes. In turn, this can influence the wider social responsibilities expected of business institutions. Throughout the 1980s, British governments acted largely as enablers for corporate social responsibility, creating, as demonstrated in Chapters 4 and 5, numerous institutional opportunities for corporate engagement in society and public policy. By contrast, the Italian state has played a limited role in terms of harnessing the private sector behind social action. However, as shown in Chapter 7, postwar governments amassed extensive interests in the economy that have allowed the state to spearhead social reforms through publicly-owned holding companies. Indeed, state-owned businesses, such as ENI and IRI, have made a significant contribution in bringing social considerations to the commercial arena.

Affirmative social action versus the negative injunction

One interesting characteristic concerning the modern era of interest in corporate responsibility, particularly in Britain, is the following assertion: that businesses can directly address social problems and contribute towards the good of society. The expansion of interest surrounding corporate social responsibility in Britain during the 1980s gained considerable momentum as prevailing orthodoxies in political thinking were radically transformed. Increasing emphasis was placed on the need to involve companies, market mechanisms and business representatives within the ambit of constructing public policy.

Chapters 4 and 5 looked at some of the areas where businesses have made social and communitarian interventions in recent years. From this analysis, it was concluded that a note of caution has to prevail in assessing the ability of the private sector to address public problems. It seems that the advocates of corporate social involvement, both in government and in business, have made exaggerated claims about the capabilities of firms to devise private-led solutions to public problems.

To begin with, private enterprises are constrained financially by what they can achieve in the social sphere. The modern corporate economy that came into being in the twentieth century revolutionised the dominant structures of ownership in the economy. In this period, the family or individually-owned enterprise was replaced by the large, shareholder-owned firm. This has introduced considerable restrictions over how company resources can be expended. Corporate executive are legally bound to use the resources at their disposal primarily to advance the interests of those who own the company — that is, the shareholders. However, charitable giving is generally seen as justifiable by shareholders and the courts alike on the grounds that they can bring goodwill to the companies making donations. Since the 1970s the social contributions of corporations have increased: in 1977 the contributions of the top 200 company donors amounted to £13.9 million; by 1991, 213 out of the 400 largest corporate donors gave about £190 million to social and non-profit activities (Lane and Saxon-Harrold, 1993, p. 24). These increases in corporate giving, though, prove to be of marginal significance when compared to the profit margins of these companies. Figures show that corporate support for the non-profit and voluntary sector as a percentage of pre-tax profits fluctuated from 0.54 per cent in 1989 to around 0.69 per cent in 1992 (Lane and Saxon-Harrold, 1993, pp. 25—6).

Such corporate support may be vitally important to some areas of voluntary and charitable work. However, the level of resources is unlikely to make serious inroads when it comes to tackling public problems such as unemployment and urban deprivation. Thus, Shell's Community Relations Department in 1992 received a budget of £6 million, which was placed into the Enterprise Unit, the education service, funds for environmental projects and donations (Fieldwork interview, Shell UK, 12.11.92). This total, though, should be set in the context of the Shell Group's pre-tax profits which totalled £7.4 billion in 1989. BT's community and social budget for 1992 came to an impressive £15 million, but this had to be spread across five different causes and 10 regional offices (Fieldwork interview, BT, 4.12.92). At the same time, the company did make a pre-tax profit of over £2 billion in 1990 (Adams *et al.*, 1991, p. 187).

The limited supply of corporate funding may jeopardise the operations of agencies that depend on corporate benefactions. For instance, it was shown in Chapter 4 how local enterprise agencies have faced difficulties in attracting corporate funds. It was the government's intention, as the main backer of the local enterprise agencies, that these organisations should be able obtain private sector resources in order to expand their operations. However, research has shown that long-term corporate funding is not necessarily guaranteed, and corporate funds tend to be concentrated in the most successful and largest agencies. This uncertainty over private funding can restrict the agencies' work. In some cases, they have either tried to rely on generating profits through private consultancy work or they have been forced to rely on public assistance to avoid insolvency.

The actual extent of corporate funds and resources set aside for social and community projects may be limited. However, during the past 15 years, the corporate sector has assumed a certain degree of influence in society and government. The efforts of recent governments to reduce the function and scope of the state have gradually caused public services to be replaced by state-sponsored private provision (Grant, 1993). Of interest have been the attempts to create opportunities for private sector involvement in policy-making. Specialist agencies, such as the urban development corporations (Chapter 4), local enterprise agencies (ibid.), the Advisory Committee on Business and the Environment (Chapter 5) and wide-ranging reforms in the public sector have transformed the social role of companies. These reforms have enabled companies and their representatives to make an influential contribution towards shaping policies across a wide variety of areas — urban rejuvenation, small firm creation and the environment. These policies have partly derived from an ideological commitment to the private sector but have also grown out of a perception that inputs from the business community can help find solutions to social problems. Research has shown, though, that commercial mechanisms and agencies may be ill-suited to dealing with public and social issues. The environment in which executives operate does not necessarily provide the specialist skills for dealing with complex social matters.

A greater concern for some commentators is that private sector involvement in government policy-making has undermined democratic institutions, especially local authorities. As shown, considerable changes have taken place in the provision of public services. These transformations, in turn, have expanded the opportunities for private sector engagement in public policy. In certain policy initiatives the interests of business predominated over those of other social groups that may have a stake in the intended strategy. As was shown in Chapter 4, some responsibilities for implementing local economic strategies were devolved from local government to unelected agencies, including urban development corporations and City Action Teams, which were often dominated by corporate representatives. Again, there are definite limits as to how far companies can influence and control public services. Indeed, there are some company executives who are critical of the way normal democratic agencies and institutions have been eroded by government efforts to privatise public policy (see Chapter 4).

From this, it could argued that corporate engagement in wider society is problematic. At the same time, there is no doubt that the private sector should be contributing in some way towards the well-being of wider society. The pertinent question, though, is what form this contribution should take. Some commentators argue that corporate resources should not be dedicated to affirmative social action — one of the dominant characteristics of contemporary corporate social responsibility in Britain. It is argued, instead, that companies concentrate on scrutinising and adjusting the impact of their commercial strategies on wider society. Simon *et al.* (1972) argue that this process involves placing a negative injunction against social injury. Parkinson makes a similar point: 'It might be argued...that the need for companies to observe moral as well as legal constraints on their conduct is more pressing than the need for them to use their resources to provide private solutions to public problems' (1994, p. 16).

There are decision-making areas in which certain strategic and commercial options may not be illegal, but will have socially detrimental consequences. Mass redundancies, transferring investment from one area to another to maintain profit, needless pollution of the environment, reducing in-house skills and occupational training schemes: such activities may not infringe the law but they are still deleterious to employees and, ultimately, to wider society. There are well documented cases where companies have infringed blatantly social considerations in the pursuit of the bottom line. On occasion this has resulted in human disaster on a considerable scale. Notable examples are the capsize of the P&O-owned *Herald of Free Enterprise* off Zeebrugge and the Union Carbide explosion at Bhopal which killed 2,500 people (Crainer, 1993). In addition, criticisms have been levelled against the long-term impact of certain industries, especially on the environment. Thus, if enterprises devise community interventions and engage in social action, yet are unwilling to subject their commercial decisions to social considerations, this can lead to stark paradoxes. As Moore *et al.* put it:

> The contributions are undoubtedly seen as significant by the companies concerned...without really impinging on the strategic decisions of companies in areas like purchasing and contracting, employment and training, or the development of new products. (1989, p. 149)

The process of shaping commercial decisions according to social considerations may require enterprises to restrict profit levels, for social and economic goals, as we have seen, are not necessarily congruent:

> ...the solutions to many of contemporary society's critical needs will require us to choose between those solutions and profitability, and to reorder our priorities in the market system, even to the extent of accepting a cutback in the private standard of living. (Simon *et al.*, 1972, p. 36)

However, the exigencies of the modern economy are likely to limit the extent to which enterprises will integrate social matters within their mainstream commercial objectives. For example, it was demonstrated in Chapter 5 that provisions for improving environmental performance, such as green auditing and product analysis, have proven to be of limited value. Overall, they have not resulted in a substantial shift from commercial to environmental objectives. These measures are implemented within a context where the commercial and financial objectives are prioritised above other points of interest. Hutton notes that the search to maintain high financial rates of return and the growth of dividends has intensified in Britain. As a result, British corporations have been ruthless in the maximisation of profit opportunities (Hutton, 1994, p. 2). This, according to a number of economists, has led to an overemphasis on short-term gain to the neglect of the longer-term interests of both business and society.

There are undoubtedly difficulties in making private businesses willing to subject their operations to social scrutiny. This does not preclude the possibility of having commercial enterprises that can fulfil communitarian objectives and avoid social harm in their decisions. In Italy, for instance, some of the state holding entities and savings banks exemplify this mode of commercial organisation. In Chapter 5, it was shown how, despite the financial strictures of finance capital, there have emerged in recent years a variety of ethical and environmental financial institutions. These organisations are not merely guided by objectives centred around the maximisation of profit, they also attempt to instil, within their commercial activities, a negative injunction to avoid social injury: they endeavour to pursue activities that are beneficial to the wider social good.

Perhaps the debate over corporate social responsibility should focus on the need for companies to avoid socially harmful consequences emanating from their commercial operations. Less emphasis should be placed on socially positive interventions. These discussions must begin to consider the type of institutional structures that will allow social objectives to be more firmly integrated within business operations.

Appendix: Research Materials

General details on fieldwork interviews

As part of the research and assessment of company involvement in society, a total number of 114 interviews were conducted with personnel from British and Italian-based organisations. The interviews can generally be divided into two categories: firstly, representative practitioners from companies that are involved in administering and coordinating social and community programmes; secondly, interviewees representing non-profit or semi-government agencies that are either supported by companies or work alongside businesses, assisting their social interventions. Multiple interviews of company personnel were conducted within the same company, particularly the larger enterprises that have several operational subsidiaries. The decision to conduct multiple interviews within single organisations was taken in order to gain a detailed picture of the social and community activities organised by companies.

These interviews were conducted over a period of some 18 months, between September 1992 and February 1994. This period of interviewing included two separate, month-long research trips to Italy between January and February 1993 and May to July 1993. In all cases, the interviews were informal, often lasting 45—60 minutes; they followed a semi-structured question schedule of topics and analytical issues which was different for each respondent, depending on the type of organisation or company being represented.

The general aim of these interviews was to obtain detailed information on companies' social action programmes, especially details which are not furnished by official company reports. The following issues were of particular interest: the historical development of social responsibility policies; the organisational structure of departments responsible for implementing social programmes; the level of resources put into social action programmes; and the expectations surrounding social interventions of company managers and executives. When interviewing respondents attached to organisations benefiting from corporate benefactions, efforts were made to elicit information about the nature and quality of these collaborations with the private sector.

Each interview was tape-recorded, transcribed verbatim and committed to computer disk. The Italian interviews were translated by the author, using his working knowledge of the language. Due to limitations of space, only a few extracts are included from the copious interview transcripts, and many of those interviewed are not quoted directly whatsoever. Although none of the respondents asked to approve the material from their interviews, the identities of each respondent has been kept anonymous. The listing of interviewees' names was considered to be unnecessary; only the organisation represented by the interviewee and the date of the interview are indicated in the extracts included in the text.

Listed below are all the organisations and companies from which relevant personnel were interviewed. For the sake of simplicity, Italian and British organisations involved in the study are listed separately. In addition, a list of details concerning the interviews is provided: this includes the interview dates, together with the position, duties and representative companies or agencies of respondents.

List of British companies and organisations that partook in the study and brief descriptions of their activities

ABSA (Association for Business Sponsorship of the Arts): business funded body to attract private sector support for the arts and culture.

Age Resource: organisation based at Age Concern offices, which attempts to promote voluntary work among 'active elders'. Shell UK played an integral part in the setting up of this organisation.

Allied Dunbar: insurance subsidiary of BAT Industries.

ARC (Action Resource Centre): agency that brokers secondments and placements of business personnel and professionals to community or voluntary organisations.

BAT Industries: one of Britain's largest companies, which has its main interests in tobacco products and financial services.

Brixton Enterprise Centre: former department store (*Bon Marché*) on the Brixton Road, which was redeveloped by BAT Industries into workshops, offices and studios for around 100 small and medium-sized businesses.

Brooke Bond: Croydon-based Unilever tea and soft drinks subsidiary.

Brunswick Enterprise Centre: Liverpool-based centre that houses workshops and offices for 120 small and medium-sized enterprises; the centre was established by BAT Industries.

BT (British Telecommunications): formerly the publicly-owned telecommunications company, which was privatised in 1984.

BT North-East Regional Centre: regional headquarters based in Leeds.

BT Northern Home Counties Regional Centre: regional headquarters based in Bedford.

BT Southern Home Counties Regional Centre: regional headquarters based in Canterbury.

Business in the Community: organisation established to coordinate business action in all aspects of society. The organisation currently has around 400 member companies.

Charities Aid Foundation: organisation set up by the NCVO to provide support for charities and generate funds from private donors, particularly companies.

City Technology Colleges Trust: organisation established to promote and find sponsors for the City Technology Colleges.

Corporate Social Responsibility Group: London-based discussion forum for large corporations involved in social action. There are some 30 companies involved.

Elida Gibbs: London and Leeds-based Unilever operational subsidiary involved in the production of cosmetics and personal hygiene commodities.

Groundwork Foundation: national environmental body, part funded by the government, which oversees a number of local trusts involved in helping companies redevelop derelict sites near factories and in trying to involve enterprises in general environmental conservation.

John West: Liverpool-based Unilever subsidiary involved in the export of sea food products.

Lambeth City Challenge: cross-representative group from Lambeth Council to organise the bid for DOE City Challenge scheme.

LENTA (London Enterprise Agency): privately-funded London-based local enterprise agency that channels private sector expertise into the tasks of tackling unemployment, encouraging enterprise awareness, and assisting small businesses.

Lever Brothers: Port Sunlight and Kingston-based Unilever subsidiary which produces domestic cleaning products.

Macmillan College: the Teesside City Technology College. This is one of fifteen secondary schools outside the state system, partly funded by the private sector, that provide a greater emphasis on technological and scientific education. This college was founded with financial assistance from BAT.

Norfolk and Waverley TEC: one of 80 quasi-public agencies managed by representatives of the private sector, which were established to organise training and school/industry links on a local basis.

PSI (Policy Studies Institute): independent social research body. Most of its research contracts are with government departments.

Shell UK: main British subsidiary of the Anglo-Dutch petroleum company, the Royal Dutch Petroleum Company.

South London Business Initiative: local enterprise agency for the south London area, providing support, through the private sector, for small businesses in areas such as Peckham and Brixton. The chairman of the organisation is the BAT Industries supremo, Sir Patrick Sheehy.

THORN EMI: electrical and technology multinational.

Unilever: British parent company of the Anglo-Dutch branded consumer multinational; Europe's largest non-oil company.

List of Italian companies and organisations that partook in the study and brief descriptions of their activities

ABI (Associazione Bancaria Italiana): the association of Italian banks.

ACRI (Associazione fra le Casse di Risparmio Italiane): representative association of the *casse di risparmio* (savings banks) and *Banche del Monte*.

AEM (Azienda Energetica Municipale Milano): the municipal electricity company for Milan, which supplies electricity for the municipal services and private consumers.

AGIP: petroleum holding company, which is owned by ENI.

Amersham Italia: Italian subsidiary of the British biotechnology and health science group.

AMI (Associazione Mecenati Italiani): support agency for companies involved in the arts and culture.

Angelini Pharmaceuticals: Ancona-based pharmaceutical company, which is still owned by the Angelini family.

Associazione Italiana per la Ricerca sul Cancro: the association for cancer research.

Banca Popolare di Milano: the cooperative bank of Milan.

Banca di Roma/Cassa di Risparmio di Roma: the public sector bank which is part owned by IRI and the foundation of the savings bank for Rome. The Cassa di Risparmio di Roma, which part owns the Banca di Roma together with IRI, distributes social funds on behalf of the bank on a yearly basis.

BIC Liguria: Genoa-based SPI subsidiary involved in the promotion and creation of small enterprises.

BIC Trieste: Trieste-based SPI subsidiary involved in the promotion and creation of small enterprises.

Cariplo (Cassa di Risparmio delle Provincie Lombarde): the savings bank for the region of Lombardy.

Cassa di Risparmio di Firenze: the savings bank of Florence.

Cassa di Risparmio di Prato: the savings bank for Prato, located near Florence.

Cassa di Risparmio di Puglia/Fondazione Cassa di Risparmio di Puglia: the savings bank for the region of Apulia and its social foundation.

Cassa di Risparmio di Reggio Emilia: the savings bank of Reggio Emilia, located near Parma.

Cirio Bertolli de Rica (Societa Generale delle Conserve Alimentari): IRI owned company involved in the production and marketing of foodstuffs.

CITER (Centro Informazione Tessile dell'Emilia-Romagna): limited liability service company for small and medium-sized textile firms in the region of Emilia-Romagna.

Comerint: training and management consultancy company owned by ENI.

Comitato (Comitato per lo Sviluppo di Nuova Imprenditorialita' Giovanile): government committee for the development of young entrepreneurs in the South of Italy. Its main function has been to implement the provisions of Law no. 44.

COMOI (Compagnia Mobiliare Investimenti): Milan based investment and portfolio company.

Coop Nordemilia: the consumer cooperative for the region of Emilia-Romagna.

Coopsette: a manufacturing cooperative based in Reggio Emilia.

Elea: training and management consultancy company owned by Olivetti.

ENEA: the national agency for new technology, energy and the environment.

ENI (Ente Nazionale Idrocarburi): state energy company involved in the extraction and distribution of gas, petroleum and chemicals.

Fiat: motor vehicle manufacturer and engineering multinational, predominantly owned by the Agnelli family.

Fondazione Adriano Olivetti: cultural foundation established in memory of the former owner, Adriano Olivetti.

Fondazione Giovanni Agnelli: the cultural and social foundation established in 1966 by Fiat in memory of Giovanni Agnelli, one of the original founders of the company.

Fondazione Italiana per il Volontariato: agency established by the Banca di Roma to support and provide services to the voluntary sector and charities in Italy.

Fratelli Dioguardi: family-owned construction company, based in Bari.

Istituto Bancario San Paolo di Torino/Fondazione Sanpaolo di Torino (Fondazione dell'Istituto Bancario San Paolo di Torino per la Cultura, La Scienza e l'Arte): Turin-based public law bank and the charitable foundation attached to the Istituto, which owns the majority of shares in the commercial bank.

Isvor Fiat (Istituto per lo Sviluppo Organizzativo): a Fiat-owned company providing services in education, training and consultancy.

Main Management: Milan-based management consultancy centre.

Monte dei Paschi di Siena: the Siena-based public law bank.

Olivetti: the Italian typewriter company, now a multinational involved in the information technology market.

Procter & Gamble Italia: Italian subsidiary of the American laundry and cleaning products manufacturer.

SIP (Societa Italiana per l'Esercizio delle Telecomunicazioni): the IRI-owned telecommunications company.

SNAM: ENI-owned holding company involved in the supply, transmission and sale of natural gas.

SNAMPROGETTI: ENI-owned holding company involved in the design and construction of petrochemical refinery and gas treatment plants.

SPI (Promozione e Sviluppo Imprenditoriale): IRI Group holding company, which promotes the development of small enterprises.

Studio Lentati: Milan-based fund raising and charity consultancy company.

Telethon — Combatti la Distrofia Muscolare e le altre Malattie Genetiche: telethon event charity established to raise funds for research into genetic diseases.

List of fieldwork interviews for the British phase (dates of when they were conducted, and the representative company or organisation of interviewees, together with their position or departmental responsibilities)

ABSA: senior official (22.4.93).

Age Resource: seconded official from Shell UK (13.12.92).

Allied Dunbar: senior manger from the community affairs department (6.10.92).

ARC: senior manager (4.11.92).

BAT Industries: head of community affairs (25.9.92).

Birds Eye Wall's: senior company manager who is the chairman of the Norfolk and Waverley TEC (21.1.94).

BITC: official that performs the role as the national information officer for education (7.4.93).

Brixton Enterprise Centre: senior manager of the centre and former BAT manager (15.9.92).

Brooke Bond: senior corporate/external affairs manager (3.12.92).

Brunswick Enterprise Centre: senior manager (4.1.93).

BT: non-commercial sponsorship manager, mainly responsible for sponsorship of the arts (23.9.92).

BT: general discussion with representatives from the Community Affairs Division (23.9.92).

BT: central education liaison officer (23.9.92).

BT: Community Affairs Division officers responsible for community and economic regeneration projects (23.9.92).

BT: external promotions manager (23.9.92).

BT: manager of Action for Disabled Customers (23.9.92).

BT: senior manager of the Community Affairs Division (4.12.92).

BT: senior Community Affairs Advisor (30.4.93).

BT: senior manager from the Environmental Policy Unit (30.4.93).

BT: Community Affairs Division officer (economic regeneration) (7.1.94).

BT North-East Regional Centre: Community/Public Affairs manager (7.1.93).

BT Northern Home Counties Regional Centre: Community Affairs manager (14.12.92).

BT Southern Home Counties Regional Centre: Corporate Relations manager (21.6.93).

CAF: senior manager (24.3.93).

Corporate Social Responsibility Group: senior representative (26.10.92).

CTC Trust: chief executive (4.5.93).

Department of the Environment Official: former senior DOE civil servant, who was involved in the setting up of BITC (23.3.93).

Elida Gibbs: national accounts manager seconded to community projects (16.12.92).

Groundwork Foundation: senior official (7.5.93).

John West: public relations officer (5.1.93).

Lambeth City Challenge: seconded official from Eagle Star Insurance, a BAT subsidiary, who promoted the Lambeth City Challenge bid (17.12.92).

LENTA: senior manager involved with the local enterprise agency movement and BITC (16.11.92).

Lever Brothers: social and public affairs officer based in Kingston (18.11.92).

Macmillan College: principal of the Teesside City Technology College (11.2.94).

Manchester Business School: environmental management expert (6.1.93).

PSI: senior researcher (24.11.92).

Shell UK: Community Relations Department manager for the environment and arts sponsorship (1.10.92).

Shell UK: management consultant of the Shell Enterprise Unit (8.10.92).

Shell UK: Community Relations Department head manager for the Shell Education Service (28.10.92).

Shell UK: head manager of the Community Relations Department (12.11.92).

Shell UK: senior official of the Shell Enterprise Unit (23.4.93).

Shell UK: former head of the Community Relations Department (30.6.93).

South London Business Initiative: executive director (5.10.92).

THORN EMI: public affairs manager (30.9.92).

Unilever: Unilever education liaison officer (8.9.92).

Unilever: head manager of Community Affairs (5.1.93).

Unilever: secretary of the Unilever Appeals Committee that administers the company's charitable giving programme (23.6.93).

Unilever: deputy head of Safety and Environment Assurance, the in-house department that oversees environmental practices (30.6.93).

List of fieldwork interviews for the Italian phase (dates of when they were conducted, and the representative company or organisation of interviewees, together with their position or departmental responsibilities)

ABI: senior official from the Italian Association of Banks (3.2.93).

ACRI: senior manger (11.2.93).

AEM: manager for the public communications department (29.1.93).

AGIP: manager from the social activities and security department (17.5.93).

Amersham Italia: director general and administrator (1.2.93).

AMI: seconded official from the Fininvest company (11.5.93).

AMI: secretary general (18.5.93).

Angelini Pharmaceuticals: senior manager involved in organising charity giving (12.2.93).

Associazione Italiana per la Ricerca sul Cancro: director general (25.5.93).

Banca di Roma/Cassa di Risparmio di Roma: senior official responsible for the distribution of charitable and social benefactions (5.2.93).

Banca Popolare di Milano: bank official and expert on the cultural and social activities of the bank (2.6.93).

BIC Liguria: senior manager responsible for providing assistance and consultancy to small enterprises (21.2.93).

BIC Trieste: senior controller and advisor to small enterprises (8.6.93).

Cariplo (Cassa di Risparmio delle Provincie Lombarde): expert on social and cultural activities (2.6.93).

Cassa di Risparmio di Firenze: external relations manager responsible for cultural and artistic activities (1.6.93).

Cassa di Risparmio di Prato: senior manager (1.6.93).

Cassa di Risparmio di Puglia: senior bank official (15.2.93).

Cassa di Risparmio di Reggio Emilia: official responsible for organising cultural activities (3.6.93).

Cirio Bertolli de Rica: senior external relations manager (11.5.93).

CITER: senior consultant involved with the Committee for Young Entrepreneurs (Comitato) (27.5.93).

Comerint: senior manager involved with the Committee for Young Entrepreneurs (Comitato) (21.5.93).

Comitato per lo Sviluppo di Nuova Imprenditorialita' Giovanile:
senior official (18.2.93).

Comitato per lo Sviluppo di Nuova Imprenditorialita' Giovanile: senior official involved in liaising with companies (13.5.93).

COMOI: senior manger that has organised fund raising events for the company (26.1.93).

Coop Nordemilia: senior manager for consumer and social activities (3.6.93).

Coopsette: official from the Employee Services Department (3.6.93).

Elea (Olivetti): senior manager involved with the Committee for Young Entrepreneurs (Comitato) (20.5.93).

ENEA: senior scientist and researcher into fuel cell plants (12.5.93).

ENI: external relations manager responsible for publications and education links (5.2.93).

ENI: human resources manager responsible for administering social programmes for employees (Iniziative Sociale Centralizzate) (5.2.93).

ENI: senior officials of the Sicurezza sul Lavoro, Igiene, Qulaita e Ambiente (Environmental Safety Department) (11.2.93).

ENI: external relations managers involved in art and cultural sponsorships (19.5.93).

Fiat: public affairs manager (29.9.92).

Fiat: senior manager form the Human and Industrial Relations Department (2.2.93).

Fiat: official involved in the education liaison scheme (Fiat per i Giovani) (2.2.93).

Fiat: senior external relations manager responsible for environmental policy (14.5.93).

Fondazione Adriano Olivetti: executive director (26.5.93).

Fondazione Cassa di Risparmio di Puglia: director of the foundation (17.2.93).

Fondazione Giovanni Agnelli: senior manager (14.5.93).

Fondazione Italiana per il Volontariato: manager responsible for external relations (19.2.93).

Fondazione Sanpaolo di Torino (Istituto Bancario San Paolo di Torino): senior official of the foundation attached to the Turin public law bank (20.5.93).

Fratelli Dioguardi: senior manager (17.2.93).

Fratelli Dioguardi: senior manager engaged in coordinating social affairs (7.6.93).

Istituto Bancario San Paolo di Torino: official responsible for cultural support (20.5.93).

Isvor Fiat: senior manager that has contributed to the Committee for Young Entrepreneurs (Comitato) (14.5.93).

Isvor Fiat: researcher involved with the Committee for Young Entrepreneurs (Comitato) (14.5.93).

Italian Communist Party: expert on the cooperative movement in Italy and Emilia-Romagna (8.2.93).

Main Management: senior consultant (27.1.93).

Monte dei Paschi di Siena: senior representative of the office of the secretary general and expert on the banks social and cultural activities (4.6.93).

Olivetti: senior manager involved in organising cultural activities for the company (9.2.93).

Olivetti: cultural and social activities manager for Ivrea (26.5.93).

Olivetti: external relations manger and expert on Olivetti's cultural activities (28.5.93).

Procter & Gamble Italia: manager involved in charitable fund raising campaigns (4.2.93).

SIP: higher education liaison officer (4.2.93).

SIP: senior manager from the External Relations, Communications and Publicity Department (11.2.93).

SIP: officials involved in establishing links with higher education institutions in Apulia (17.2.93).

SIP: industrial relations, research and projects manager (19.2.93).

SIP: senior manager for external relations responsible for social telecommunications initiatives (21.5.93).

SIP: external relations for the region of Apulia, responsible for liaising with schools (31.5.93).

SNAM: senior manager involved in social activities (17.5.93).

SNAMPROGETTI: senior manager for administering social activities (24.5.93).

SPI: executive director (4.2.93).

SPI: executive director (12.5.93).

Studio Lentati: head of the management consultancy group (29.1.93).

Telethon: organisational director (18.5.93).

University of Ancona University: expert on the Italian voluntary sector (18.2.93).

References

(For clarity, business documents are separated from non-business related texts, mainly references to academic and government publications)

British company documents and publications

BAT Industries (n.d.), *Factfile BAT Industries: Community Involvement* (London: BAT Industries).

Bowtell, M. (1991), 'BT environmental policy', typescript of address to the National Communications Union Environment Conference, 10 April 1991.

BT (British Telecommunications) (1991), *BT in the Community* (London: BT).

BT (1992), *BT and the Environment: Environmental Performance Report 1992* (London: BT).

Groundwork Today (1992), *Groundwork Today*, Issue 19 (Winter) (Birmingham: Groundwork National Office).

Lambeth City Challenge (1992), *Lambeth City Challenge* (Brixton, London: Lambeth City Challenge Team).

Livewire Bulletin (1992), *Livewire Bulletin* (Winter) (Newcastle: Livewire).

Livewire (1992/93), The Link — *Newspaper for the Youth Enterprise Network from Livewire*, Issue 16 (Winter) (Newcastle: Livewire).

Livewire (1993), The Link — *Newspaper for the Youth Enterprise Network from Livewire*, Issue 17 (Spring) (Newcastle: Livewire).

PNE (Project North East) (1990), *Project North East — 10 Years* (Newcastle: Project North East).

Shell Better Britain Campaign (1988), *Getting Help for Community Environmental Projects* (Birmingham: SBBC).

Shell UK (1992), *Shell UK Review: Business and Social Report*, no. 2 (London: Shell UK).

Skelly, B. (1993), 'Throwing a lifeline to the environment', *Unilever Magazine*, no. 87, pp. 18—21 (London: Unilever External Affairs).

Tuppen, C. (n.d.), 'Devising and implementing a corporate environmental policy for BT', environmental briefing typescript for BT.

Unilever (n.d. (a)), *Unilever and the Environment* (London and Rotterdam: Unilever External Affairs).

Unilever (n.d. (b)), *Unilever Worldwide* (London and Rotterdam: Unilever External Affairs).

Unilever (1992a), *Annual Review 1992 and Summary Financial Statement* (London and Rotterdam: Unilever).

Unilever (1992b), *Review 1992: Research, Engineering and Patents* (London and Rotterdam: Unilever).

Italian company documents and publications

Banca di Roma (1992), 'Il restauro del Colosseo', *Gli Speciali della Lettera Finanziaria* 29 November 1992, pp. 21—3.

Banca Popolare di Milano (n.d.), *A Profile of Group Activities* (Milan: Banca Popolare di Milano).

Banca Popolare di Milano (1990), *Statuto: Aggiornato con le Modifiche Deliberate dalla Assemblea Straordinaria dei Soci del 28 Aprile 1990* (Milan: Banca Popolare di Milano).

BIC Liguria (n.d.), *B.I.C. Liguria: Business Innovation Centre* (Genoa: BIC Liguria).

BIC Trieste (n.d.), *BIC Trieste S.p.A: Business Innovation Centre* (Trieste: BIC Trieste).

Cassa di Risparmio di Reggio Emilia (1991), *Il Battistero di Reggio Emilia* (Reggio Emilia: Cassa di Risparmio di Reggio Emilia).

Fiat (n.d.(a)), La Fabbrica Integrata a Melfi, typescript.

Fiat (n.d.(b)), Fiat Group's Cultural Policy, internal Fiat document.

Fiat (1992a), *Fiat Policies for the Environment* (Turin: Fiat External Relations and Communications Department).

Fiat (1992b), *Fiat and the Arts* (Turin: Fiat External Relations).

Fondazione Sanpaolo di Torino (n.d.), The Sanpaolo Foundation for the Promotion of Culture, Science and Art, promotional document (Turin: Sanpaolo).

Fondazione Sanpaolo di Torino (1991), *La Fondazione* (Turin: Sanpaolo).

IRI (Istituto per la Ricostruzione Industriale) (1992), *IRI Gruppo: 1991—92 Yearbook* (Rome: IRI General Administration and Public Relations Office).

Monte dei Paschi di Siena (n.d.), *Historical Notes* (Siena: Monte dei Paschi di Siena).

Olivetti (n.d.), *A Story of Patronage in the Arts: Olivetti* (Ivrea: Olivetti Cultural Relations).

Olivetti (1983), *Design Process: Olivetti 1908—1983* (Milan: Olivetti Direzione di Corporate Image).

Olivetti News (1992), 'A company in the arts', *Olivetti News — International Edition*, vol. 32, no. 1, pp. 33—6.

Sanpaolo (n.d.), *A Profile* (Turin: Istituto Bancario San Paolo di Torino).

SPI (Promozione e Sviluppo Imprenditoriale) (n.d.), *Promozione e Sviluppo Imprenditoriale Gruppo IRI* (Rome: SPI).

References of texts, articles and government publications

Aaronovitch, S. (1955), *Monopoly: a Study of British Monopoly Capitalism* (London: Lawrence and Wishart).

Abrate, M. (1981), 'La politica economica e sindicale della Confindustria', in S. Zaninelli (ed.), *Il Sindicator Nuovo: Politica e Organizzazione del Movimento Sindacale in Italia negli Anni 1943—55* (Milan: Fondazione Agnelli).

Ackerman, R. W. (1975), *The Social Challenge to Business* (Cambridge, Mass.: Harvard University Press).

Adams, R., Carruthers, J., and Hamil, S. (1991), *Changing Corporate Values: a Guide to Social and Environmental Policy and Practice in Britain's Top Companies* (London: Kogan Page).

Adamson, C. (1975), 'The CBI view', *CBI Review*, no. 18, pp. 34—42.

Advisory Committee on Business and the Environment (1993), *Third Progress Report to and Response from the Secretary of State for the Environment and the President of the Board of Trade* (London: DTI and DOE).

Aldag, R. J., and Bartol, K. M. (1978), 'Empirical studies of corporate social performance and policy: a survey of problems and results', in L. E. Preston (ed.), *Research in Corporate Social Performance and Policy: a Research Annual*, volume 1 (Greenwich, Conn.: JAI Press).

Alibrandi, T., Natoli, G., and Silvestro, E. (1983), *I Beni Culturali ed Ambientali: Legislazione Statale ed Organizzazione Regionale* (Florence: Le Monnier).

Allen, K., and Stevenson, A. (1974), *An Introduction to the Italian Economy* (London: Martin Robertson).

Allen, M., and Ward, A. (1990), *Sponsoring the Arts: New Business Strategies for the 1990s*, special report, no. 2069 (London: Economist Intelligence Unit).

Amato, G. (ed.) (1972), *Il Governo dell'Industria in Italia* (Bologna: Il Mulino).

Amato, G. (1976), *Economia, Politica e Istituzioni in Italia* (Bologna: Il Mulino).

Andrews, F. E. (1950), *Philanthropic Giving* (New York: Russell Sage Foundation).

Antonini, E. (1991), 'Italy — cultural heritage', in A. Cutrera (ed.), *European Environmental Yearbook* (London: DocTer International).

Armytage, W. H. G. (1955), *Civic Universities: Aspects of a British Tradition* (London: Ernest Benn).

Arthur Andersen (1991), *Business Support for the Arts in Europe: a Guide through the Fiscal Maze* (London: Arthur Andersen and CEREC).

Ashley, W. J. (1894), *An Introduction to English Economic History and Theory: Part 1 — the Middle Ages* (London: Longmans, Green and Co.).

Ashley, W. J. (1914), *The Economic Organisation of England: an Outline History* (London: Longmans, Green and Co.).

ABSA (Association for Business Sponsorship of the Arts) (1993), *A Survey of Arts Sponsorship in the UK 1992/1993* (London: ABSA).

ACRI (Associazione fra le Casse di Risparmio Italiane) (n.d.), *Il Sistema delle Casse di Risparmio e delle Banche del Monte Italiane* (Rome: ACRI).

Baglioni, G. (1974), *L'Ideologia della Borghesia Industriale nell'Italia Liberale* (Turin: Einaudi).

Bamford, J. (1987), 'The development of small firms, the traditional family and agrarian patterns in Italy', in R. Goffee and R. Scase (eds), *Entrepreneurship in Europe: the Social Processes* (London: Croom Helm).

Barberis, C. (1980), *L'Artigianato in Italia e nella Comunità Economica Europea* (Milan: F. Angeli).

Barnekov, T., Boyle, R., and Rich, D. (1989), *Privatism and Urban Policy in Britain and the United States* (Oxford: Oxford University Press).

Beck, J. (1983), 'Accountability, industry and education — reflections on some aspects of the educational and industrial policies of the Labour administrations of 1974—79', in J. Ahier and M. Flude (eds), *Contemporary Education Policy* (London and Canberra: Croom Helm).

Becker, M. B. (1981), *Medieval Italy: Constraints and Creativity* (Bloomington: Indiana University Press).

Beesley, M. E. (1974), 'The context of social responsibility in business', in M. E. Beesley (ed.), *Productivity and Amenity: Achieving a Social Balance* (London: Croom Helm/New York: Crane Russak).

Beesley, M. E., and Evans, T. (1978), *Corporate Social Responsibility: a Reassessment* (London: Croom Helm).

Benn, C. (1992), *Keir Hardie* (London: Hutchinson).

199

Benn, T. (1989), *Against the Tide: Diaries 1973—76* (London: Hutchinson).

Bennett, R. (1990), *Leadership in the Community: a Blueprint for Business Involvement in the 1990s* (London: BITC).

Berle, A. A. (1959), *Power Without Property: a New Development in American Political Economy* (New York: Harcourt, Brace and Company).

Biorcio, R. (1988), 'Ecologia politica e liste verdi', in R. Biorcio and G. Lodi (eds), *La Sfida Verde* (Padua: Liviana).

Birch, R. C. (1974), *The Shaping of the Welfare State* (Harlow: Longman).

Birnie, A. (1955), *An Economic History of the British Isles* (London: Methuen).

Board of Trade, (1909), *Railway Companies (Charitable and Other Contributions, 1908): Showing in Detail the Amounts Contributed by the Railway Companies of the United Kingdom, during the Year 1908, to Institutions and Associations of Various Character, not Directly Controlled by the Companies, and not for the Exclusive Benefit of the Companies' Servants*, Parliamentary Papers, 19 Aug, 1909, vol. LXXVII (London: HMSO).

Bodo, C. (1984), 'Financing the arts and culture in Italy', in J. Myerscough (ed.), *Funding the Arts in Europe*, Studies in European Politics 8 (London: Policy Studies Institute).

Bodo, C. (1989), 'The boom of cultural sponsorship in Italy', in C. R. Waits, W. S. Hendon and J. M. Davidson Schuster (eds), *Cultural Economics 88: a European Perspective* (Ottawa: Association for Cultural Economics).

Booth, C. (1902—03), *Life and Labour of the People in London*, 17 Volumes (London: Macmillan).

Bowen, H. R. (1953), *Social Responsibilities of the Businessman* (New York: Harper and Brothers).

Bradley, I. C. (1987), *Enlightened Entrepreneurs* (London: Weidenfeld and Nicolson).

Bremmer, R. H. (1988), *American Philanthropy*, 2nd edition (Chicago: University of Chicago Press).

BIM (British Institute of Management) (1974), *The British Public Company: its Role, Responsibilities and Accountability*, Occasional Paper — New Series OPN 12 (London: BIM).

Brosio, G., and Santagata, W. (1992), 'Beni e stili culturali', in G. Brosio and W. Santagata (eds), *Rapporto sull'Economia delle Arti e dello Spettacolo in Italia* (Turin: Fondazione Giovanni Agnelli).

Brown, E. J. (1953), *The Private Donor in the History of the University* (Leeds: The University of Leeds).

Browne, A. (1983), *Tony Benn: the Making of a Politician* (London: W. H. Allen).

Brusco, S. (1982), 'The Emilian model: productive decentralisation and social integration', *Cambridge Journal of Economics*, vol. 6, no. 2, pp. 167—84.

Bruyn, S. T. (1987), *The Field of Social Investment* (Cambridge: Cambridge University Press).

Bunce, J. T. (1882), *Josiah Mason: a Biography* (Birmingham: The 'Journal' Printing Works — printed for private circulation).

BITC (Business in the Community) (1987), *Small Firms: Survival and Job Creation — the Contribution of Enterprise Agencies —* a report by Enterprise Dynamics for Business in the Community (London: BITC).

Cafagna, L. (1973), 'The industrial revolution in Italy 1830—1914', in C. M. Cipolla (ed.), *The Emergence of Industrialised Societies: The Fontana History of Europe* (London: Collins/Fontana Books).

Campa, G., and Bises, B. (1980), *La Spesa della Stato per Attivita Culturali in Italia* (Milan: Giuffre).

Campbell, C. (1987), *The Romantic Ethic and the Spirit of Modern Consumerism* (Oxford: Basil Blackwell).

Cannon, T. (1992), *Corporate Responsibility* (London: Pitman Publishing).

Caracciolo, A. (1977), *Stato e Societa Civile: Problemi dell'Unificazione Italiana* (Turin: Einaudi Editore).

Caraman, M. (1993), 'Silvio Berlusconi', typescript research paper, Harvard Business School.

Carley, M. (1991), 'Business in urban regeneration partnerships: a case study in Birmingham', *Local Economy*, vol. 6, no. 2, pp. 100—15.

Carmichael, S., and Drummond, J. (1989), *Good Business: a Guide to Corporate Responsibility and Business Ethics* (London: Business Books).

Carpanetto, D., and Ricuperati, G. (1987), *Italy in the Age of Reason 1685—1789*, trans. C. Higgitt (London and New York: Longman).

Casiccia, A. (1989), 'Lo sponsor privato di arte e cultura', in G. Bechelloni (ed.), *Il Mutamento Culturale in Italia 1945—1985* (Naples: Liguori Editore).

Castronovo, V. (1975), *La Storia Economica Storia d'Italia*, volume IV, part I (Turin: Einaudi).

Castronovo, V. (1981), 'Cultura e sviluppo industriale', in C. Vivanti (ed.), *Storia d'Italia. Annali 4. Intellettuali e Potere* (Turin: Einaudi).

Ceriani, L. (1962), 'Italy: the commercial banks and financial institutions', in R. S. Sayers (ed.), *Banking in Western Europe* (Oxford: Clarendon Press).

Chapman, A. W. (1955), *The Story of a Modern University: a History of the University of Sheffield* (London: Oxford University Press).

Chiesi, A., and Martinelli, A. (1989), 'The representation of business interests as a mechanism of social regulation', in P. Lange and M. Regini (eds), *State, Market, and Social Regulation: New Perspectives on Italy* (Cambridge: Cambridge University Press).

Christie, I., Carley, M., Fogarty, M., and Legard, R. (1991), *Profitable Partnerships: a Report on Business Investment in the Community* (London: Policy Studies Institute).

Clark, J. M. (1957), *Economic Institutions and Human Welfare* (New York: Alfred A. Knopf).

Clark, M. (1984), *Modern Italy 1871—1982* (London and New York: Longman).

Clune, G. (1943), *The Medieval Gild System* (Dublin: Browne and Nolan).

Clutterbuck, D. (1981), *How to be a Good Corporate Citizen: a Manger's Guide to Making Social Responsibility Work — and Pay* (London: McGraw Hill).

Clutterbuck, D., and Snow, D. (1990), *Working with the Community: a Guide to Corporate Social Responsibility* (London: Weidenfeld and Nicolson, in association with Kingfisher Plc).

Cochrane, E. (1988), *Italy 1530—1630* (London: Longman).

Cohen, J. S. (1967), 'Financing industrialisation in Italy, 1894—1914: the partial transformation of a late-comer', *The Journal of Economic History*, vol. XXVII, no. 3, pp. 363—82.

Colenutt, B. (1988), 'Local democracy and inner city regeneration', *Local Economy*, vol. 3, no. 2 (August), pp. 119—25.

Comitato (Comitato per lo Sviluppo di Nuova Imprenditorialita Giovanile) (n.d.), Tutoring, internal typescript document.

Comitato (1988), *Building the Future: Youth Enterprise Creation in Southern Italy* (Rome: Istituto della Enciclopedia Italiana).

Comitato (1991), *Nuove Imprese e Rapporti tra Imprese: l'Esperienza della Legge 44* (Turin: ISEDI Petrini Editore).

Comitato (1993), Dati Generali, internal document 19.1.93.

CBI (Confederation of British Industry) (1973), *The Responsibilities of the British Public Company*, final Report of the Company Affairs Committee (London: CBI).

CBI (1988), *Initiatives Beyond Charity: Report of the CBI Task Force on Business and Urban Regeneration* (London: CBI).

Confindustria (1988), *Il Matrimonio fra Impresa e Cultura* (Rome: Confindustria).

Costanzo, G. (1923), 'The principal types of agricultural co-operative society in Italy', *International Review of Agricultural Economics*, vol. 7, no. 1, pp. 50—80.

Cottino, G. (ed.) (1978), *Ricerca sulle Partecipazioni Statali*. vol. II, *L'ENI da Mattei a Cefis: La Politica del Petrolio tra Mito e Realta* (Turin: Einaudi).

Cragg, G. R. (1968), 'Introduction', in G. R. Cragg (ed.), *The Cambridge Platonists* (New York: Oxford University Press).

Craig, G., Mayo, M., and Sharman, N. (1979), *Jobs and Community Action* (London: Routledge and Kegan Paul).

Craig Smith, N. (1990), *Morality and the Market: Consumer Pressure for Corporate Accountability* (London: Routledge).

Crainer, S. (1993), *Zeebrugge: Learning from Disaster: Lessons in Corporate Responsibility* (London: Herald Charitable Trust).

Crowther, S., and Garrahan, P. (1988), 'Corporate power and the local economy', *Industrial Relations Journal*, vol. 19, no. 1, pp. 51—9.

Cunningham, W. (1922), *The Growth of English Industry and Commerce During the Early and Middle Ages*, 5th edition (London: Cambridge University Press).

Currie, D. (1983), 'World capitalism in recession', in S. Hall and M. Jacques (eds), *The Politics of Thatcherism* (London: Lawrence and Wishart).

Cutrera, A. (ed.) (1991), *European Environmental Yearbook* (London: DocTer International).

Davidson, R., and Roche, D. C. (1993), *Global Strategy and Economics: European Privatisation*, International Investment Research 21 May (London: Morgan Stanley).

Davidson Schuster, J. M. (1986), 'Tax incentives as arts policy in Western Europe', in P. J. Di Maggio (ed.), *Nonprofit Enterprise in the Arts: Studies in Mission and Constraint* (New York: Oxford University Press).

Davies, P., and Freedland, M. (1993), *Labour Legislation and Public Policy: a Contemporary History* (Oxford: Clarendon Press).

Deakins, D. (1993), 'What role for support agencies? A case study of UK enterprise agencies', *Local Economy*, vol. 8, no. 1, pp. 57—68.

De Chalander, J., and De Brebisson, G. (1987), *Mecenat en Europe* (Paris: La Documentation Francaise).

De Grazia, V. (1981), *The Culture of Consent: the Mass Organisation of Leisure in Fascist Italy* (Cambridge: Cambridge University Press).

De Groot, L. (1992), 'City challenge: competition in the urban regeneration game', *Local Economy*, vol. 7, no. 3, pp. 196—209.

DOE (Department of the Environment) (1977), *Policy for the Inner Cities*, Cmnd. 6845 (London: HMSO).

DOE (1980), *Anglo-American Conference on Community Involvement: Papers and Proceedings*, Sunningdale 9—10 April 1980 (London: DOE).

DOE (1990), *This Common Inheritance*, Cmnd. 1200 (London: HMSO).

DOE (1991), *City Challenge*, Action for Cities (London: DOE).

DTI (Department of Trade and Industry) (1973), *Company Law Reform*, Cmnd. 5391 (London: HMSO).

Diani, M. (1990), 'The Italian ecology movement: from radicalism to moderation', in W. Rudig (ed.), *Green Politics* (Edinburgh: Edinburgh University Press).

Dierkes, M. (1980), 'Corporate social reporting and performance in Germany', in L. E. Preston (ed.), *Research in Corporate Social Performance: a Research Annual*, vol. 2 (Greenwich, Conn.: JAI Press).

Ditchfield, P. H. (1904), *The City Companies of London and their Good Works: a Record of their History, Charity and Treasure* (London: J. M. Dent and Co.).

Dobkin Hall, P. (1989), 'Business giving and social investment in the United States', in R. Magat (ed.), *Philanthropic Giving: Studies in Varieties and Goals* (New York: Oxford University Press).

Donnelly, G. (1987), *The Firm in Society*, 2nd edition (London: Pitman).

Dunham, R. (1988), 'Virtue rewarded?', *Accountancy*, June, pp. 103—5.

Dunham, R. (1990), 'Ethical funds no bar to profit', *Accountancy*, June, p. 111.

Earle, J. (1986), *The Italian Cooperative Movement: a Portrait of the Lega Nazionale delle Cooperative e Mutue* (London: Allen and Unwin).

Eckaus, R. S. (1961), 'The North-South differential in Italian economic development', *The Journal of Economic History*, vol. XXI, no. 3, pp. 285—317.

The Economist (1993), 'On sale in Italy', *The Economist*, 16 October, p. 17.

Economist Intelligence Unit (1957), *Business and the Community: a Study of Industry's Contribution to Science, the Arts, Education and the Nation's Welfare* (London: The Economist Intelligence Unit).

Eden, F. M. (1928), *The State of the Poor: a History of the Labouring Classes in England, with Parochial Reports* (London: George Routledge and Sons).

Elkington, J., and Hailes, J. (1988), *The Green Consumer Guide: High Street Shopping for a Better Environment* (London: Victor Gollancz).

Elkington, J., Knight, P., and Hailes, J. (1991), *The Green Business Guide* (London: Victor Gollancz).

Epstein, E. M. (1976), 'The social role of business enterprise in Britain: an American perspective: part I', *The Journal of Management Studies*, vol. 13, no. 3, pp. 213—33.

Epstein, E. M. (1977), 'The social role of business enterprise in Britain: an American Perspective: part II', *The Journal of Management Studies*, vol. 14, no. 3, pp. 281—316.

Epstein, E. M. (1989), 'Business ethics, corporate good citizenship and the corporate social policy process: a view from the United States', *Journal of Business Ethics*, vol. 8, no. 8, pp. 583—95.

EIRIS (Ethical Investment Research Service) (1989), *Choosing an Ethical Fund: the EIRIS Guide*, 2nd edition (London: EIRIS).

EIRIS (1993), Ethical Funds, typescript (London: EIRIS).

Evans, K. (1975), *The Development and Structure of the English Educational System* (London: University of London Press).

Ewing, B. (1970), 'The good goldfish: a case study in the corporate conscience', in C. Perrow (ed.), *Organisational Analysis* (London: Tavistock).

Fabbri, M., and Greco, A. (eds) (1988), *La Comunità Concreta: Progetto ed Immagine, I Pensiero e le Iniziative di Adriano Olivetti nella Formazione della Cultura Urbanistica ed Architettonica Italiana* (Rome: Fondazione Adriano Olivetti).

Farooq Khan, A., and Atkinson, A. (1987), 'Managerial attitudes to social responsibility: a comparative study in India and Britain', *Journal of Business Ethics*, vol. 6, no. 6, pp. 419—32.

Farrell-Vinay, G. (1989), *The Old Charities and the New State: Structures and Problems of Welfare in Italy 1860—1890*, PhD thesis, University of Edinburgh, 1989.

Fogarty, M. (1966), 'Wider business objectives: American thinking and experience', *Political and Economic Planning*, vol. 32, no. 495, pp. 42—76.

Fogarty, M. (1975), *Company Responsibility and Participation: a New Agenda*, PEP Broadsheet, vol. XLI, no. 554 (London: PEP).

Fogarty, M., and Christie, I. (1990), *Companies and Communities: Promoting Business Involvement in the Community* (London: Policy Studies Institute).

Forester, T. (1978), 'How Labour's industrial strategy got the chop', *New Society*, vol. 45, no. 822, 6 July, pp. 7—10.

Forgacs, D. (1990), *Italian Culture in the Industrial Era 1880—1980: Cultural Industries, Politics and the Public* (Manchester: Manchester University Press).

Forrester, S. (1990), *Business and Environmental Groups: a Natural Partnership?* (London: Directory of Social Change).

Fothergill, S., and Guy, N. (1990), *Retreat from the Regions: Corporate Change and the Closure of Factories* (London: Jessica Kingsley Publishers and Regional Studies Association).

Frankel, P. H. (1966), *Mattei: Oil and Power Politics* (London: Faber and Faber).

Frazer, D. (1979), *Power and Authority in the Victorian City* (Oxford: Basil Blackwell).

Friedman, M. (1962), *Capitalism and Freedom* (Chicago: University of Chicago Press).

Fry, L. W., Keim, G. D., and Meiners, R. E. (1982), 'Corporate contributions: altruistic or for-profit?', *Academy of Management Journal*, vol. 25, no. 1, pp. 94—106.

Galbraith, J. K. (1974), *The New Industrial State*, second edition (Harmondsworth: Penguin).

Gambetta, D. (ed.) (1988), *Trust: Making and Breaking Cooperative Relations* (Oxford: Basil Blackwell).

Gerschenkron, A. (1962), *Economic Backwardness in Historical Perspective: a Book of Essays* (Cambridge, Mass.: Harvard University Press).

Gianni, F., and Giuliani, A. (1990), 'Italy', in J. C. F. Lufkin and D. Gallagher (eds), *International Corporate Governance* (London: Euromoney Books).

Gibb, A. A., and Durowse, H. (1987), 'Large business support for small enterprise development in the UK', *Leadership and Organisation Development Journal*, vol. 8, no. 1, pp. 3—16.

Gillies, C. S. (1992), *Beyond Charitable Giving: Board Policy on Community Involvement* (London: BITC).

Gist, R. R. (1971), *Marketing and Society: a Conceptual Introduction* (New York: Holt, Rinehart and Winston).

Goldsmith, E., and Hildyard, N. (1986), 'Introduction', in E. Goldsmith and N. Hildyard (eds), *Green Britain or Industrial Wasteland?* (Cambridge: Polity Press).

Goss, D. (1991), *Small Business and Society* (London: Routledge).

Goyder, G. (1987), *The Just Enterprise* (London: Andre Deutsch).

Grant, W. (1993), *Business and Politics in Britain*, 2nd edition (Basingstoke: Macmillan).

Gray, R., Bebbington, J., and Walters, D. (1993), *Accounting for the Environment (The Greening of Accountancy, Part II)* (London: Paul Chapman Publishing).

Gray, R., and Morrison, S. (1992), 'The physical environment, accounting and local development', *Local Economy*, vol. 6, no. 4, pp. 336—50.

Gray, R. H., Owen, D. L., and Maunders, K. T. (1987), *Corporate Social Reporting: Accounting and Accountability* (New Jersey: Prentice-Hall).

Graziani, A. (1972), *L'Economia Italiana, 1945—70* (Bologna: Il Mulino).

Green, I., and Murphy, G. W. (1954), 'The income of voluntary social services of Manchester and Salford in 1951 and a comparison with 1938', *Social Welfare*, vol. 9 (IX), no. 4, pp. 78—96.

Green, M. (1973), 'The corporation and the community', in R. Nader and M. J. Green (eds), *Corporate Power in America* (New York: Grossman Publishers).

Gruppo Prospettive (1992), *Arte & Sponsor: Manifestazione Nazionale delle Sponsorizzazioni Culturali* (Rome: Edizioni Gruppo Prospettive).

Guiotto, L. (1979), *La Fabbrica Totale: Paternalismo Industriale e Citta Sociale in Italia* (Milan: Feltrinelli).

Hambleton, R. (1981), 'Implementing inner city policy: reflections from experience', *Policy and Politics*, vol. 9, no. 1, pp. 51—71.

Hammersley, M. (1992), *What's Wrong with Ethnography? Methodological Explorations* (London and New York: Routledge).

Handel, G. (1982), *Social Welfare in Western Society* (New York: Random House).

Hannah, L. (1983), *The Rise of the Corporate Economy*, 2nd edition (London and New York: Methuen).

Harding, A. (1990), 'Public-private partnerships in urban regeneration', in M. Campbell (ed.), *Local Economic Policy* (London: Cassell Education Ltd.).

Hargreaves, J., and Dauman, J. (1975), *Business Survival and Social Change: a Practical Guide to Responsibilities and Partnership* (London: Associated Business Programmes).

Harris, N. (1983), *Of Bread and Guns: the World Economy in Crisis* (Harmondsworth: Penguin).

Harrison, B. (1982), *Peaceable Kingdom: Stability and Change in Modern Britain* (Oxford: Clarendon Press).

Hart, P. E., and Prais, S. J. (1956), 'The analysis of business concentration: a statistical approach', *Journal of the Royal Statistical Society*, Series A (General), vol. 119, part 2, pp. 150—91.

Harte, G., Lewis, L., and Owen, D. (1991), 'Ethical investment and the corporate reporting function', *Critical Perspectives on Accounting*, vol. 2, no. 3, pp. 227—53.

Harte, G., and Owen, D. (1991), 'Environmental disclosure in the annual reports of British companies: a research note', *Accounting, Auditing and Accountability Journal*, vol. 4, no. 3, pp. 51—61.

Hartridge, R. A. R. (1930), *A History of Vicarages in the Middle Ages* (London: Cambridge University Press).

Harvey, B., Smith, S., and Wilkinson, B. (1984), *Managers and Corporate Social Policy: Private Solutions to Public Problems?* (London: Macmillan).

Hawkins, K. (1983), 'Bargaining and bluff: compliance strategy and deterrence in the enforcement of regulation', *Law and Policy Quarterly*, vol. 5, no. 1, pp. 35—73.

Hayek, F. A. (1969), 'The corporation in a democratic society: in whose interest ought it and will it be run?', in H. I. Ansoff (ed.), *Business Strategy: Selected Readings* (Harmondsworth: Penguin).

Heald, D. (1983), *Public Expenditure: its Defence and Reform* (Oxford: Martin Robertson).

Heald, M. (1970), *The Social Responsibilities of Business: Company and Community, 1900—1960* (Cleveland and London: The Press of Case Western Reserve University).

Hearder, H. (1983), *Italy in the Age of the Risorgimento 1790—1870* (London and New York: Longman).

Hearder, H. (1990), *Italy: a Short History* (Cambridge: Cambridge University Press).

Hearder, H., and Waley, D. P. (1963), *A Short History of Italy: from Classical Times to the Present Day* (Cambridge: Cambridge University Press).

Heseltine, M. (1987), *Where There's a Will* (London: Hutchinson).

Hickson, C. R., and Thompson, E. A. (1991), 'A new theory of guilds and European economic development', *Explorations in Economic History*, vol. 28, no. 2, pp. 127—68.

Hodder, E. (1887), *The Life of Samuel Morley* (London: Hodder and Stoughton).

Hodson, H. V. (1991), 'Introduction', in H. V. Hodson (ed.), *The International Foundation Directory 1991* (London: Europa Publishers).

Humble, J. (1976), 'Social responsibility: the heart of business', *Unilever Topics*, no. 4, November/December, pp. 1a—2a.

Hutton, W. (1994), 'Bad times for the good life', *The Guardian 2*, Tuesday, August 2, pp. 2—3.

Hyde, J. K. (1973), *Society and Politics in Medieval Italy: the Evolution of the Civil Life, 1000—1350* (London: Macmillan Press).

Ingram, R. W., and Frazier, K. B. (1980), 'Environmental performance and corporate disclosure', *Journal of Accounting Research*, vol. 18, no. 2, pp. 614—22.

International Labour Office (1932), *The F.I.A.T. Establishments*, Studies in Industrial Relations II, Studies and Reports Series A, no. 35 (Geneva: International Labour Office, League of Nations).

Irvine, S. (1989), *Beyond Green Consumerism*, discussion paper, no. 1 (London: Friends of the Earth).

Irvine, S. (1991), 'Beyond green consumerism', in C. Plant and J. Plant (eds), *Green Business — Hope or Hoax?* (Devon: Green Books).

IRES (Istituto Ricerche Economico-Sociale del Piemonte) (1992), *Relazione sulla Situazione Economica, Sociale e Territoriale del Piemonte 1992* (Turin: Rosenberg and Sellier).

Ivens, M. (ed.) (1970), *Industry and Values: the Objectives and Responsibilities of Business* (London: George G. Harrap).

Jeremy, D. J. (1991), 'The enlightened paternalist in action: William Hesketh Lever at Port Sunlight before 1914', *Business History*, vol. 33, no. 1, pp. 58—81.

Johnson, D. A. (1986), 'Confronting corporate power: strategies and phases of the Nestle boycott', in L. E. Preston (ed.), *Research in Corporate Social Performance and Policy: a Research Annual*, vol. 8 (Greenwich, Conn.: JAI Press).

208

Jones, B., and Saren, M. (1990), 'Politics and institutions in small business development: comparing Britain and Italy', *Labour and Society*, vol. 15, no. 3, pp. 287—300.

Jones, K. (1974), *The Human Face of Change: Social Responsibility and Rationalization at British Steel* (London: Institute of Personnel Management).

Jones, T. M. (1980), 'Corporate social responsibility revisited, redefined', *California Management Review*, vol. 22, no. 3, pp. 59—67.

Jones, T. M. (1983), 'An integrating framework for research in business and society: a step toward the elusive paradigm?', *The Academy of Management Review*, vol. 8, no. 4, pp. 559—64.

Jordan, W. K. (1961), 'The English background of modern philanthropy', *The American Historical Review*, vol. 66, no. 2, pp. 401—8.

Jordan, W. K. (1964), *Philanthropy in England 1480—1660: a Study of the Changing Pattern of English Social Aspirations*, 2nd edition (London: George Allen and Unwin).

Joyce, P. (1982), *Work, Society and Politics: the Culture of the Factory in Late Victorian England*, 2nd edition (London: Methuen).

Judge, D., and Dickson, T. (1987), 'The British state, governments and manufacturing decline', in T. Dickson and D. Judge (eds), *The Politics of Industrial Closure* (Basingstoke: Macmillan).

Kavanagh, D. (1990), *Thatcherism and British Politics: the End of Consensus?*, 2nd edition (New York: Oxford University Press).

Kaysen, C. (1957), 'The social significance of the modern corporation', *American Economic Review*, vol. 47, no. 2, pp. 311—19.

Kelly, A. (1991), 'The enterprise culture and the welfare state: restructuring the management of the health and personal social services', in G. Burrows (ed.), *Deciphering the Enterprise Culture: Entrepreneurship, Petty Capitalism and the Restructuring of Britain* (London: Routledge).

Kempner, T., MacMillan, K., and Hawkins, K. (1974), *Business and Society: Tradition and Change* (London: Allen Lane).

Kicherer, S. (1990), *Olivetti: a study of the Corporate Management of Design* (London: Trefoil Publications).

King, D. S. (1987), *The New Right: Politics, Markets and Citizenship* (Basingstoke and London: Macmillan Education).

King, R. (1985), *The Industrial Geography of Italy* (London: Croom Helm).

Kitsuse, J. I., and Spector, M. (1989), 'The labeling of social problems', in E. Rubington and M. S. Weinberg (eds), *The Study of Social Problems: Six Perspectives*, 4th edition (New York and Oxford: Oxford University Press).

Knox, J., and Ashworth, M. (1985), *An Introduction to Corporate Philanthropy* (London: BIM/CAF).

Kropotkin, P. (1907), *Mutual Aid: a Factor of Evolution* (London: William Heinemann).

Lane, F. C. (1966), *Venice and History: the Collected Papers of F. C. Lane* (Baltimore: John Hopkins Press).

Lane, J., and Saxon-Harrold, S. K. E. (1993), 'Corporate philanthropy in Britain', in S. K. E. Saxon-Harrold and J. Kendall (eds), *Researching the Voluntary Sector* (Tonbridge: Charities Aid Foundation).

La Palombara, J. (1966), *Italy: the Politics of Planning* (Syracuse, N.Y.: Syracuse University Press).

Lawless, P. (1987), 'Urban development', in M. Parkinson (ed.), *Reshaping Local Government* (Hermitage: Policy Journals).

Lawrence, D. (1988), *The Third Way: the Promise of Industrial Democracy* (London: Routledge).

Law Reports (1883), *Hutton v. West Cork Railway Company*, *Law Reports*, vol. 23, Chancery Division, pp. 654—84 (London: Council of Law Reporting).

Lawson, N. (1992), *The View from No. 11: Memoirs of a Tory Radical* (London: Bantam Press).

Lentati, B. (1991), 'Company giving in Italy: an overview', in B. Dabson (ed.), *Company Giving in Europe: a Survey of Different Approaches to Community Involvement by Companies in each of the Member States of the European Community with Case Studies of Good Practice* (London: Directory of Social Change).

L'Etang, J. (1994), 'Public relations and corporate social responsibility: some issues arising', *Journal of Business Ethics*, vol. 13, no. 2, pp. 111—23.

Levitt, T. (1979), 'The dangers of social responsibility', in T. L. Beauchamp and N. E. Bowie (eds), *Ethical Theory and Business* (Englewood Cliffs, NJ: Prentice-Hall).

Lipson, E. (1937), *The Economic History of England, Volume 1: the Middle Ages* (London: Adam and Charles Black).

Lloyd, E. A. (1925), *The Co-operative Movement in Italy, with reference to Agriculture, Labour and Production* (London: Fabian Society and George Allen and Unwin).

Logsdon, J. M. (1985), 'Organizational responses to environmental issues: oil refining companies and air pollution', in L. E. Preston (ed.), *Research in Corporate Social Performance and Policy: a Research Annual*, vol. 7 (Greenwich, Conn.: JAI Press).

Logsdon, J. M., Reiner, M., and Burke, L. (1990), 'Corporate philanthropy: strategic responses to the firm's stakeholders', *Nonprofit and Voluntary Sector Quarterly*, vol. 19, no. 2, pp. 93—109.

Lowe, P., and Goyder, J. (1983), *Environmental Groups in Politics* (London: George Allen and Unwin).

Lowe, P. D., and Rudig, W. (1986), 'Review article: political ecology and the social sciences — the state of the art', *British Journal of Political Science*, vol. 16, part 4, pp. 513—50.

Lumley, R. (1990), 'Challenging tradition: social movements, cultural change and the ecology question', in Z.G. Baranski and R. Lumley (eds), *Culture and Conflict in Postwar Italy: Essays on Mass and Popular Culture* (Basingstoke: Macmillan).

Lutz, V. (1962), *Italy: a Study in Economic Development* (Oxford: Oxford University Press).

McAdam, T. W. (1973), 'How to put corporate social responsibility into practice', *Business and Society Review*, no. 6, pp. 8—16.

McCarthy, K. D. (1982), *Noblesse Oblige: Charity and Cultural Philanthropy in Chicago 1889—1929* (Chicago: University of Chicago Press).

MacKenzie, D. (1989), 'It makes money, being green', *New Scientist*, 7 October (Special Greening of Industry Supplement), pp. 6—7.

Magini, M. (1992), *La Cassa di Risparmio di Firenze: Breve Compendio di Una Lunga Storia* (Florence: Leo S. Olschki Editore).

Maraffi, M. (1980), 'State/economy relationships: the case of Italian public enterprise', *British Journal of Sociology*, vol. 31, no. 4, pp. 507—24.

Martin, J. (1991), 'Information technology: Ing. C, Olivetti and C., S.P.A.', in A. Hast (ed.), *International Directory of Company Histories*, volume III (Chicago and London: St. James Press).

Martinelli, A. (1979), 'Organised business and Italian politics: Confindustria and the Christian Democrats in the postwar period', *West European Politics*, vol. 2, no. 3, pp. 67—87.

Martinelli, A., Chiesi, A. M., and Chiesa, N. D. (1981), *I Grandi Imprenditori Italiani: Profilo Sociale della Classe Dirigente Economica* (Milan: Feltrinelli).

Martinelli, A., and Treu, T. (1984), 'Employers associations in Italy', in J. P. Windmuller and A. Gladstone (eds), *Employers Associations and Industrial Relations: a Comparative Study* (Oxford: Clarendon Press).

Martines, L. (1979), *Power and Imagination: City-States in Renaissance Italy* (New York: Alfred A. Knopf).

Marx, K. (1976), *Capital: a Critique of Political Economy Volume 1* (Harmondsworth: Penguin Books/ New Left Review).

Massey, D., and Meegan, R. (1982), *The Anatomy of Job Loss: the how, why and where of Employment Decline* (London and New York: Methuen).

Mauksch, M. (1982), *Corporate Voluntary Contributions in Europe* (New York: The Conference Board).

Meakin, B. (1905), *Model Factories and Villages: Ideal Conditions of Labour and Housing* (London: T. Fisher Unwin).

211

Melrose-Woodman, J., and Kverndal, I. (1976), *Towards Social Responsibility: Company Codes of Ethics and Practice*, Management Survey Report, no. 28 (London: British Institute of Management).

Merenda, M. J. (1981), 'The process of corporate social involvement: five case studies', in L. E. Preston (ed.), *Research in Corporate Social Performance and Policy: a Research Annual*, vol. 3 (Greenwich, Conn.: JAI Press).

Merli, S. (1972), *Proletariato di Fabbrica e Capitalismo Industriale*, volume 1 (Florence: La Nuova Italia).

Metcalf, H., Pearson, R., and Martin, R. (1989), *Stimulating Jobs: the Charitable Role of Companies* (Brighton: Institute of Manpower Studies).

Miller, A. (1992), 'Green investment', in D. Owen (ed.), *Green Reporting: Accountancy and the Challenge of the Nineties* (London: Chapman Hall).

Mitchell, B. R. (1988), *British Historical Statistics* (Cambridge: Cambridge University Press).

Mitchell, N. J. (1989), *The Generous Corporation: a Political Analysis of Economic Power* (New Haven: Yale University Press).

Mitchell, N. J. (1990), 'The decentralization of business in Britain', *Journal of Politics*, vol. 52, no. 2, pp. 622—37.

Monasta, A. (1994), 'Italy', in C. Brock and W. Tulasiewicz (eds), *Education in a Single Europe* (London and New York: Routledge).

Moore, C. (1988), 'Enterprise agencies: privatisation or partnership?', *Local Economy*, vol. 3, no. 1, pp. 21—30.

Moore, C., and Booth, S. (1986), 'Urban policy contradictions: the market versus redistributive approaches', *Policy and Politics*, vol. 14, no. 3, pp. 361—87.

Moore, C., Richardson, J. J., and Moon, J. (1985), 'New partnerships in local economic development: a case study of local entrepreneurship', *Local Government Studies*, vol. 11, no. 5, pp. 19—33.

Moore, C., Richardson, J. J., and Moon, J. (1989), *Local Partnership and the Unemployment Crisis in Britain* (London: Unwin Hyman).

Moratto, G. (ed.) (1986), *L'amministrazione dei Beni Culturali ed Ambientali* (Naples: Simone).

Mueller, A. (1985), 'A civil servant's view', in D. Englefield (ed.), *Today's Civil Service* (Harlow: Longman).

Murray, R. (1983), 'Pension funds and local authority investments', *Capital and Class*, no. 20, Summer, pp. 89—102.

Myers, K. (1991), 'Selling green', in C. Squiers (ed.), *The Critical Image: Essays on Contemporary Photography* (London: Lawrence and Wishart).

Neubeck, K. J. (1974), *Corporate Response to Urban Crisis* (Toronto: D. C. Heath and Company).

Neufeld, M. F. (1961), *Italy: School for Awakening Countries: the Italian Labour Movement in its Political, Social and Economic Setting from 1800 to 1960* (Ithaca: New York State School of Industrial and Labour Relations, Cornell University).

New Society (1973), 'Loaning pros', *New Society*, vol. 25, no. 568, 23 August, p. 463.

Nichols, T. (1969), *Ownership, Control and Ideology: an Enquiry into Certain Aspects of Modern Business Ideology* (London: George Allen and Unwin).

Niven, M. N. (1978), *Personnel Management 1913—63: the Growth of Personnel Management and the Development of the Institute*, 2nd edition (London: Institute of Personnel Management).

Norton, M. (1987), *The Corporate Donor's Handbook* (London: Directory of Social Change).

Norton, M. (1989), *Major Companies and their Charitable Giving* (London: Directory of Social Change).

Oakey, R. P. (1985), 'Innovation and regional growth in small high technology firms: evidence from Britain and the USA', in D. J. Storey (ed.), *Small Firms in Regional Economic Development: Britain, Ireland and the United States* (Cambridge: Cambridge University Press).

Ogus, A. (1983), 'The regulation of pollution', in G. Richardson, A. Ogus and P. Burrows, *Policing Pollution: a Study of Regulation Enforcement* (Oxford: Clarendon Press).

O'Hagan, J. W., and Duffy, C. T. (1989), 'Tax concessions to the arts: importance and impact', in C. R. Waits, W. S. Hendon, J. M. Davidson Schuster (eds), *Cultural Economics 88: a European Perspective* (Ottawa: Association for Cultural Economics).

Orpen, C. (1987), 'The attitudes of US and South African managers to corporate social responsibility', *Journal of Business Ethics*, vol. 6, no. 2, pp. 89—96.

Owen, D. (1964), *English Philanthropy 1660—1960* (Cambridge Mass.: The Belknap Press of Harvard University Press).

Owen, D. L. (1990), 'Towards a theory of social investment: a review Essay', *Accounting, Organisations and Society*, vol. 15, no. 3, pp. 249—65.

Palma, G., and Clemente, G. (1987), 'State intervention in the arts in Italy from 1945 to 1982', in M. C. Cummings and R. S. Katz (eds), *The Patron State: Government and the Arts in Europe, North America, and Japan* (New York and Oxford: Oxford University Press).

Parkinson, J. (1994), 'The legal context of corporate social responsibility', *Business Ethics — A European Review*, vol. 3, no. 1, pp. 16—22.

Parkinson, M. (1988), 'Urban regeneration and development corporations: Liverpool style', *Local Economy*, vol. 3, no. 2, pp. 109—18.

Pasquino, G. (1979), 'Italian Christian Democracy: a party for all seasons?', *West European Politics*, vol. 2, no. 3, pp. 88—109.

Payne, P. L. (1967), 'The emergence of the large-scale company in Great Britain, 1870—1914', *The Economic History Review*, Second Series, vol. 20 (XX), no. 3, pp. 519—42.

Peacock, A. (1984), *The Regulation Game: how British and West German Companies Bargain with Government* (Oxford: Basil Blackwell).

Penrose, E. T. (1968), *The Theory of the Growth of the Firm* (Oxford: Basil Blackwell).

Perks, R. W., Rawlinson, D. H., and Ingram, L. (1992), 'An exploration of ethical investment in the UK', *British Accounting Review*, vol. 24, no. 1, pp. 43—65.

Pettigrew, A. M. (1985), *The Awakening Giant: Continuity and Change in Imperial Chemical Industries* (Oxford: Basil Blackwell).

Petrilli, G. (1967), *Lo Stato Imprenditore: Validita e Attualita di una Formula* (Bologna: Cappelli).

Plant, C., and Albert, D. H. (1991), 'Green business in a grey world — can it be done?', in C. Plant and J. Plant (eds), *Green Business — Hope or Hoax?* (Devon: Green Books).

Podbielski, G. (1974), *Italy: Development and Crisis in the Postwar Economy* (Oxford: Clarendon Press).

Pollard, S. (1965), *The Genesis of Modern Management: a Study of the Industrial Revolution in Great Britain* (London: Edward Arnold).

Por, O. (1923), *Guilds and Cooperatives in Italy*, trans., E. Townshend (London: The Labour Publishing Company).

Posner, M. V., and Woolf, S. J. (1967), *Italian Public Enterprise* (London: Gerald Duckworth).

Post, J. E., and Andrews, P. N. (1982), 'Case research in corporation and society studies', in L. E. Preston (ed.), *Research in Corporate Social Performance and Policy: a Research Annual*, volume 4 (Greenwich, Conn.: JAI Press).

Prochaska, F. (1988), *The Voluntary Impulse: Philanthropy in Modern Britain* (London: Faber and Faber).

Prodi, R. (1974), 'Italy', in R. Vernon (ed.), *Big Business and the State: Changing Relations in Western Europe* (London: Macmillan).

Prodi, R., and De Giovanni, D. (1993), 'Forty-five years of industrial policy in Italy: protagonists, objectives and instruments', M. Baldassarri (ed.), *Industrial Policy in Italy 1945—90* (Basingstoke: Macmillan/ New York: St. Martin's Press/ in assoc. Rome: Rivista di Politica Economica).

Pullan, B. (1971), *Rich and Poor in Renaissance Venice: the Social Institutions of a Catholic State to 1620* (Oxford: Basil Blackwell).

Putnam, R. D. (1993), *Making Democracy Work: Civic Traditions in Modern Italy* (Princeton, NJ.: Princeton University Press).

Raistrick, A. (1993), *Quakers in Science and Industry: Being an Account of the Quaker Contributions to Science and Industry During the Seventeenth and Eighteenth Centuries*, 2nd edition (York: Sessions Book Trust).

Rey, F. (1980), 'Corporate social performance and reporting in France', in L. E. Preston (ed.), *Research in Corporate Social Performance and Policy: a Research Annual*, vol. 2 (Greenwich, Conn.: JAI Press).

Richardson, J. J. (1983), *The Development of Corporate Responsibility in the UK*, Strathclyde Papers on Government and Politics, no. 1 (Glasgow: Department of Politics, University of Strathclyde).

Richardson, J. J. (1989), 'Britain: changing policy styles and policy innovation in response to economic crisis', in E. Damgaard, P. Gerlich, and J. J. Richardson (eds), *The Politics of Economic Crisis: Lessons from Western Europe* (Aldershot: Avebury).

Roberts, C. B. (1991), 'Environmental disclosures: a note on reporting practices in mainland Europe', *Accounting, Auditing, and Accountability Journal*, vol. 4, no. 3, pp. 62—71.

Robertson, J. (1974), *Profit or People? The New Social Role of Money* (London: Calder and Boyars).

Robinson, F., and Shaw, K. (1991), 'Urban regeneration and community involvement', *Local Economy*, vol. 6, no. 1, pp. 61—73.

Robinson, M. (1992), *The Greening of British Party Politics* (Manchester and New York: Manchester University Press).

Rockness, J., and Williams, P. F. (1988), 'A descriptive study of social responsibility mutual funds', *Accounting, Organizations and Society*, vol. 13, no. 4, pp. 397—411.

Roll, E. (1992), *A History of Economic Thought*, 5th edition (London and Boston: Faber and Faber).

Ronci, D. (1980), *Olivetti, Anni '50: Patronalsocialismo, Lotte Operaie e Movimento Comunità* (Milan: Franco Angeli Editore).

Rowntree, B. S. (1922), *Poverty: a Study of Town Life* (London: Longmans, Green and Co.).

Sabel, C. F. (1981), 'The internal politics of trade unions', in S. Berger (ed.), *Organising Interests in Western Europe: Pluralism, Corporatism and the Transformation of Politics* (Cambridge: Cambridge University Press).

Sanderson, M. (1972), *The Universities and British Industry 1850—1970* (London: Routledge and Kegan Paul).

Saraceno, P. (1976), 'Le radici della crisi economica', *Il Mulino*, no. 243, January/February, pp. 3—26.

Sasso, G. (1978), 'Partecipazioni statali e politica del lavoro', in G. Cottino (ed.), *Ricerca sulle Partecipazioni Statali*, vol. I: *Studi sulla Vicenda Italiana* (Turin: Einaudi).

Sassoon, D. (1986), *Contemporary Italy: Politics, Economy and Society since 1945* (London and New York: Longman).

Schoyen, A. R. (1958), *The Chartist Challenge: a Portrait of George Julian Harney* (London: Heinemann).

Scott, J. (1985), *Corporations, Classes and Capitalism*, 2nd edition (London: Hutchinson).

Scott, J. (1986), *Capitalist Property and Financial Power: a Comparative Study of Britain, the United States and Japan* (Brighton: Wheatsheaf).

Senin, A. (1976), 'Monte di pegno', in *Enciclopedia del Diritto: Estratto dal Ventiseiesimo Volume* (Milan: Giuffre Editore).

Sheikh, S. (1990), 'Judicial policy on corporate giving', *The Law Society's Gazette, no. 25,* 4 July, pp. 16—18.

Shenfield, B. (1969), *Company Giving* (London: PEP).

Shenfield, B. (1971), *Company Boards: their Responsibilities to Shareholders, Employees, and the Community* (London: George Allen and Unwin/Political and Economic Planning).

Shimmin, A. N. (1954), *The University of Leeds: the First Half Century* (Cambridge: Cambridge University Press).

Shutt, J., and Whittington, R. (1987), 'Fragmentation strategies and the rise of small units: cases from the North West', *Regional Studies*, vol. 21, no. 1, pp. 13—23.

Siegfried, J. J., Maddox McElroy, K., and Biernot-Fawkes, D. (1983), 'The management of corporate contributions', in L. E. Preston (ed.), *Research in Corporate Social Performance and Policy: a Research Annual*, volume 5 (Greenwich, Conn.: JAI Press).

Simon, J. G., Powers, C. W., and Gunnemann, J. P. (1972), *The Ethical Investor: Universities and Corporate Responsibility* (New Haven: Yale University Press).

Simpson, A. (1991), *The Greening of Global Investment: how the Environment, Ethics and Politics are Reshaping Strategies*, special report, no. 2108 (London: The Economist).

Smallbone, D. (1990), 'Enterprise agencies in London: a public private sector partnership?', *Local Government Studies*, vol. 16, no. 5, pp. 17—32.

SSRC (Social Science Research Council) (1976), *The Social Responsibilities of Business*, a Report to the Social Science Research Council by an SSRC Advisory Panel (London: SSRC).

Staley, E. (1906), *The Guilds of Florence* (London: Methuen).

Storey, D. (1982), *Entrepreneurship and the New Firm* (London: Croom Helm).

Storey, D. (1985), 'The implications for policy', in D. J. Storey (ed.), *Small Firms in Regional Economic Development: Britain, Ireland and the United States* (Cambridge: Cambridge University Press).

Storey, D., Keasey, K., Watson, R., and Wynarczyk, P. (1987), *The Performance of Small Firms: Profits, Jobs and Failures* (London: Croom Helm).

Strong, P., and Robinson, J. (1990), *The NHS — Under New Management* (Milton Keynes: Open University Press).

Supple, B. (1973), 'The state and the industrial revolution 1700—1914', in C. M. Cipolla (ed.), *The Industrial Revolution: Fontana Economic History of Europe* (London: Fontana/Collins Books).

Tabacco, G. (1989), *The Struggle for Power in Medieval Italy: Structures of Political Rule*, trans., R. Brown Jensen (Cambridge: Cambridge University Press).

Tawney, R. H. (1920), *The Acquisitive Society* (New York: Harcourt Brace Jovanovich).

Tawney, R. H. (1967), *The Agrarian Problem in the Sixteenth Century* (New York: Harper Torchbooks).

Tawney, R. H. (1984), *Religion and the Rise of Capitalism: a Historical Study*, Penguin Books reissue (Harmondsworth: Penguin).

The Times (1968), 'Less high street money for charities', *The Times*, September 3, p. 2.

Toniolo, G. (1977), 'Effective protection and industrial growth: the case of Italian engineering, 1898—1913', *The Journal of European Economic History*, vol. 6, no. 3, pp. 659—73.

Toniolo, G. (1990), *An Economic History of Liberal Italy 1850—1918* (London: Routledge).

Tudor, A. (1989), *Monsters and Mad Scientists: a Cultural History of the Horror Movie* (Oxford: Basil Blackwell).

Ullmann, A. A. (1985), 'Data in search of a theory: a critical examination of the relationships among social performance, social disclosure, and economic performance of U.S. firms', *Academy of Management Review*, vol. 10, no. 3, pp. 540—57.

Useem, M. (1984), *The Inner Circle: Large Corporations and the Rise of Business Political Activity in the U.S. and U.K.* (New York: Oxford University Press).

Useem, M. (1987), 'Corporate philanthropy', in W. W. Powell (ed.), *The Nonprofit Sector: a Research Handbook* (New Haven: Yale University Press).

Usher, A. P. (1934), 'The origins of banking: the Primitive bank of deposit, 1200—1600', *The Economic History Review*, vol. 4, no. 4, pp. 399—428.

Utton, M. A. (1982), *The Political Economy of Big Business* (Oxford: Martin Robertson).

Varni, A., Gobbo, F., and Mosconi, F. (1991), *La Cassa di Risparmio di Cesena 1841—1991* (Rimini: Bruno Ghigi Editore).

Villa, M. L. (1991), 'Adesso l'industria sponsorizza la voglia di studiare', *Corriere della Sera* 16 November.

Villari, L. (ed.) (1975), *Il Capitalismo Italiano de Novecento* (Rome and Bari: Laterza).

Vogel, D. (1986), *National Styles of Regulation: Environmental Policy in Great Britain and the United States* (Ithaca: Cornell University Press).

Wagner, G. (1987), *The Chocolate Conscience* (London: Chatto and Windus).

Waley, D. (1969), *The Italian City-Republics* (London: Weidenfeld and Nicolson).

Walton, C. C. (1967), *Corporate Social Responsibilities* (California: Wadsworth).

Walton, C. C. (1982), 'Corporate social responsibility: the debate revisited', *Journal of Economics and Business*, vol. 34, no. 2, pp. 173—87.

Ward, S. (1991), *Socially Responsible Investment: a Guide for those Concerned with the Ethical and Social Implications of their Investments* (London: Directory of Social Change).

Ward, W. (1990), *Getting it Right in Italy: a Manual for the 1990s* (London: Bloomsbury).

Weber, M. (1985), *The Protestant Ethic and the Spirit of Capitalism* (London: Counterpoint).

Webley, S. (1974), *Corporate Social Responsibility: Report on a Survey Conducted on Behalf of the Public Relations Consultants Association* (London: PRCA).

Webster, R. A. (1961), *Christian Democracy in Italy 1860—1960* (London: Hollis and Carter).

Weiss, L. (1984), 'The Italian state and small business', *The European Journal of Sociology*, vol. XXV, no. 2, pp. 214—41.

Weiss, L. (1988), *Creating Capitalism: the State and Small Business since 1945* (Oxford: Basil Blackwell).

Williams, I. A. (1931), *The Firm of Cadbury 1831—1931* (London: Constable).

Willmott, P., and Hutchison, R. (eds) (1992), *Urban Trends 1: a Report on Britain's Deprived Urban Areas* (London: PSI).

Wilson, P. R. (1987), *Women Workers, Scientific Management and Workers Welfare: the Magneti Marelli in the Fascist Period*, PhD thesis, University of Essex, 1987.

Woolf, S. (1979), *A History of Italy 1700—1860: the Social Constraints of Political Change*, 1991 edition (London and New York: Routledge).

Woollett, S. (1993), *Environmental Grants: a Guide to Grants for the Environment from Government, Companies and Charitable Trusts* (London: Directory of Social Change).

Worsley, P. (1983), 'One world or three? A critique of the world-system theory of Immanuel Wallerstein', in D. Held, J. Anderson, B. Gieben, S. Hall, L. Harris, P. Lewis, N. Parker, B. Turok (eds), *States and Societies* (Oxford: Martin Robertson in association with The Open University).

Yearley, S. (1992), *The Green Case: a Sociology of Environmental Issues, Arguments and Politics* (London: Routledge).

Author Index

222

Subject Index

26, 34, 171
early studies and statistics, 32
relief, 21, 23, 29, 111, 112
predestination, 23, 25
preservation of cultural heritage
business contribution to, 152,
157—62
fiscal assistance, 153—4
and Italian banks, 162—9
promotion of sponsorship for,
155—6
state contribution to, 149—54,
169
private charity, 22, 23—4, 26, 29
Procter & Gamble, 155
product analysis, 87, 97—8
Protestant Ethic, 23
Prudential Insurance Co., 43
Public Health Act (1872), 34
public law banks, 163—4
Publitalia, 155, 156
Puritanism, 23, 24, 25

Quakers (the Society of Friends),
25—6, 27
businessmen and charitable
action, 28—9
qualitative analysis, 11, 13

RAI, 154—5
Reading University, 40
the Reformation, 21, 22
Renaissance, 103, 109
research methodology, 10—13
the Restoration, 25
Reynolds, Richard, 28—9
Risorgimento, 109
Roman Catholicism, 105
Rome, 109, 114, 155
Rossi, Alessandro, 120
Rowntree, John Stevenson, 29

Rowntree, Joseph, 29—30
Royal Holloway College, 31

Sawfield chemical factory, 33
Second World War, 8, 35, 39, 43,
45, 47, 125, 128, 171, 172,
163
service sector, 12—13
shareholders, 36, 39, 40, 46, 49
Sheffield university, 41
Shell Small Business Unit, 63, 64,
69
Shell UK, 9, 12, 52, 54, 57, 59,
60, 62, 63—4, 69, 70, 71,
79, 83,85, 93, 146, 173, 177
Shore, Peter, 58—9
small and medium enterprises
corporate support, 52, 58,
60—4, 68—71, 76, 138
job creation, 71
managed work spaces, 72—4
venture capital funds for, 75—6
Smith, Adam, 1
social reforms, 130—4
social responsibility, 30, 44, 87
Social Science Research Council,
49
sottogoverno, 130
SPI, 136, 137, 138, 144, 175
Staveley Coal and Iron Co., 41
Stock Exchange, 37, 38—9
Supreme New Jersey Legislature, 2
SustainAbility, 91

Taunton v. Royal Insurance Co.
(1864), 39
Technical and Enterprise Councils,
138
Tesco, 59, 60, 83, 92
Tetley, Dr Charles, 41
textile industry, 37, 42, 120

232

Thatcher, Margaret, 61
Third Italy, 135, 144
the Third World, 88, 99
The Times, 45
traditional industries, 37
the Treasury, 84
Trident Trust, 51—2
Trippier, David, 62
Trustee Investment Act (1961), 95
TSB, 83
Tuscany, 106, 109

unemployment, 34, 35, 38, 47, 58,
    171
Unilever, 9, 12, 39, 54, 62, 79,
    92, 155, 173
  and environmental performance,
    93, 96—8
United Steel Company, 41
university education, 40—3, 42—3
urban policy
  Action for Cities, 66
  City Action Teams, 77, 178
  City Challenge, 66—8, 173
  Conservative influence, 64—6,
    77

effectiveness of policy, 76—8
private sector involvement,
    64—8, 72, 76,
Single Regeneration Budget, 68
Task Forces, 77
urban development corporations,
    65—6
Urban Programme, 58—9, 60,
    61, 66, 70
urban poverty, 26, 60—1, 76—8

Vickers Ltd., 41
Victorian period, 26, 29, 30—2,
    34, 46

welfare state, 35, 36
Western capitalism, 44
Wills tobacco producers, 34
workplace conditions, 33
World Wide Fund for Nature, 84,
    85, 86, 151

Yorkshire industry, 42

Zeebrugge, 179
Zorzi, Renzo, 157, 159, 160